Palm & Pocket PC Programming

Vadim Kalinin
Vladimir Rafalovich

alist

Copyright (c) 2003 by A-LIST, LLC
All rights reserved.

No part of this publication may be reproduced in any way, stored in a retrieval system of any type, or transmitted by any means or media, electronic or mechanical, including, but not limited to, photocopy, recording, or scanning, *without prior permission in writing* from the publisher.

A-LIST, LLC
295 East Swedesford Rd.
PMB #285
Wayne, PA 19087
702-977-5377 (FAX)
mail@alistpublishing.com
http://www.alistpublishing.com

This book is printed on acid-free paper.

All brand names and product names mentioned in this book are trademarks or service marks of their respective companies. Any omission or misuse (of any kind) of service marks or trademarks should not be regarded as intent to infringe on the property of others. The publisher recognizes and respects all marks used by companies, manufacturers, and developers as a means to distinguish their products.

Palm & Pocket PC Programming

By Vadim Kalinin, Vladimir Rafalovich

     ISBN: 1-931769-20-6

Printed in the United States of America

03 04 7 6 5 4 3 2 1

A-LIST, LLC titles are distributed by Independent Publishers Group and are available for site license or bulk purchase by institutions, user groups, corporations, etc.

Book Editors: Jessica Mroz, Peter Morley

LIMITED WARRANTY AND DISCLAIMER OF LIABILITY

A-LIST, LLC., INDEPENDENT PUBLISHERS GROUP AND/OR ANYONE WHO HAS BEEN INVOLVED IN THE WRITING, CREATION OR PRODUCTION OF THE ACCOMPANYING CODE ("THE SOFTWARE") OR TEXTUAL MATERIAL IN THE BOOK, CANNOT AND DO NOT WARRANT THE PERFORMANCE OR RESULTS THAT MAY BE OBTAINED BY USING THE CODE OR CONTENTS OF THE BOOK. THE AUTHORS AND PUBLISHERS HAVE USED THEIR BEST EFFORTS TO ENSURE THE ACCURACY AND FUNCTIONALITY OF THE TEXTUAL MATERIAL AND PROGRAMS CONTAINED HEREIN; WE HOWEVER MAKE NO WARRANTY OF ANY KIND, EXPRESSED OR IMPLIED, REGARDING THE PERFORMANCE OF THESE PROGRAMS OR CONTENTS.

THE AUTHORS, THE PUBLISHER, DEVELOPERS OF THIRD PARTY SOFTWARE, AND ANYONE INVOLVED IN THE PRODUCTION AND MANUFACTURING OF THIS WORK SHALL NOT BE LIABLE FOR DAMAGES OF ANY KIND ARISING OUT OF THE USE OF (OR THE INABILITY TO USE) THE PROGRAMS, SOURCE CODE, OR TEXTUAL MATERIAL CONTAINED IN THIS PUBLICATION. THIS INCLUDES, BUT IS NOT LIMITED TO, LOSS OF REVENUE OR PROFIT, OR OTHER INCIDENTAL OR CONSEQUENTIAL DAMAGES ARISING OUT OF THE USE OF THE PRODUCT.

THE USE OF "IMPLIED WARRANTY" AND CERTAIN "EXCLUSIONS" VARY FROM STATE TO STATE, AND MAY NOT APPLY TO THE PURCHASER OF THIS PRODUCT.

Contents

ACKNOWLEDGEMENTS _____ 1

INTRODUCTION _____ 2

PART I: POCKET PC AND PDA _____ 5

Chapter 1: The World of Portable Devices _____ 7

Classifying Portable Devices _____ 9
Models of Portable Devices _____ 10
Standard Software _____ 44

Chapter 2: Operating Systems of Pocket PCs and PDAs _____ 49

Features of Palm OS _____ 50
Features of Pocket PC _____ 53

Chapter 3: Overview of Palm/Pocket PC Development Tools _____ 57

A Brief Overview of the Main Development Environments for Pocket Computers ___ 57
Why Did We Choose AppForge MobileVB and eVB? _____ 63

PART II: PROGRAMMING PALM OS WITH
    APPFORGE MOBILEVB _____ 77

Chapter 4: Installing the AppForge MobileVB
Development Environment _____ 79

Versions of AppForge MobileVB 3 _____ 80
The AppForge MobileVB Installation Procedure _____ 80
Integration with Visual Basic _____ 82
Compatibility with Visual Basic _____ 84
Booster _____ 84
Ingots _____ 85
Libraries _____ 86

IV Contents

Testing 87
Porting a Ready Application to a Pocket Computer 87
Project Settings 88
Additional Features 89
Application Compatibility for Palm OS and Windows CE 89
Databases in AppForge MobileVB 90

Chapter 5: Introduction to AppForge MobileVB 91

Creating a New Project 91
Debugging and Testing the Application 93
Compilation 93
Copying the Application to the Pocket Computer 95
The Limitations of the AppForge MobileVB Developing Environment 97
Utilities 99
Palm Emulator 101
Obtaining an Emulator 103
Installing the ROM File 104
Installing the Booster 105
Installing the Application on the Emulator 106
Gremlins 106

Chapter 6: Working with Ingots 109

Project Description 111
The *AFMovie* Ingot 123
The *AFFilmstrip* Ingot 124
The *AFSignatureCapture* Ingot 124

Chapter 7: Databases in AppForge MobileVB 127

The Database Converter Utility 128
Functions of the Module Created During Conversion 131
The Universal Conduit 134

Chapter 8: Developing an Application with a Database 141

Displaying Records 143
Deleting Records 145

Sorting Data 147
Adding a New Record 147
Editing a Record 152
Creating a Report 152
Compiling the Application 155

Chapter 9: Internet Programming 159

Project Description 159
Creating the User Interface 160
Creating the Code 162

Chapter 10: Creating Web Clipping Applications 169

The Technological Concept 169
The Limitations of Web Clipping 174
Specific Tags 174
Illustrated Examples 176

PART III: PROGRAMMING POCKET PC WITH EMBEDDED VISUAL BASIC 181

Chapter 11: Installing eMbedded Visual Tools 3.0 183

Chapter 12: Introduction to eMbedded Visual Basic 193

Creating a Demo Application 193
The Type of Variables in eVB 197
All Variables Are *Variants* 198
Other Differences between VB and eVB 199
Using Windows CE Emulators 201
And More Differences between VB and eVB 203
Note 204

Chapter 13: Working with Controls 205

Developing a Demo Application 206
Working with the Menu 217
Working with Files and the File System 222

Events, Properties, Methods, and Additional Controls
in eMbedded Visual Tools 3.0 227

Chapter 14: Database Access Programming in eMbedded Visual Basic 3.0 Using ADOCE 3.0 241

The Distinctive Features of Database Programming for Pocket PC. ADOCE Objects ___ 241
Structure of a Windows CE Database 242
Using ActiveSync 242
Currency Calculator: an Example of Using ADOCE 244

Chapter 15: Database Access Using ADOCE 3.1, ADOXCE, and SQL Server CE 1.0 285

Setting up Microsoft SQL Server 285
One Way of Installing on a Computer with Enterprise SQL Server 287
Installing SQL Server 2000 Windows CE on a Portable Device 288
Creating and Manipulating Databases Using SQL Server Tools 294
Interaction with the External MS SQL Server 302
Additional Features of SQL Queries Supported by SQL Server CE 306

Chapter 16: Communication and the Infrared WinSock Control in Windows CE 309

Project Description 309
Creating the Interface 311
Infrared Port 311
Creating the Code 312
Properties, Methods, and Constants of the WinSock Control 320

CONCLUSION 325
APPENDIX A: LIST OF USEFUL WEB SITES FOR PALM AND POCKET PC DEVELOPERS 326
APPENDIX B: ADVICE ON FURTHER ACTIONS 327
REFERENCES 328
INDEX 329

To my parents, Igor and Vera Rafalovich. Thank you for raising me with such great care. Thank you for loving me so much.

Vladimir Rafalovich

To Svetlana Dementieva who inspired me.

Vadim Kalinin

Acknowledgements

Books are like movies. Whereas actors dominate the big screen, authors claim the front cover, in either case grabbing most of the attention. But behind the authors and actors lies a large team of endless inspiration, without whom no book or movie would ever make it print or celluloid. This book is no exception. The authors are forever thankful to Svetlana Vokhmina of St. Petersburg, Russia, and Tatiana Davydova of Yaroslavl, Russia, for their technical and tireless organizational help. Thanks also go to Vladimir Nevzorov of Moscow for his research materials for the overview of Part I.

We wish to thank everyone at A-LIST Publishing, especially Natalia Tarkova and Vadim Sergeev, who managed to keep things moving smoothly.

Lastly, I would like to thank my parents, Vera and Igor Rafalovich, for their permanent interest, love and encouragement, and my daughter, Jennifer Mariah, to whom I could not dedicate as much time as I would have liked while busily working on this book.

Introduction

Portable and pocket computers are becoming available to more and more businessmen, as prices come down and the possibilities they offer increase. The ability to exchange data with a desktop PC, as well as Internet capability, make portable and pocket computers indispensable tools for daily business. As the demand for such tools grows, so does the demand for new software.

This book is one of the first manuals to deal with portable-computer programming. As not all programmers possess a portable computer, the book is illustrated as copiously as possible, to explain the use of pocket-computer emulators, and to describe in detail portable devices and the history of their development.

At the same time, the book takes a dialectic approach, describing two tools from approximately the same starting point — using them in the first steps of creating simple software, to creating databases and Internet applications. The bibliography contains a list of useful Internet sites for readers to follow up on themes of interest. Procedures for copyrighting new software ase also described, so readers can make a profit by applying the methods described here.

What Is the Purpose of This Book?

So, what is this book about and what is its target audience? The book describes two tools for developing portable-device software: AppForge's AppForge and Microsoft's eMbedded Visual Basic. Both programs are similar to Visual Basic, and can be used to create applications in the space of a few days, or even hours. AppForge is universal — in other words, it can be used to write software for devices running the Palm operating system or Windows CE — but is rather expensive. eMbedded Visual Basic, on the other hand, is limited to creating software for Windows CE devices, but is free. Both products, however, can be downloaded from the relevant web sites, although AppForge is only available as a trial version.

It is assumed that readers have at least a minimal understanding of Visual Basic. In addition, some knowledge of SQL is required for the sections working with database software.

The main aim of this book is to provide a sense of the spirit and capabilities of portable-device programming, which differs somewhat from traditional programming in being limited by technical parameters (e.g., a small display, modest processing power, limited memory, etc.). Another aim is to provide a basic guide to the two products under consideration. For example, since AppForge is a comprehensive product, but rather expensive, by demonstrating some of its features, the book aims to help readers decide whether or not to purchase AppForge for further programming work. Although the book is well illustrated, the only real way to master any application is to use it in practice. Both AppForge and eMbedded Visual Basic can be downloaded from the Internet but, since they are both fairly expansive programs, just their key features are described here.

How To Read This Book?

The book is divided into three parts, the first part is an overview, the second part is devoted to AppForge, with the third part for eVB. Naturally, the second and third sections stand alone, and can be read separately. While the techniques, functions and methods used are naturally different, the structure is the same. First, the application's general characteristics are considered, followed by simple tasks. Then, the book examines the creation of database-base applications and, finally, programs using the Internet. Below is a brief outline of the chapters that make up the book.

Chapter 1 provides a historical overview of the origin and development of portable devices, including now-defunct operating systems, e.g., Newton, and systems, such as EPOC, that are not considered further in this book. The overview starts from the very first portable devices, which were more like programmable calculators. As well as history, some manufacturers' most popular models are considered, providing illustrations and technical parameters. Also included is a classification of pocket computers by operating systems.

Chapter 2 examines the Palm and Windows CE operating systems in more detail.

Chapter 3 looks at existing software-development tools for both operating systems, classified both functionally with respect to each operating system and by the programming language on which the tool is based. For example, ToolBox can be used to create database-based applications for Palm without a single line of code; it doesn't even include a code editor. NS Basic is also considered, a product that deserves more detailed examination, which is, unfortunately, beyond the scope of this book.

The second part of the book is devoted to AppForge.

Chapters 4 and *5* describe software installation and general concepts. Additional AppForge applications — supplied with the product to help create portable-device applications — are also considered, as is the option of converting an application created for Palm to Pocket PC and vice versa.

Chapter 6 deals with specific AppForge controls, and creates a more or less functional application.

Chapter 7 demonstrates database work with AppForge, explaining each function in detail. Also examined is the concept of a conduit — a utility responsible for synchronizing a portable device's database with one on a desktop computer.

Chapter 8 provides a practical example of using databases; *Chapter 7* should be studied first.

Chapter 9 demonstrates the use of AppForge to create an Internet application, including methods of connecting to web sites. Most examples are applicable to creating Palm applications.

Chapter 10 deals with the creation of Web Clipping applications, widely used with Palm devices. A basic knowledge of HTML is required.

The third part examines Windows CE programming using eMbedded Visual Basic.

Chapter 11 deals with installing eVB on a PC, possible problems, and how to solve them.

Chapter 12 describes the differences between eVB and Visual Basic, including the limitations and specific nature of eVB. The lack of a debugging environment in eVB makes this chapter particularly important.

Chapter 13 discusses various eVB features, using them to create a calculator application. Also considered are menu procedures, working with the file system, etc.

Chapters 14 and *15* outline database work in eVB, and should be read together. *Chapter 14* gives an example using Pocket Access, whereas *Chapter 15* uses the portable-device version of SQL, which must be downloaded. Reference material is also provided.

Finally, *Chapter 16* examines using eVB for Internet work. WinSock is examined, and an application to obtain stock-exchange information from a web server is created. Also discussed is the infrared port.

The authors welcome comments on the book by e-mail: tihiydon@yahoo.com

Part I

Pocket PC and PDA

Chapter 1: The World of Portable Devices

Chapter 2: Operating Systems of Pocket PCs and PDAs

Chapter 3: Overview of Palm/Pocket PC Development Tools

Chapter 1

The World of Portable Devices

In the last thirty years, the electronic assistant of the human being — the computer — has been considerably reduced in size. In the late '70s a computer would take up an entire room, and in the 80s it would fit quite well on a table. In the late '90s, the computer felt comfortable in your palm. Many people already can't imagine their lives without such companions as their cell phone, pager, or electronic planner. Along with the evolution of the computer, new devices that we could not even have dreamt of in the recent past have appeared. For example, digital cameras that work without film appeared, cell phones became the norm, cars are built with orientation components, etc. There is an evident trend of merging portable devices with various communication devices. So-called smart phones may serve as an example, being a hybrid of a cell phone and an electronic planner.

So, what is a portable device? It seems to be something in between an electronic planner and a full-fledged notebook. Each new version of a portable device gets closer to full-size notebook computers in its functions, but their "pocket" size and relatively economical power consumption remain — a portable device can run 2–5 times longer than a notebook without being recharged.

Modern portable devices can not replace real PCs, but can perform a wide range of tasks: work with the Internet, e-mail, databases, spreadsheets, files, documents, etc. Regular applications are not suited for work on portable devices, but there are "pocket" versions developed for many of them.

Thus, a portable device is a device that gives the user quick access to necessary information, is equipped with a means of communication, and requires regular connection to a PC to synchronize the user's data and to install new applications.

A few years ago, portable computers were treated as electronic planners, or organizers, and this was pretty much the truth. Today, portable devices (Pocket PC, Handheld PC, Palm-size PC) are full-fledged computers that are much more powerful and multipurpose than simple electronic planners, and for which there are a large number of applications.

Let's trace the history of portable computers and outline these trends, revealing the rises and falls of various models of portable devices.

There is no agreed date for the invention of the Personal Digital Assistant (PDA). Some are sure that the tiny machines sprang from "intelligent calculators": In the early '80s, calculator manufacturers created dozens of models that were programmed in Basic.

Others are convinced that the ancestors of the contemporary PDA were electronic organizers. Although they appeared later, these devices were intended not only for calculation, but also for personal data management.

We mentioned in the *Introduction*, however, that portable devices are a combination of two different concepts. One is a computer based on the Palm platform, which looks like desktop planners, and has evolved from the simplest forms with a minimal memory, storing no more than two pages of typescript, into the modern devices, with a memory storing several thousands of addresses, and with a life of several years. Such devices are constantly striving to enlarge their capacity. The other branch is the attempt to reduce the PC to a tiny size. The Windows CE operating system, specially created for this purpose, which soon developed into Pocket PC 2002, is a highly pared-down version of desktop Windows. Gradually, though, these computers also expand their capacities. One thing that unites these branches is the size of the computers.

The ancestors of portable devices were the intelligent calculators that were put on the market in the late '70s and early '80s. Some had not only a numeric keypad, but also a keyboard to enter commands of the integrated Basic language interpreter. Such devices were manufactured by Canon, Hewlett-Packard and other companies.

Classifying Portable Devices

There are no strict rules about the classification of portable devices. First of all, let's clear up the terms. Palm-size PC, Palm-top PC, Handheld PC, Pocket PC, and PDA are the notions that are most often used to describe personal digital assistants. The first four models run the Windows CE operating system, while the last one runs Palm OS. Although Palm-size or Palm-top PCs are compact devices without a keyboard, handled via a press-sensitive display, and Handheld PC, on the other hand, is equipped with a small folding keyboard, they differ only slightly, especially since Palm Computing officially calls Palm (according to the Palm-size PC classification) a Handheld PC. Even more strange is the definition of "Pocket PC" that was used before the Microsoft Pocket PC operating system was put on the market.

From the programmer's point of view, the most reasonable classification is, of course, classification according to the operating system. The majority of portable devices use only one of three software cores: Palm OS, EPOC, or Windows CE; the Pocket PC operating system is a version of Windows CE.

As a rule, a company manufacturing a portable computer sticks to one operating system. Therefore, knowing the name of the device (or, rather, the manufacturer) you can predict its operating system. Only Symbol manufactures portable devices on both platforms, and only the British company Psion manufactures portable devices with a keyboard and their own EPOC operating system that stands apart from the others. These computers occupy just a few percent of the market, and are not considered in this book, other than a few words in the historical review.

Table 1.1 below demonstrates the platforms to which a certain device is related, and the companies that manufacture them.

Table 1.1. Systematization of Portable Devices

Company	Operating system	Devices
Palm computing	Palm	Palm III, IIIc, IIIx, IIIe, V, Vx, VII, VIIx, m100, m105, m125, m130, m500, m505, m515
Symbol	Palm	SPT-1500, SPT-1700, SPT-1733, SPT-1734, SPT-1740, SPT-1800
Handspring	Palm	Visor, Visor Deluxe, Visor Platinum, Visor Prism, Visor Edge, Visor Pro, Visor Neo, Treo

continues

Table 1.1 Continued

Company	Operating system	Devices
Sony	Palm	CLIE PEG-N760C, CLIE PEG-N6101C, CLIE PEG-N710C, CLIE PEG-S300, CLIE PEG-S320, CLIE PEG-S500C, CLIE PEG-T615C, CLIE PEG-T415
Kyocera	Palm	Smartphone QCP-6035
HandEra	Palm	330, TRGpro
IBM	Palm	Workpad, WorkPad c3, WorkPad C500
Samsung	Palm	1300
Compaq	Win CE	iPAQ H3100 series, iPAQ H3600 series, iPAQ H3700 series, iPAQ H3800 series
Hewlett Packard	Win CE	Jornada 520 series, Jornada 540 series, Jornada 560 series
Casio	Win CE	Cassiopeia E-200, Cassiopeia E-125, Cassiopeia EM-500, Cassiopeia EG-800
Toshiba	Win CE	e570
Symbol	Win CE	PPT-2700, PPT-2800, PDT-8100, SPS-300

Models of Portable Devices

The historical and model review offered below is aimed not only at satisfying the reader's curiosity, but also, if possible, at demonstrating the technical features of the most popular models of portable devices from various manufacturers. This review is not exhaustive; moreover, we don't claim that our review is any kind of reference. The idea here is that, for example, a programmer developing a multimedia game would be glad to know that the relatively new Palm VII portable device has a monochrome display, or that Cassiopeia E-125, thanks to its original constructive solution, enables you freely to scroll the screen top down and vice versa. Therefore, the applications developed for such a portable device can have one long form, instead of many standard ones.

One of the first popular models of semi-portable device — the semi-calculator — was the **Sharp PC-1500**, manufactured in the early 1980s. It had a liquid-crystal display with a resolution of 7×156 pixels (a 26-character capacity), an 8-bit LH5801 processor, 16 KB ROM, of which almost 6 KB were allotted for applications, and a socket for additional memory modules. It was rather small, and a number of special additional devices were developed for it.

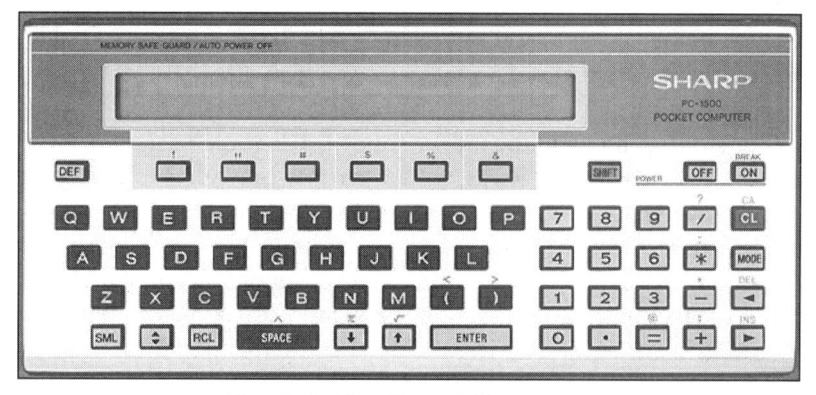

Fig. 1.1. The Sharp PC-1500

There were also special props created so that it could be connected to a tape recorder, printing devices, additional memory, etc.

At approximately the same time, however, the British company **Psion** actively made a name for itself on the market by launching its first portable device — Psion Organizer 1 — based on its own operating system, the first version of which was named SIBO.

Portable devices from Psion even now enjoy popularity as reliable, very convenient to work with, economical devices, and they have always been able to boast of exceptional design as well.

Psion was founded in 1980 by David Potter. He once recalled that he had drawn the design for the first portable device on a napkin during lunch in a Greek restaurant on Edgeware Road in London. The first portable devices from Psion were put on the market in 1984, and were aimed at both corporate and "regular" users. For example, Marks & Spencer successfully used them for inventory and control of its goods. The first organizer looked just like a calculator, had only 1 KB of memory, and a one-line liquid-crystal display.

Initially, Psion was planned by its founder as a software-development company, and Psion made its first steps (starting in 1980) in the direction of rather successful software development. Having established itself in the computer world and made back its original capital, the company turned to conquering other markets, which were practically unexplored at that time. Mr. Potter managed to see something that was not obvious to others, since the capabilities of the electronic industry and technology of that time never supposed extraordinary miniaturization, although many electronic manufacturers (such as Sharp) had started developing programmable calculators, and even a kind of micro-computer with integrated Basic interpreters.

But, in the contemporary meaning of the term, the first portable device is considered **Psion Organizer** I, created by Psion in 1984. Psion Organizer I was conceived not as just a powerful calculator with a programming language, but as a device for storing and handling information. The first model — Psion Organizer CM — had 2 KB RAM, 4 KB ROM, and a processor with a clock speed of 0.92 Hz. Outwardly, the device recalled a massive calculator with a moving hard cover, which hid a keyboard with 37 keys underneath (some models had 36 keys). The screen enabled a display of only one string of 16 characters. Applications were stored on memory cards that were inserted into two slots. The main application integrated in the computer was the database. Organizer I was very usable as a portable device: it weighed 225 g, and fit in the palm of your hand. With average use, one set of batteries served for 5 months. At $200, it was also affordable. Thus, Organizer I was the first portable information device on the market.

Psion Organizer II

Two years after the first model was put on the market, the second model, **Psion Organizer** II, appeared. Who could have predicted that this computer, which was first manufactured in 1988, is still being produced even now? This is possibly the most long-lived portable computer in the world (Fig. 1.2).

Fig. 1.2. Psion Organizer II

Table 1.2. Main Characteristics of Psion Organizer II

Parameters	Value
Manufacturer	PSION Computers
Operating system	SIBO
Processor	HD6303X 0.92 MHz
Memory	32 or 64 KB RAM (models LZ and LZ64)
Display	Alpha-numeric, 2 or 4 strings of 20 characters
Highlight	None
Power supply	9 V
Ports	2 slots for Data Pack cards, port compatible with RS232
Dimensions, weight	14.2 x 7.8 x 2.9 cm, 250 g

The larger memory size and the two-string display made it different from the first model (Table 1.2). Certain specialized computers, such as point-of-sale terminals, were based on Organizer II. It is this computer with which cashiers read barcodes.

The use of these devices in various industries urged the appearance of industrial portable devices.

By the mid-'80s, interest in portable devices receded, and the new stage of their development started only in 1989, when the **Portfolio** computer was put on the market by Atari.

The size of an average book, it was a full-fledged PC XT (Intel 8086 processor) with an operating system compatible with MS-DOS 2.2. This computer had 128 KB RAM (upgradable to 512 KB), a 40 × 8 character display, serial and parallel ports, and a power supply from three AA batteries. Among the applications, there was a spreadsheet (compatible with Lotus 1–2–3), a text editor, an organizer, etc. It was this computer that determined the appearance of all subsequent pocket machines.

Two years later, another portable device was released that became very popular — Psion Series 3. It is remarkable in the design of its elements (a folded case: one part is the display, the other is the keyboard, with a system board hidden underneath, and a sensor panel between them with 8 buttons for shortcuts to the integrated applications). This became standard for most portable devices with a keyboard produced by various companies. On both sides of the case, there are slots for expanding the memory (the SSD — Solid State Disk). Psion Series 3 portable devices won their popularity thanks to being very reliable, undemanding system resources, and having a well-thought-out SIBO operating system. The main omission of the developers of this operating system was probably the lack of support for the sensor display. Since an Intel 8086-compatible processor architecture was used, another drawback was the impossibility of compiling applications that exceeded 64 KB (fortunately, the volume of data was limited only by the size of the memory, thanks to efficient segmentation). A graphic liquid-crystal display with a resolution of 240 × 80 pixels was used.

At approximately the same time, work on the **Companion PC** (a keyboard-less organizer) was started. Companies including Microsoft, Phoenix, Lotus, and Chips and Technology tried to create a device with the Lotus Works software package integrated. Very soon, however, Microsoft issued a version of Windows 3.1 for computers with touch input, and launched its own WinPad project, which was supposed to lead to the creation of a universal keyboard-less platform. The development of the WinPad computer was based on an Intel 80386 processor, an integrated, abridged version of Windows 3.1, and was intended for manual entering of text. This project, however, has remained unfinished.

So, why have none of these portable devices become massively popular? The most difficulty turned out to be determining how they would be used.

The developers wanted to make a universal computer that would operate without having to connect to a desktop computer. Pocket machines were inconvenient for office work due to their small keyboards, and the tiny monochrome displays hampered working with the Internet, which was developing extremely quickly. This is all even more understandable taking into account the high price of the first portable devices, their incompatibility with desktop-computer software, and the instability of the operating systems.

In 1992, Apple Computer undertook the development of a new portable device with touch information input. The idea of handwritten input was implemented by this company in 1993, with the release of the **Newton MessagePad**, which for many years established the guidelines for the development of super-portable computers (Fig. 1.3).

During five years of production, the market saw the appearance of two main MessagePad families. These were models of the 1 × 0 series, numbered 100, 110, 120, and 130, and models of the 2 × 0 series, numbered 2000 and 2100.

The first Newton was a rather big and heavy device. It weighed about 400 g including batteries, which could work for about 14 hours. This portable device had a fast (relative to the time) 20 MHz ARM 610 processor, a display with a resolution of 40 × 336 pixels, 640 KB RAM (482 KB of which was allotted for the system requirements), 4 MB ROM, COM and IR ports, as well as a PCMCIA socket (type II) for various extension cards, including a modem. The processor did not cope well with resource-consuming tasks, and was very slow when the recognition system was working. The Calligrapher recognition application was developed in Russia, and worked as follows: the user wrote a phrase in cursive on the display, and the computer recognized the letters, simultaneously searching for the corresponding words in the integrated dictionary, thus automatically correcting recognition errors. The information was displayed on the monochrome touch screen by means of a special stylus kept in a groove on the computer's case.

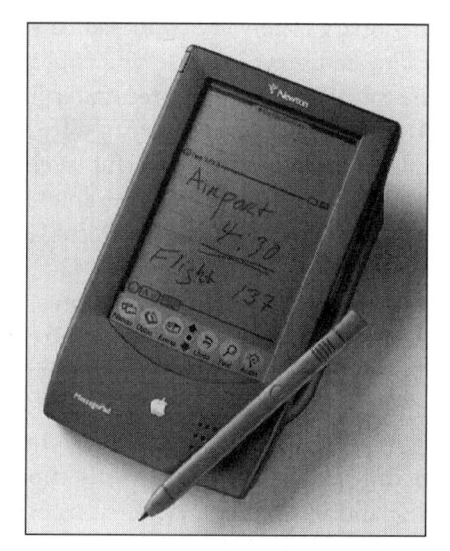

Fig. 1.3. Newton MessagePad

Beginning with Newton, the stylus became a necessary part of any keyboard-less portable device.

A bit later, a new model of this computer appeared — **MessagePad 100** — which differed from the previous one only in an improved operating system (Newton OS 1.3).

In November 1995, MessagePad 120 computers were replenished with a new version of the operating system — Newton OS 2.0 — which was a real event in the world of portable devices.

The new operating system featured a printed-symbols-recognition system that did not require a long process of handwriting recognition or a dictionary (the old version was in use alongside the new one, and users could decide which one to choose). By this time, the quality of recognition was fairly high. Later versions of Newton OS were equipped with the function of automatic image reorientation (after pressing a button in the menu, the image turned 90 degrees, which was very convenient for input, or for reading a lot of text).

This model also featured the ability to connect a special external keyboard, fax reception (previously, it was only possible to send faxes), connection to the Internet using Newton Internet Enabler, etc.

The next model, based on Newton OS 2.0, was put on the market in March 1996, and was named **MessagePad 130**. It differed from the previous model in extra lighting for the display, a new anti-glare display covering (the display had a dull luster), an expanded dictionary (from 15,000 to 93,000 words) and a larger memory (2.5 MB RAM), which allowed users to start several applications simultaneously.

In a few months, **MessagePad 2000** appeared, and a little later, **MessagePad 2100**.

MessagePad 2000 differed significantly from all of the previous portable devices produced by Apple. It included the powerful Intel StrongARM-110 processor with a clock speed of 160 MHz, which considerably enhanced the system's efficiency: text was recognized almost instantaneously. RAM was increased up to 5 MB, and the display resolution increased up to 480 × 320 pixels. The option of simultaneously using two PCMCIA cards and an integrated microphone was provided. The range of the integrated software was expanded: Internet browser, spreadsheet (not in all portable devices), etc. The design was also changed: the protective covering was not thrown back as before, but opens to the side, recalling a book. The case also got bigger (210.3 × 118.7 mm) and heavier (640 g).

MessagePad 2100 differed from the previous model by having more RAM (4 MB instead of 1 MB) and in the updated versions of the communication applications.

Apart from MessagePad, Apple also released the unusual **eMate 300**, based on Newton OS, and mainly aimed at high school students. Its design resembles a semi-transparent seashell made of bottle-green plastic. eMate was smaller than a standard notebook, but bigger than a portable device. Technically, it hardly differs from MessagePad. Its construction has interesting features: there are no electric circuits under the keyboard, and the solid case stands shocks well, but if the display or the keyboard are somehow damaged, they can be easily taken out and replaced with new ones.

The general feature of all Newton devices is the Newton OS operating system (versions 1.0, 1.3, 2.0, and 2.1). At that time, the new computer was equipped with all necessary means for efficiently working with it. Later, the handwriting-recognition system was so much improved (compared to the first models), that even now it remains an unattainable peak even for computers of the most recent generation.

The creator of the **Palm Pilot** computer — Jeff Hawkins, a former engineer at Intel and a specialist on human memory and consciousness — left his job as a programmer at GRiD Systems, having only $1 million at his disposal that he received from Tandy (founder of GRiD Systems) and from two venture companies. In eighteen months, with an additional $2 million dollars, Palm Computing released its first product: the **Zoomer** microcomputer, sold as a Tandy product. By that time, Palm was already cooperating with Casio in the hardware-development area, with Geoworks in creating the operating system, and with Intuit and America Online in developing supplementary software. Then, Palm made use of its connections with Casio and Tandy to expand the distributional channels of its products.

Until the mid-'90s, Palm Computing was involved in developing the manual-input Graffiti system, which got the cold shoulder from portable-device manufacturers.

In 1995, Palm Computing decided to start developing its own portable device, and in just a year, the **Palm (Pilot–1000)** organizer appeared. It was an extremely simple device with limited functionality. The small size, convenient system of manual input, and reasonable price (about $300) made this device very popular compared to other portable devices.

Fig. 1.4. The most popular Palm models

The range of Palm models is very diverse. Outwardly, all models of portable devices, beginning from the very first Palm Pilot, look similar (Fig. 1.4). In the course of time, only the case's form has changed, from strictly rectangular to narrowed in the lower part, and later rounded. The most popular and affordable Palm model is Palm m100. Palm m105 is a little bit more expensive, and features an expanded RAM. Palm Vx models are aimed at well-off customers: they have a solid aluminum case and an integrated lithium accumulator. Unlike the above models, Palm IIIc is equipped with a color display. All these models work with the Palm operating system, which was specially developed for portable devices. This operating system, however (or rather its core), is not the in-house design of Palm Computing, but was licensed from the implemented-systems developer Kadak.

Recently, these models of portable devices have been replaced by more up-to-date ones with the new PalmOS 4.0 operating system and the option of working with removable solid-state data carriers — memory cards.

Palm VII

On May 24, 1999, 3Com/Palm Computing put the Palm VII organizer (Fig. 1.5 and Table 1.3) with an integrated radio modem, onto the market. The release of the new device was met with enthusiasm among adherents of the Palm platform who used the Palm IIIx and Palm V models.

Outwardly, Palm VII looks similar to Palm IIIx. The new model, however, is a little bit heavier (by 10 g) than its predecessor. Apart from the previous advantages (wonderful technical characteristics, the possibility of storing a lot of useful information — addresses, telephone numbers, notes, expenses, etc.), the new model featured a completely new function — wireless communication — not only via the regular infrared, but also through a radio channel.

Fig. 1.5. Palm VII

Table 1.3. The Main Characteristics of Palm VII

Parameters	Value
Manufacturer	Palm Computing / 3Com
Operating system	Palm OS 3.1 / 3.5

continues

Table 1.3 Continued

Parameters	Value
Processor	Motorola DragonBall EZ 16 MHz
Memory	2 MB RAM, 2 MB ROM
Display	160 × 160 pixels, touch screen
Highlight	Yes
Power supply	2 AAA batteries, spare battery CP1620.
Average life of batteries	35–40 hours of continuous work
Duration of work	Up to 40 hours
Ports	COM (RS232C), Infrared (IrDA)
Dimensions	13.65 × 8.45 × 1.95 cm
Application package for the device	Date Book, Address Book, Desktop e-mail connectivity, To Do List, Memo Pad, Expenses, Calculator, Security, Games, HotSync® technology for local and remote PC synchronization
Application package for the desktop PC	Date Book, Address Book, To Do List, Memo Pad, Expenses, Desktop e-mail connectivity, Desktop import and export formats: CSV, TAB delimited, and TXT, Palm OS® 3.1 software
Additional information	Integrated radio transmitter supporting TCP/IP

The debut of Palm VII was another step ahead for the 3Com company in the area of wireless-connection technology. However, the device, generated as a hybrid of the original Palm concept and the strategic plans of 3Com, turned out to be unsuccessful. When the developers attempted to create such device, they were not able to get around the platform's limitations. The small display hampered the viewing of web pages, the relatively small memory limited options of working with information, the low-power CPU did not allow the viewing of graphics (the power was insufficient even for quick unpacking), and the "single-tasking" of the device limited the options of working on the Internet.

The new Palm VII was a sort of medley of an electronic organizer, a portable Internet browser with wireless access, and a tool for figuring out codes of car alarms and public telephones. The uses of the first item are clear, while the last one is more for criminals (3Com simplified their work by equipping Palm VII with a long-range infrared port and the options of a good computer), but wireless access to the Internet requires more attention. Palm VII combines three important qualities necessary for a portable device to work with the Internet: compactness, lightness, long-lasting batteries (two batteries should last for several weeks), and a long-range radio channel (to be able to connect to the Internet from remote places).

This model does not provide any hardware improvements compared to Palm III, except for a short folding antenna for wireless connection, which simultaneously works as a switch.

The main drawback of Palm VII was not so much in its construction as in the fact that the device could be connected only in 260 large regions of the United States (access was provided by the BellSouth Wireless Data network) and, despite the promises of 3Com, no models for GSM were created.

Palm m100

This can be considered the most popular model of all the portable devices from Palm (Fig. 1.6 and Table 1.4). While Palm m100 was being created, it had the code name Calvin.

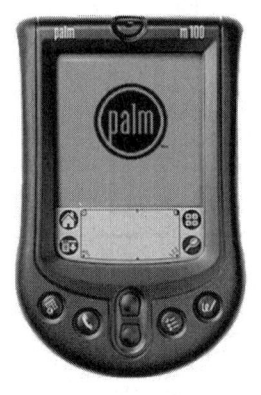

Fig. 1.6. Palm m100

Table 1.4. The Main Characteristics of Palm m100

Parameters	Value
Producer	Palm Computing
Operating system	Palm OS 3.5
Processor	Motorola DragonBall EZ 16 MHz
Memory	2 MB RAM

continues

Table 1.4 Continued

Parameters	Value
Display	160 x 160, touch screen
Highlight	Yes
Power supply	2 AAA batteries
Duration of work	Up to 30 hours
Ports	RS232, IrDA
Dimensions, weight	11.84 × 7.92 × 1.83 cm, 125 g
Software	Address Book, Date Book, Clock, To Do List, Memo Pad, Note Pad, Calculator, HotSync for synchronization with the desktop PC, other applications and utilities
Additional information	Year of production: 2000; removable front panel can be substituted for one of another color

Palm m100's original design, maximum usability, and reasonable price distinguish it from other pocket-size devices. This Palm model does not look like any of the previous ones. You have everything you need here, and even more: all standard applications (addresses, diary, calculator, and a new Notepad), an integrated, high-quality speakerphone, an infrared port to transmit data to the other devices, and even a clock that can be viewed without opening the protective cover.

The new Palm has a streamline case, as well as a cover that has the same contours and that opens easily.

The main novelty of this model is the option of using Palm m100 as a fashionable pocket watch. If you wanted to know the time with previous models of Palm, you had to open the case and switch on the device. Thanks to an original technical solution, in Palm m100, it is sufficient to press the scroll-up button (for this purpose there is an opening on the case in the form of a button (Fig. 1.7)) and see the current time and date in a special D-shaped window on the device's case. During the operation, the computer is switched on for just a couple of seconds, and then returns to a standby state. Therefore, you can see the current time in one operation, and this function makes Palm a good substitute for a pocket watch.

Actually, Palm m100 is the same Palm IIIc with several internal additions, a completely new case, and the option of changing its appearance using multicolored frames.

Fig. 1.7. Palm m100, view with closed case

The dimensions of Palm m100 are almost the same as Palm V, although the new device is twice as thick. The power is supplied by two AAA batteries hidden under the cover on the back panel. This cover is bigger than for the other Palm models, and it is more difficult to open. According to the developers' concept, such a cover should prevent the batteries from falling out if the organizer is dropped.

Palm m100's on/off switch is above the display in the middle. This is not necessarily the best place for it, but in this case the possibility of turning the computer on by accident is minimized. The scroll buttons located in the bottom are divided, as on the IIIc model. Pressing the upper scroll button activates the clock. While the device is working, pressing this button activates the highlight. The rightmost fast-start button activates not Memo Pad, as in previous versions, but the new Notepad application. Unlike Memo Pad, which is also installed on the organizer, Notepad enables you to make notes right on the display. As a result, you can quickly write down something without using Graffiti.

The buttons of Palm m100 are rather flat and slightly recessed, which practically eliminates any chances of pressing them accidentally. The labels on the buttons are done in a more "youthful" style. There is no display-contrast regulator on the side of this device, but in the Graffiti symbols input area, there is a small circle consisting of two halves — white and black — that you can press on to show the contrast regulation slider on the display.

The standard method of data exchange between a Palm portable device and a desktop PC is via a special serial cable. One end of this cable is connected to the COM port of the PC, and there is a special synchronization cradle on the other end of the cable. The portable device is set in the cradle, and the data-exchange procedure is initialized with the press of a button. In Palm m100, the old principle was violated for the first time: there is only a cable for the COM port in its kit. One end of the cable is connected to the portable device, and the other to the PC, and the button is then pressed.

A range of special products was also manufactured for m100: a connectable modem and applications for work with e-mail.

In the race for miniaturization of the new computer, the developers were compelled to reduce the size of the display yet again. Whereas the original PalmPilot and the subsequent Palm III had a diagonal length of 8 cm, in Palm V it was already 7.6 cm. The diagonal length of the new Palm m100 is 7 (!) centimeters. The feeling you get when working with it leaves much to be desired. The standard fonts integrated in Palm look even smaller than usual, and, of course, this does not increase information readability on the display.

Palm m100 runs the Palm 3.5.1 operating system. The main novelties of this model are the following:

- A very detailed integrated Help system, enabling even a novice user to master the device quickly.
- The new Notepad application. Text can be written directly on the display, without using Graffiti. You can set a timer for each note, which lets you know that a specified event is being executed by playing a sound.
- Support of quick operations with data in the applications. When the service slash "/" is entered, the panel with the icons of the main operations ("delete", "send", etc.) appears in the bottom part of the display, depending on the type of operation with data supported by this application.

Software disadvantages include the following:

- The impossibility of upgrading the operating system, as well as writing the user's applications in the free part of the system flash memory.
- In all other models, you could start the Address application and skim through the list of addresses looking for a certain name using the scroll buttons. Now you can do this only with the stylus and the scrollbar of the application. Previously, you could open any record of the Address book and look the next or previous records using the scroll buttons, but now this option is also unavailable, as is looking through a long record that doesn't fit on the screen using the buttons.

Palm m505

This is another member of the Palm family (Fig. 1.8 and Table 1.5). Palm m505 is a further (and successful) development of the Palm V-series computers. While retaining all the conveniences of Palm V, such as a light and solid case and integrated accumulators, m505 has acquired many new and even revolutionary features for the Palm family.

Fig. 1.8. Palm m505

Table 1.5. The Main Characteristics of Palm m505

Parameters	Value
Manufacturer	Palm Computing
Operating system	Palm OS 4.0
Processor	Motorola DragonBall VZ 33 MHz
Memory	8 MB RAM
Display	160 × 160 pixels, 65,536 colors, touch screen
Highlight	Yes
Power supply	Li-Ion accumulator
Duration of work	Up to 30 hours
Ports	USB, IrDA, SD
Dimensions, weight	11.43 × 7.87 × 1.27 cm, 139 g
Software	Date Book, Graffiti, Address Book, Find, To Do List, Memo Pad, HotSync Notepad, Calculator, Clock
Additional applications	AOL for Palm OS, Palm Reader, Documents To Go v3.0, MGI PhotoSuite, AvantGo, Mobile Connectivity Software, powerOne Calculator, PocketMirror v3.0, Palm Desktop Software v4.0 for Windows
Additional information	Year of production: 2001; reliable, solid metal case

Palm m505 has a new type of clear, easily readable display, which supports 65,536 colors.

First, 505 differs from its predecessors in the availability of a USB, which considerably accelerates data exchange with a desktop PC. The availability of an expansion slot for a MultiMedia Card, the first time in Palm devices, allows memory expansion, since 8 MB is very often insufficient. The reflective color display is a little too dim when working with the highlight, but perfect with bright external light. Palm m505 was equipped with a new operating system — Palm OS, version 4.

It is the background that makes the display of the m505 model completely different from all other portable devices with color displays. The background in m505 is not white, but rather a "light-gray metallic". Consequently, the color icons look as if they were pastel. All colors on the m505 are bright and well discernable. The light-gray background provides a feeling of "color depth". Most importantly, such a color display strains the eyes much less, and among all the available color devices, it is probably the most readable.

Indoors, the display of the m505 (without the highlight) looks different. For example, under a luminous tube it looks monochrome (the icons look as if they were drawn with colored chalk). Nearer to a window, the general appearance of the display changes: the background becomes brighter, and the icon colors reveal themselves more brightly. In both cases, the m505's display is easily readable.

You can use the highlight in the m505 both in the dark and in the light. In the first case (twilight, darkness, etc.) the display looks like those of color portable devices: bright, with an almost white background. The color of the icons changes as well: the "pastels" disappear, and become simply color. When used in the light, the highlight also behaves differently, depending on the general conditions of illumination. Under some conditions, nothing is changed, while under others, the "light angle" issue must be dealt with — i.e., with average illumination, you can slightly turn the device to have the light falling on the display, or simply switch on the highlight (the display will not become brighter, but it will be very clear).

The only drawback of the m505's display is the lack of brightness and contrast regulators.

There is only one application in the m505 for work with MMC/SD cards: Card Info. It performs several simple functions (including giving information concerning the free space on the memory card and enabling formatting and renaming). Copying the application from the main memory of the device to MMC/SD card (and back) is done using the standard launch menu. Starting the applications is implemented as follows: select the **Card** category from the drop-down list of the standard launch categories (in the top right corner). A window will be opened in which the icons of the applications on the MMC/SD card will appear. If there are many applications written on the card, then the process of opening the **Card** window may take a long time, since to execute this query, the device must scan the whole card. There is another inconvenience: you can select the **Card** category only from the standard Palm launcher, since it may be invisible in other launchers (e.g., LaunchEM).

Among the variety of software for the memory cards, there are three particularly interesting applications: McFile, PowerRun, and MSMount.

McFile is simply a multi-functional file manager for RAM//MMC/SD cards.

The interface is a tree of the directories, subdirectories, and files. Naturally, there are new/copy/move/rename/delete options. There is also the integrated Text Viewer for .txt files. You can send files saved on MMC/SD cards as attachments to e-mails. You also have the option of backing up all data from the main memory on MMC/SD cards.

There are many settings in the application that enable it to be customized for a specific user: it can show either everything available in the open directory, or applications that have been launched, installed hacks, DF applications, texts in DOC format, etc.

This application is necessary for quickly moving files from the main memory to the memory card (and back), as well as for creating special directories on the memory card that will be required by applications that have access to MMC/SD cards.

Another interesting application in Palm m505 is Power Run.

First, a few words about the basic way of starting applications on MMC/SD cards. An application recorded on an MMC/SD card cannot be started directly. First, the launcher copies the application to the main memory, and only then starts it. This process is hidden from the user, and takes about a second. After work with the application is completed, it is automatically copied back to the MMC/SD and deleted from the main memory. There are a lot of subtleties there, but this is basically how it is done.

Power Run fully automates the starting process from the MMC/SD card. PowerRun does this much quicker than the software integrated for this purpose and — also important — it is performed "by addresses", meaning that when you work with PowerRun, you don't need to wait until the full list of applications on the MMC/SD card is loaded to start just one application.

The PowerRun application creates real "labels" that can be seen and started from any launcher. The label looks like a regular icon, but with a square in the bottom left corner of the icon, and an asterisk in the right corner. You can move the labels to any category of the launcher, and any label — like any application in the main memory of the device — can be assigned a hardware button.

Therefore, by their functionality, the labels are the same as icons of common applications. To start an application, just push the label with the stylus.

There is another nuance of PowerRun. The application has the option of controlling the automatic deletion of the application from the main memory after it has been used. At the start of the label/application, PowerRun gives the message: "Loading ...". After exiting the application, PowerRun gives the message: "Cleaning ...". If for some reason PowerRun cannot delete the application from the main memory, it will inform the user.

It is also interesting to note that PowerRun works not only with applications, but with their databases as well. In other words, when an application is copied from the main memory to the MMC/SD card, PowerRun copies both the application and its associated databases. Later, when the "label" is started, the application and the databases are copied to the main memory. After the work is completed, the application is returned to the MMC/SD card with updated databases (as a result of working with them).

Using PowerRun, you not only have the option of starting applications from the MMC/SD cards "with a press of a button" and of freeing up the main memory of the computer, but also of solving the task of saving data, since even if the power is off, both the applications and the databases on the MMC/SD card remain secure.

PowerRun considerably simplifies the user's life, but still works according to the rules set by the developers of the m505 (starts applications by the system MMC/SD card -> RAM -> MMC/SD card). In another application — **MSMount** — a completely approach to using data on the memory cards is implemented. The application allows you to work with large, non-updated databases located on the MMC/SD cards *without copying them into the main memory*.

Here, by "non-updated databases", we mean those associated with a particular application, but not updated in the course of work with them. These are, for example, dictionaries, encyclopedias, books or databases containing pictures, etc.

The uniqueness of MSMount lies not only in that it can work with data located on the MMC/SD card without transferring it to the main memory, but also that many applications originally not intended for work with memory cards can now cope with this task perfectly.

MS Mount was successfully tested with the following applications: iSilo, Tomb Raider, KDIC, Dictionary, and Liberty.

So, after installing McFile, PowerRun, and MSMount on your Palm m505 (with a total size of only 151 KB), you can considerably expand the functionality of the MMC/SD cards with the option of starting the applications from the memory cards "with just one push", the option of working with large databases without copying them into the main memory of the computer, and the option of making use of applications that could not work with the MMC/SD cards before.

So far, we have considered several models of the wide range of portable devices that run the Palm operating system. Now let's consider another group of portable devices, running the Windows CE operating system.

The Windows CE operating system is used in many devices, from Pocket PC and Handheld PC up to gas stations and microwave ovens. It cannot be compared with Windows for desktop PCs or servers. You can not install it yourself on your computer from a CD ROM. Windows CE is a built-in system for certain hardware platforms, and is compiled from various modules, e.g., from the user interface, the application programming interface (API), drivers, the processor, etc.

The developers take Windows CE, and according to the Pocket PC's reference design, create a unique version of the software (the reference design describes the availability or absence of the keyboard, the display size and resolution, the hardware buttons, and much more). So, the Pocket PC software consists of the Windows CE operating system, the Pocket PC user interface, the API, drivers, and applications (Pocket Word, etc.).

"An efficient, scalable operating system for a very wide range of applications" said Bill Gates about the new operating system.

The fundamental difference between the portable devices based on the Microsoft Windows CE operating system and those based on Palm is in their higher functionality. The Pocket PC computer features many more options than Palm.

The variety of Pocket PC computers is no less diverse than that of Palm, but apart from keyboardless devices with touch screens, there are also models that have keyboards.

The Windows CE operating system has a micro-core created with NT technology, and a graphic interface that is a simplified version of the Windows GUI. The first versions of Windows CE supported processors of many types (Hitachi SH3/SH4, NEC 41xx, MIPS, Motorola PowerPC, ARM, and Intel 486 and later). Hardware/software sets based on the Windows CE operating system are called PalmSize PC (with Windows CE 2.0 installed), and were initially equipped with monochrome displays. The next version — Windows CE 2.1x — introduced color displays to the world of portable devices. Since the end of 2000, Microsoft has been promoting a new platform, Pocket PC (Pocket PC 2000), also based on the Windows CE operating system, this time version 3.0. The complex software for Pocket PC consists of a Windows CE operating system, the Pocket PC user interface, the API, drivers, and a package of user applications (Pocket Word, Excel, etc.). Windows CE is quite reliable, since it is a multithread system with displaced multitasking, similar to Windows NT. One of the main advantages of this system is the compatibility of documents created on the portable device with Office 97/2000 applications. Devices that work on this platform provide full access to the Internet, mainly thanks to the simplified version of the standard IE Pocket Internet Explorer integrated into the ROM, and make it possible to send or receive e-mail via two standard protocols: POP3 or IMAP4. There are many applications created for Windows CE, but many of them are not thought out well enough to compete with the standard software of this operating system.

One of the big disadvantages of Pocket PC portable devices is their high power consumption and relatively short working time (7–8 hours), due to their integrated accumulators. The use of lithium batteries, however, will rectify the situation, but, compared to portable Palm devices, the autonomy of the Pocket PC is very limited.

Let's consider some models of these portable devices.

The most popular portable devices are manufactured by Casio, and combine the functions of a business organizer and those of a pocket entertainment center. They achieved their status thanks to their very fast, bright, and high-contrast liquid crystal TFT display, which reproduces more than 65,000 colors. All models of Casio portable devices are equipped with a very simple but ingenious cursor control device — the Action wheel — which performs several functions. By turning the wheel in a certain direction, you can emulate the Up and Down buttons, and pressing on the wheel is like pressing Enter. The convenience of such a control is appreciated when you only have one hand free to use the portable device, and such situations are not uncommon when working with portable computers.

Cassiopeia E-125 Pocket PC

This is a rather advanced device similar in appearance to a Palm device that works with Windows CE 3.0 (Fig. 1.9 and Table 1.6). Cassiopeia E-125 is equipped with COM, infrared, and USB ports, which makes connecting to many peripheral devices possible. You can also work well with more or less up-to-date cell phone models.

Table 1.6. The Main Characteristics of Cassiopeia E-125

Parameters	Value
Manufacturer	Casio
Operating system	Windows CE 3.0
Processor	32-bit processor NEC Vr4122 Mips 150 MHz

continues

Table 1.6 Continued

Parameters	Value
Memory	32 MB RAM + 16 MB ROM
Display	Hyper Amorphous Silicon TFT, 65,536 colors, 320 × 240 pixels
Highlight	Yes
Power supply	Li-Ion accumulator, AC adapter, standby power supply: battery RS2032
Duration of work	8 hours
Ports	RS232C, IrDA 1.2, USB
Dimensions, weight	13.1 × 8.35 × 1.99 cm, 255 g
PDA software package	Mobile Calendar (ROM), Mobile Address Book (ROM), Menu (ROM), CF Backup (ROM), Mobile Video Player (CD), E-Mail Set-Up Tool (ROM), AOL Dialer (ROM), AOL (MAIL) (WEB), ZIO Golf Demo 3D (CD), MS: Pocket Word (ROM), Pocket Excel (ROM), Pocket Outlook (ROM)
PC software package	Palm Data Converter (CD), Mobile Video Converter (PC) (CD), Mobile Video Picture Viewer (PC) (CD), Audible (CD), MS: Mobile Favorites Synch Provider (CD), Notes Synch Provider (CD), Transcriber (CD), USB Synch Component (CD), Outlook 2000 (CD)
Additional information	Extension slots: Compact Flash Type I/II, sound: integrated microphone, speakerphone, headphones socket

Fig. 1.9. Cassiopeia E-125

The software supplied with the computer supports audio reproduction (MP3 and WMA) and video files. Cassiopeia E-125 has an integrated speakerphone and a microphone, as well as a headphones socket, and can work without recharging for 8 hours. Also, working from an AC socket is possible (the batteries are charged simultaneously). It weighs 255 g.

If you compare Cassiopeia E-125 with its predecessors — E-100, E-105, and E-115 — you will see that there is practically no physical difference between them. All models have the same form, weight, and size.

The case color and USB support not withstanding, one definite improvement in the new model was the processor. The previous NEC Vr4121 MIPS processor had a clock speed of 131 MHz. Now, Cassiopeia has an NEC Vr4122 processor with a clock speed of 150 MHz. Users may not notice the difference in the performance of this portable device compared to previous models when working with the standard Pocket Outlook applications, but this model works twice as fast when using Microsoft Reader, Pocket Word, or Pocket Excel. Cassiopeia E-125 possesses enough power to start several applications simultaneously, but if you start 4 or 5 applications simultaneously, its efficiency falls abruptly. However, this is a problem with practically all portable devices.

Cassiopeia could always boast of its perfect display, since it has the brightest and clearest liquid-crystal display of any portable device, and the E-125 model is no exception. Moreover, it was equipped with an improved display (Hyper Amorphous Silicon TFT), which was first tried on the EM-500. The display became a little brighter and more readable in daylight than that of the E-100 and E-105.

Cassiopeia E-125, with its fast processor, colorful display, and the CompactFlash Type II slot, has recently been one of the most popular models, but even this third-generation product has some disadvantages.

The E-125's angular form can't exactly be called up-to-date, since it strongly resembles the first Handhelds.

One representative of a very fashionable trend is the multimedia **Cassiopeia EM-500** portable device, based on the E-125 business model. This positioning of the computer is stressed by the letter "M" in the name, and a case with corners slightly more rounded than in other Casio models, made in various colors: dark blue, green, yellow, and red. There is a special insert of soft, semi-transparent plastic provided on the right side of the case, which not only improves the appearance, but provides additional comfort for your fingers. The stereo headphones socket in the upper part of the EM-500 makes it very convenient to listen to music when walking with the portable device placed in the cover on your belt or in your pocket. There were only two changes introduced from the E-125: the memory size was reduced by 50% (down to 16 MB), and the more compact SD/MMC slot took the place of the Compact Flash slot, which made it possible to decrease the price slightly.

Another model, the **Cassiopeia E-200**, specially developed for the latest Pocket PC 2002 platform from Microsoft, is one of the latest in Casio's range of portable devices. In this model, Casio rejected its perfect HAST TFT display, giving up its live and rich colors for the option of reading outdoors and prolonging battery life. The cursor-control joystick in the new model was moved from the corner (which distinguished all older Cassiopeas from models of other manufacturers) to the lower middle part of the case. The E-200 has a CompactFlash Type II extension slot covered by a plastic plug positioned on the upper edge of the device, and a SecureDigital/MultiMediaCard (SD/MMC) slot on the left side. One very interesting feature of the E-200's synchronization and recharging cradle that no other competitors yet have is the USB Host interface for connecting peripheral devices (mostly) printers and standard keyboards, as well as mouses, DVD/CD ROM drives, and much more. No doubt the availability of the integrated hub even in the cradle allows this portable device to take one step closer to the functionality of desktop computers.

The mid-price pocket manager **Cassiopeia BE-300** is aimed at filling in the niche between the very cheap Pocket Viewer models and the more expensive Pocket PCs. It is based on the 64-bit NEC VR4131 processor with a clock speed of 166 MHz, capable of executing up to 280 million operations per second. When the BE-300 was developed, the main idea was to reduce the price, while retaining the maximum number of functions. To achieve this, the infrared port and the loudspeaker were sacrificed. The BE-300 is equipped with a color display (a passive STN matrix) with a resolution of 240 × 320 pixels, reproducing 32,768 colors. It measures 8.13 cm diagonally, slightly less than that of typical Pocket PC displays. The pause before the display gains its nominal brightness after switching on may also be considered a disadvantage. Apart from the integrated CompactFlash Type II slot, the additional module, which is mounted on the case of the device and recalls the jackets used in the Compaq iPAQ, can be used for PC Card extension cards.

Lately, portable devices from Compaq have become more and more popular. Compaq offers compact, but at the same time powerful-computers (it was the first to use Intel Strong ARM processors with a clock speed of 206 MHz in a portable device). The range of Compaq models contains many iPAQ models, which are based on the Pocket PC platform and differ only in numbers.

iPAQ H-3630 is a color model, with 32 MB ROM. **iPAQ H-3660** has 64 MB. **iPAQ H-3130** differs from its "color relatives" in that it has black control buttons.

Chapter 1: The World of Portable Devices

In all iPAQ models, the operating system and installed software are stored in the 16 MB Flash ROM, which drastically simplifies the procedure for upgrading the operating system. The touch display in the color iPaq models can reproduce up to 4,096 colors at a maximum resolution of 240 × 320 pixels, and it is perfectly readable even in direct sunlight, thanks to its reflective matrix. The adjustable, milky-colored highlighter makes iPaq screens readable under any illumination, be it indoor light or pitch darkness. The brightness of the display is either set automatically, using the sensor on the front panel, or manually, via the settings panel.

All iPAQ models, however, suffer from the fact that dust can easily get under the glass protecting the display. Unlike Palm, which has a special section for text entry, with iPAQ — like all portable devices running Windows CE — the entire display is intended for showing graphics, considerably expanding the visible area of the display but reducing the lifetime of its cover, which is subject to scratches from the stylus. Also, it is the first series of portable devices to use integrated lithium-polymer accumulators, which provide for extended operation without having to recharge. At the same time, the impossibility of having the power supplied by batteries may also be considered a certain disadvantage, when added to the lack of a spare battery for feeding the memory when the main batteries are completely dead — data can easily be lost.

Compaq rejected integrated slots for extension cards of any type in order to reduce the weight of the device and the case's dimensions, especially its thickness. Instead, it decided to use special Expansion Jackets, which provide the device with considerable power to support peripheral devices of various types. Currently, these include a universal PCMCIA adapter, for connecting many PC Card-format devices, the slot for CompactFlash Type II cards, a GSM telephone module, a GPRS satellite-navigation-system receiver, and even a TV tuner. All this, however, costs a lot of money.

The latest series of Compaq iPAQ H-38xx portable devices, running the Pocket PC 2002 operating system, feature additional flash memory (Intel StrataFlash, 32 MB), which is used to avoid data loss from the RAM when there is no power, and for storage of a backup of the user's most important information. Currently, the series includes two models: **H-3850** and **H-3870**. The second device is almost the same as the first one, but includes a Bluetooth wireless-connection port.

The Compaq 38xx series differs from the previous devices only in some slight superficial changes, a more powerful accumulator (1500 mA/h, as compared to 950 mA/h in the H-36xx models), and, what is more, the new models now have an extension slot for the SD/MMC memory cards, since the extension jackets did not prove successful. The separate socket for the circuit AC adapter was also eliminated, and moved to the cradle. However, iPAQ models can be charged independently via the synchronization port; for this purpose, there is a special adapter provided in the package that is inserted into the power adapter.

Another representative of the Pocket PC class worth mentioning is **Jornada 420**. This portable device has a color touch display that is narrower than regular portable devices, and a keyboard that is positioned vertically. Because of this, the Windows screen is "squeezed" on the sides, and the menus appear to overlap each other.

Jornada 420 is a useful tool for heavy PC users who want to have all the necessary addresses, telephone numbers, notes, texts, e-mail, and web sites always on hand. New information entered in Jornada during the day can by synched onto the desktop computer in the evening. To do this, insert the portable device into the cradle, and the new information (telephone book, diary, calendar, notes, e-mail) will be automatically copied into the corresponding sections of Outlook (or Schedule 7a+). The information from the desktop computer is similarly synchronized with the portable device. Using this approach, the information on the portable device and on the desktop PC is always identical, and no manual work is needed to synchronize the data. When the portable device is placed in the cradle, the Li-Ion battery is automatically recharged.

The interface of many Jornada applications replicates the appearance of Outlook. For all its outward simplicity, Jornada 420 is an efficient and convenient computer. It features a color display, a processor with a 100 MHz clock speed, the option of remote access to the modem via cell phones, many third-party applications, an upgradable memory, and standard In/Out ports.

Jornada 525

In spring of 2001, Hewlett Packard released a new model of a portable device based on Windows CE.

This device is a miniature computer that easily fits into your pocket, so you can carry it with you anywhere. The HP Jornada 525 (Fig. 1.10 and Table 1.7) allows you to work pretty much anywhere. It not only enables you to keep your everyday business schedule, but also to perform any job when you are out of the office.

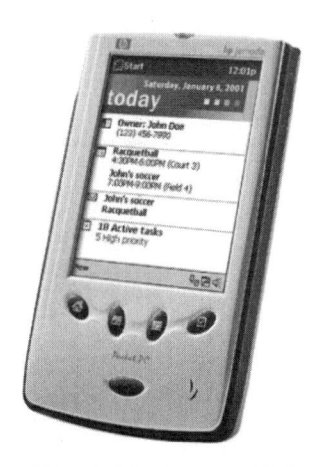

Fig. 1.10. Jornada 525

Table 1.7. The Main Characteristics of Jornada 525

Parameters	Value
Manufacturer	Hewlett Packard
Operating system	Microsoft Pocket PC (Windows CE 3.0)
Processor	32-bit Hitachi 7709 SH3 133 MHz processor
Memory	16 MB RAM, 16 MB ROM
Display	(Diagonal 95 mm) color CSTN, 256 colors, resolution 320 × 240, highlight
Highlight	Yes
Power supply	Non-detachable Li-Ion accumulator (8 hours of continuous work), spare power source (5 days), AC adapter
Duration of work	8 hours
Software for pocket operating system	Outlook, Pocket Inbox, Pocket Word, Pocket Excel, Pocket Internet Explorer, Microsoft Reader with ClearType (Audible Support), Notes, Windows Media Player, Channel, Calculator, Active Sync 3.1, File Explorer, Voice Recorder, Windows Media Manager for Pocket PC. Software: ROM Landware Omnisolve, Socket Communications Ethernet Driver, Peacemaker, HP Settings, Backup, Home, Task Switcher, game buttons, HP Security. Software on CDAOL: Mail, Yahoo Messenger, Music Match (desktop), Sierra Image Expert CE 2.0, Phatware HPC Notes 3.03 lite edition, HP Jetsend 2.0, Inso QuickView Plus 2.0, Microsoft Expedia Pocket Streets

continues

Table 1.7 Continued

Parameters	Value
Ports	serial (RS232C), infrared (IrDA)
Dimension, weight	7.8 × 13.2 × 1.77 cm, 226.8 g
Additional information	Extension slots: 1 for CompactFlash type I
Sound	Speakerphone and microphone, socket for headphones
Synchronization	Serial cable (540), USB Cradle (545), Serial Cable and USB Cradle (548)

Jornada 525 is equipped with the special "pocket" versions of Microsoft Outlook, Word and Excel packages, so you can edit spreadsheets on a plane, for example, or enter text in Word on the beach listening to your favorite compositions in MP3 while simultaneously recording voice comments as some useful ideas come to mind. In addition, this computer is equipped with everything necessary for an Internet connection. You can send and receive e-mails, find out the latest news, currency exchange rates, and much more. Finally, when relaxing, HP Jornada allows you to read a book on its perfect display with rich, clear colors, play a game, or surf the web. Moreover, to upgrade the portable device, you can add memory or additional accessories using the integrated Compact Flash slot.

The composed design, the powerful 133 MHz SH-3 processor, 16 MB memory, the 256-color touch-screen display, the digital dictaphone, and the entire set of the software demonstrate that, on the one hand, Jornada 525 is merely a simplified version of Jornada 545 but, on the other hand, that it is one of the cheapest color PDAs that possess the necessary minimum of features and efficiency.

Apart from the regular controls of a portable device, including a stylus (a pen and four shortcut buttons), Jornada features a wheel button almost identical to Casio's. The developers, though, failed to provide the convenient joystick ring. The integrated digital dictaphone, traditional for all devices based on the Pocket PC platform, is also very convenient. Recording is activated by pressing a button on the side, but any kind of manipulation of the recording can only be done by programming methods.

The more up-to-date **Jornada 545/548** portable devices, which differ only in the size of the memory — 16 and 32 MB, respectively — is a logical development of

Jornada 525. Although the number of colors supported by the CSTN display reached 4,096, this is insufficient for models that claim the title multimedia. Jornada 545/548 weighs 260 g, making it the heaviest of the models under consideration. At the same time, it has a solid case made of metal, and not of cheap, brittle plastic. In addition, only Jornada devices possessn the incontestable advantage of a tip-up removable cover, protecting a non-working display from being damaged.

Jornada 565/568 are new-generation portable devices from Hewlett Packard running Pocket PC 2002, and became pioneers in the promotion of this new Microsoft product. They differ only in the size of the memory: the older model has 32 MB, whereas the latest one has 64 MB. The display of the new model does not yield to its competitors in either the number of colors reproduced or in the availability of the supported functions, one of the most important of which is the option of switching it off completely, which makes the batteries last longer when, say, listening to MP3 files. The microphone is positioned on the lower end of the case. Here it is more convenient to work with the applications on the display using the navigation joystick. The upgrade options, however, are the same as previous models'. The considerable reduction in the weight and dimensions of Jornada 565/568 was gained by giving up the metal case and by using a lithium-polymer battery, which is removable (unlike the Compaq battery) and is located on the rear side of the device. The sides and lower end of the device are equipped with the rubber strips (like bumpers on a car) preventing the computer from slipping out of your hand.

Like Pocket PC portable devices, Handheld PC pocket computers also run Windows. To meet various user needs, there are four types of Handheld PC, which differ in their design and size: devices with a half VGA screen and integrated keyboard ("shells"), devices with a full screen and integrated keyboard, plotting boards, and enhanced-reliability devices. All Handheld PCs support wireless-access technology. There are many companies involved in the production of such portable devices, of which the most recent is **Handheld PC 2000**.

Handheld PC 2000 is a device from Microsoft. The basis of Handheld PC 2000 is the Windows CE 3.0 operating system with expanded functionality. Users of Handheld PC 2000 have "pocket" versions of Word, Excel, PowerPoint, Access, and Outlook available to them, as well as an integrated client of Windows 2000 Terminal Services, enabling them to work with the full-scale desktop versions using wire and wireless connections, a browser compatible with Internet Explorer 4.0, and Windows Media Player, supporting the Windows Media and MP3 formats.

Usually, Handheld PC portable devices are used both for collection of form-based data and full-scale desktop applications, and as portable web devices. This class of devices features the following:

- The option of instantaneous switching on and off.
- The battery provides power during the workday, and while using a wireless connection.
- Higher reliability due to the absence of traveling components.
- Simplified support thanks to protection of the basic operating system and applications from accidental shock (they are located in the ROM).
- The option of working access to all business information, e-mail, documents, calendar, contacts and tasks outside the office, as well as the option of further synchronization. Handheld PC computers provide a platform for corporate portable applications, and do not replace laptop devices.

The advantages of Handheld PCs include:

- The execution of form-based business applications provides a range of advantages compared to the paper carriers: faster and more accurate data collection, enhanced efficiency, accelerated creation of business reports required for decision making, reduction of operational costs, such as reduced data-entry time.
- Using a Handheld PC as a "thin" client for access to full-scale applications that work on the connected Windows 2000 Terminal Server reduces workload and costs thanks to centralized application support for mobile users.
- The viewer installed on Handheld PC 2000 is compatible with Internet Explorer 4.0, and provides mobile users with access to the Internet and its applications anywhere, which considerably enhances efficiency.
- The Microsoft Windows CE operating system has a familiar interface.
- Handheld PC portable devices running Windows CE come with popular Microsoft applications in portable-device versions. Such applications provide continuous working access to information and corporate resources, providing employees with considerable competitive advantages.

Cassiopeia A-11 is one of the first Handheld PC portable devices running Windows CE. It was released in November 1996.

Cassiopeia A-11

One of the novelties of Cassiopeia A-11 (Fig. 1.11 and Table 1.8), which is also available in the Compaq PC Companion, is the blinking indicator to remind users, for example, about the time of a planned appointment. The notification key switches off the warning signal. Compaq PC Companion is clearly not as good as Cassiopeia A-11, even before taking into account the latter's "switch on" and "switch off" keys. It also features a perfect keyboard with backlined keys. This device is easily opened, and is slightly smaller and lighter than the HP 320LX.

Fig. 1.11. Cassiopeia A-11

Table 1.8. The Main Characteristics of Cassiopeia A-11

Parameters	Value
Manufacturer	Casio
Operating system	Windows CE 2.0, supports MS Office files
Processor	Hitachi SH-3, 40 MHz
Memory	6 MB RAM, 8 MB ROM
Display	Monochrome, 480 × 240 pixels, 16 gradations of gray
Highlight	Yes
Power supply	Ni-MH accumulators or 2 alkaline batteries
Duration of work	20 hours

continues

Table 1.8 Continued

Parameters	Value
Ports	Serial (RS232C); Casio Data Port, infrared (IrDA 1.0)
Dimension, weight	175 × 91 × 25 mm, 380 g
Software package	BFAX, QV Camera Connection, SkyTel Messenger, PageCard for Windows CE, Virtual Courier, LandWare Financial Consultant, Maple for Windows CE. Standard Microsoft Windows CE 2.0 applications
Additional information	Extension slots: 1 for PC cards (PCMCIA). Integrated microphone, speakerphone, headphone socket, integrated modem

Like the Compaq system, this model is equipped with a socket for connecting a digital camera (an additional cable is needed). To exchange data with a Casio QV Digital Camera, separate software is needed (we did not test this function).

The main advantages of Cassiopeia A-11 are: perfect sensitivity to the stylus, the display highlight, the bright and contrast symbols.

The small size of the display is one of the disadvantages of this device. Like its Compaq equivalent, Cassiopeia A-11's contrast regulator is external, requiring frequent adjustment. There are also additional styluses — since the stylus is attached on the outside, it is easily lost.

If you need to write down information and make appointments in places unsuitable for work with a regular computer, this device will come in handy, especially if you can use a wireless modem.

Hewlett Packard was one of the first manufacturers of portable devices running DOS, with models such as HP 95LX, 100LX, and 200LX. Then, multiple improvements took place in both hardware and software, and were implemented in the Pocket PC and Handheld PC portable devices.

In the new version, Windows CE applications look the same as in Pocket PC, but the interface has become simpler and clearer. Along with additional applications, Hewlett Packard added an updated version of its HP Viewer, which shows contacts, a diary, and a calendar on one screen.

Compared to modern portable devices, the first HP 300-series Palmtop had rather modest performance specifications and a high price, but nevertheless was very popular. After the 300 series, the HP 360 LX model appeared, in which the far-from-perfect Windows CE 1.0 operating system was replaced with the streamlined Windows CE 2.0.

The next step for HP was implementing color support, based on Windows CE 2.0. As a result, the HP 620 LX model appeared — the first portable device with a liquid-crystal display, supporting 256 colors. The HP 660 LX model, equipped with a special PC Card-standard modem with reduced power consumption, came to take its place. Both models had a dictaphone with a loudspeaker integrated as a standard option. Among peripheral devices, a card for connecting an external monitor was introduced. Also, touch keys for opening an application and a special settings panel were provided. A little later, a new generation of the portable devices based on the Windows CE 2.11 operating system appeared. The range of portable devices from HP was supplemented by the promising Jornada family, all of which run the integrated Microsoft Windows CE 2.11 operating system. Some of them are described below.

The Hewlett Packard Jornada 600 series PDA is a large, heavy device. It more likely fits in with briefcase computers than with pocket ones, since it weighs almost as mush as a notebook computer.

At the same time, HP Jornada 680 is the smallest device based on Windows CE Professional Edition. Jornada 680 is a pocket-size device running Windows CE that has a convenient keyboard and integrated modem. It also has a very elegant design. The front panel contains silvery buttons for controlling the dictaphone (you can use it when the computer is switched off). A sliding lock protects these buttons from being accidentally pressed while in a pocket or bag. The main difference between Jornada 680 and previous models is the integrated V.90-standard hardware modem, and good upgrade potential. Apart from the serial RS232 and infrared ports standard for such devices, Jornada has Compact Flash Type I and PC Card Type II slots.

Power is supplied either by the ion-lithium accumulators (up to 8 hours of continuous work) or the AC adapter. The cradle is used for synchronization with the desktop computer.

Jornada 720 is another model of this class.

Jornada 720

While HP Jornada 720 was being developed (Fig. 1.12 and Table 1.9), Hewlett Packard in part used the solutions tested on the previous-generation model, Jornada 690. Jornada 720 is much faster than its predecessor. It has an improved operating system and faster hardware. The sound that comes from the loudspeaker is much better in quality than in the 690 model, but seems somewhat muted, since it comes from beneath the device. The sound in the headphones is much better, richer, and louder than in Jornada 545.

Fig. 1.12. Jornada 720

Table 1.9. The Main Characteristics of Jornada 720

Parameters	Value
Manufacturer	Hewlett Packard
Operating system	Windows for Handheld PC 2000, v.3.0
Processor	High-efficiency 32-bit RISC processor Intel StrongArm SA1110 206 MHz
Memory	32 MB RAM
Display	640 × 240 pixels, 256 colors, 2D accelerator
Highlight	Yes
Power supply	Rechargeable Li-Ion battery. One spare tablet battery 3B CR2032. AC adapter
Duration of work	9 hours
Software package Microsoft Windows 2000 for portable devices	Version 3.0. of the operating system, Microsoft Word, Microsoft Excel, Microsoft PowerPoint, Microsoft Access for portable devices. Microsoft Outlook (calendar, ToDo, contacts, Inbox) for portable devices. Version 4.01 of Internet Explorer for portable devices. Microsoft Windows Media Player for portable devices, Microsoft Voice Recorder, Microsoft Terminal Server Client, HP Jornada viewer, remote access, settings, backup, shortcuts, quick access panel, power supply, security, and data exchange. HP ChaiVM 4.1.2. LandWare OmniSolve business calculator. Online chat client. Yahoo! Messenger for instant message exchange with friends and colleagues, as well as for receiving news, exchange rates, etc.

continues

Table 1.9 Continued

Parameters	Value
Ports	RS232, Fast IrDA, RJ11
Dimensions, weight	18.9 × 9.5 × 3.4 cm, 510 g
Additional information	Extension slots: 1 for PCMCIA II, 1 for Compact Flash type 1, 1 for SmartCard Reader
Modem	56 bit/sec v.90
Sound	Integrated microphone, loudspeaker, headphone jack

The power of this portable device comes from the 206 MHz 32-bit RISC processor Intel StrongArm. HP Jornada 720 runsMicrosoft Windows for Handheld PC 2000, version 3.0. It is equipped with a 6.5-inch LCD display with a 2D graphics accelerator and 32 MB SDRAM. Jornada 720 has perfect upgrade options. For this purpose, there is one slot provided for PC Cards Type II and one slot for CompactFlash Type I cards. A very interesting solution is the availability of a socket for a portable device for reading special smart cards (Smart Card Reader), used to refuse anyone not possessing the corresponding smart card to access data. The enhanced multimedia options of Jornada 720 made it appropriate to install sockets for stereo headphones, to play, for example, MP3 files. The standard modem is 56,000 bit/sec (V.90). Apart from the operating system, the software includes: Pocket Office (Outlook, Word, Excel, Access, and PowerPoint), Microsoft Internet Explorer for Handheld PC (version 4.01), Microsoft Windows Media Player for Handheld PC, Microsoft Voice Recorder, Microsoft Terminal Server Client, Yahoo! Messenger (message exchange in real time), and other applications. ActiveSync is used to synchronize data between the portable device and a desktop computer, and the synchronization itself is performed via the USB or serial port on the docking cradle. Users can also synchronize data via the infrared port or via the network, if there is a network card available. The connection to the network can be either wired or wireless.

HP Jornada 720 allows storage of the most recent versions of files, which provides the necessary flexibility and power, regardless of time or location.

A highly efficient processor, a high-speed data bus, and a 2D graphics accelerator provide quick access to important information. To accelerate performance, there are shortcut icons for opening applications, as well as programmable hotkeys, and synchronization with a desktop or portable PC to actualize the working data.

Thanks to Microsoft Internet Explorer, version 4.01, it is very easy to navigate the web. For intensive work with the web, there is a special power-control function provided, which maintains the connection with the display switched off, receives notifications of new e-mail messages, and lets the user continue working. HP Jornada 720 weighs about 500 g, and can be carried in a pocket or in bag.

To prevent unauthorized access to confidential information, the portable device is equipped with a password option. File security is maintained by the integrated HP backup application that saves data on the memory card.

Despite the small size of the keyboard, it is convenient for typing. The light plastic stylus fits perfectly in the hand, although it could have been heavier. The display is readable under any illumination, except for bright and direct sun, but even then is quite operable.

Standard Software

Let's take a brief look at the applications usually supplied with a portable device. For illustration, we'll use a portable device running the Pocket PC operating system. To start applications, navigate between windows, and to perform other operations, you need to press only once on the display with the stylus. Since the display is small, it is impossible to have several windows opened in cascade or beside each other. Therefore, only full-screen mode is used.

The display of a device running Windows CE 2.11 resembles Windows 95, with the **Start** button in the bottom left corner, and with an X and/or OK button in each application. However, this design is not particularly convenient for a portable device. The operating system does not provide integrated office applications, since they must be installed additionally. The version 3.0 interface is friendlier, but with some changes to the design. To close the application, the OK button in the upper right corner is used. A button analogous to **Start** is in the upper left corner, marked with the Windows logo. Most application menus are in the lower part of the display, along with the **New** menu, to start certain applications specified in the control panel settings quickly. The applications are a simplified version of the MS Windows software, and perform most office functions.

First, the device can serve as an organizer. After booting up, the **Today** window appears, with tips on the main tasks to be done during the current day, and with "one-click" access to the applications specified by the user. The first time the device is started, these are the calendar, user info, a list of tasks, and sent or received mail (Fig. 1.13). The main menu is called by pressing the Win sign (Fig. 1.14). In this menu, the user can change the settings of the **Today** panel that will appear when

Chapter 1: The World of Portable Devices   45

the computer is loaded. To set the main menu, use the **Start-Settings-Personal-Menus-Start** Menu (Fig. 1.14).

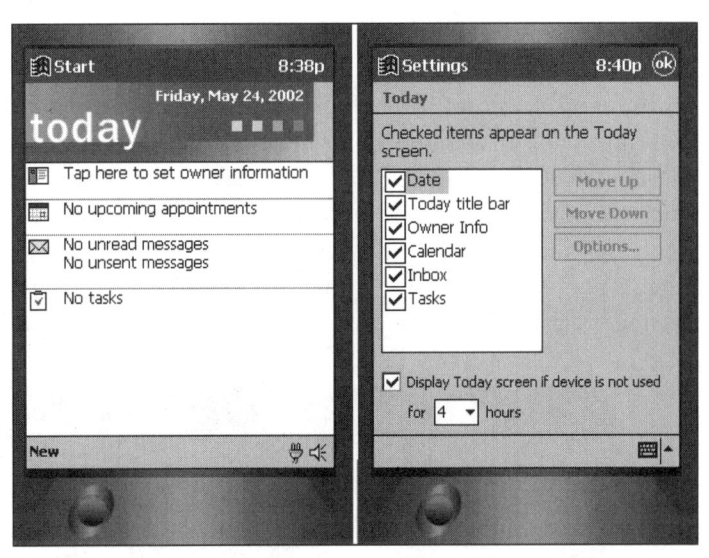

Fig. 1.13. The appearance of the display with Windows CE 3.0. On the left — when loading, and on the right — the settings of the **Today** panel

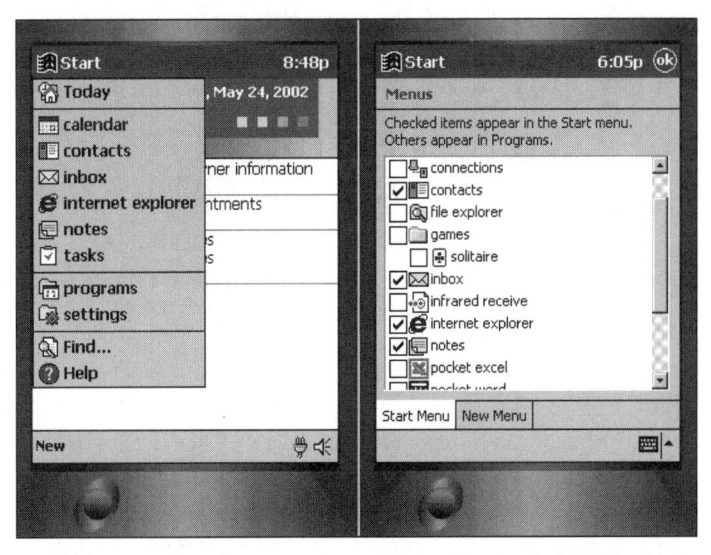

Fig. 1.14. The appearance of the display with Windows CE 3.0. On the left is the main menu, and on the right is the main menu settings panel

Fig. 1.14 shows the applications selected by default in the main menu. Most of these applications are electronic-organizer components — the calendar, notes, tasks, a notebook with a file search system, help, and the applications specified in the main menu — as well as Internet Explorer (Fig. 1.15) and a mail application (Fig. 1.16). The latter is simple, but features many useful functions. In its setting options, Internet Explorer resembles Internet Explorer 3.0 for a desktop PC. The user can establish a connection with the Internet, choose a homepage, select the time for which links and visited pages are archived, choose a language, and reproduce sounds, pictures, and applets. It is also possible to specify the size of the image and the address display. The application is simple, but, considering the limited options of a portable device, rather advanced. Users are not limited to only viewing special web sites, as with a Palm or a second-generation cell phone.

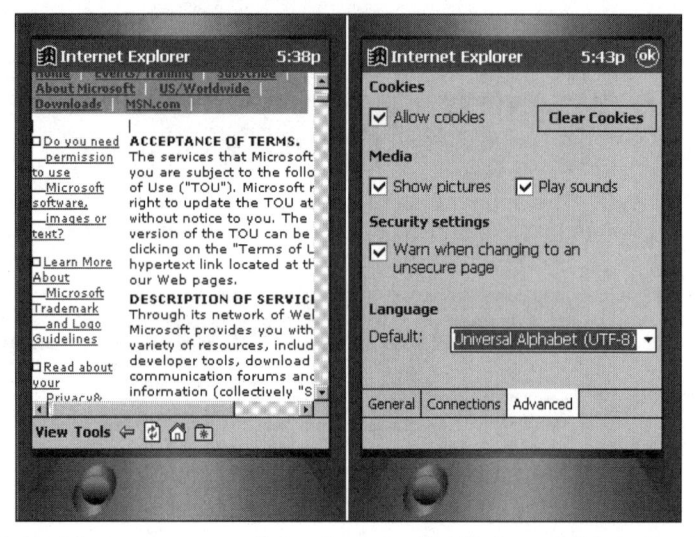

Fig. 1.15. The appearance of the display with Windows CE 3.0. On the left is Internet Explorer browser window, and on the right are the settings

The **Programs** menu is used to access other applications specified in the menu. File Explorer (Fig. 1.17), a simplified version of Explorer for a desktop PC, is used to access all other applications and files. MS Office 2.11 is not supplied, but version 3.0 and later is. The office applications are selected by the manufacturer. If Microsoft applications were chosen, or Pocket MS Office was purchased separately, Pocket Word and Pocket Excel are present (Fig. 1.18). These applications are reduced but operable versions of the equivalent desktop programs. Many Compaq devices are

Chapter 1: The World of Portable Devices   47

equipped with software from Compaq and third-party manufacturers. One version includes Audible, an audio-book player, and Picture Viewer, for viewing graphic files, etc.

Fig. 1.16. Windows CE 3.0: Letter editing

Fig. 1.17. Windows CE 3.0: File Explorer

Fig. 1.18. Windows CE 3.0: Pocket Excel

The design and purpose of all the above applications correspond to those for desktop PC, and data exchange with the desktop PC is performed via the synchronization tools. Pocket Outlook and MS Reader are supplied separately. Pocket Access comes only with Handheld PC Pro. For other portable devices, database access is performed with the help of user-created applications.

One of the most important components of the portable computer is ActiveSync, used to establish a connection with a desktop PC via a cable or an infrared port and use information stored on it, or, on the other hand, to copy information onto the desktop PC. While this application is working (which is possible only if the same application is running on the desktop PC, and a cable, modem, or infrared connection is established), data from Word, Excel, Access, etc., is converted from the portable-device format into that of the desktop PC, and vice versa, enabling users to use texts, spreadsheets, and databases, and to enter or read fragments of information for the desktop PC.

Of the other applications, the calculator, solitaire, and the graphics editor are also worth mentioning. The control panel (**Settings**) is used for setting the portable-device software. This component is used to establish a connection, set menu types, change the appearance of the **Today** panel, and make other changes to the available menus and applications. One feature of a portable devices is that the operating system and hardware settings are installed in the flash memory, and can't be changed simply by going into the **Control Panel**. This enhances the foolproof characteristics of the system, since all unwanted changes can be cancelled by simply resetting the device, but it reduces its flexibility, hampering updating of both hardware and software.

Chapter 2

Operating Systems of Pocket PCs and PDAs

This chapter will concentrate on the Windows CE (Pocket PC) and Palm operating systems, and specifically their differences and characters.

The availability of only two main types of portable devices (Palm Pilot and similar PDAs, and Pocket PC) has long been the situation. Even a user unaware of the details, or a passer-by who wandered into an electronics store to wait out the rain and decided to fiddle with some of these devices, would easily be able to tell the difference between them. These differences are seemingly not going away, nor are they insignificant or accidental.

These two families of pocket devices have absolutely different origins. If Palm descends from electronic organizers (or PDAs — Personal Digital Assistants) and is aimed at being utterly simple, intuitive, and compact (fitting in both your hand and in your pocket), the Pocket PC (or Windows CE) family is more like a diminished version of a real PC, with the same power and versatility, but much smaller.

It was only a few years ago that the Palm operating system was installed in 90% of all pocket devices, but these statistics changed quickly after Microsoft launched its new, compact operating system — Pocket PC. First, many users who were used to their PCs found no problems with the familiar interface. In addition, the wide variety of new business tasks required varied software, as well as relative power and processor speed. As well as this, there appeared users who, like moths fluttering toward the light, were attracted by the color display and the various multimedia options offered by Pocket PC.

Nevertheless, there are many specialists who need to use typical procedures everyday, and who thus value simplicity, speed, and usability more highly. For example, doctors prefer to have simple Palm devices with an automated search function, instead of delving into volumes of reference literature in search of the right dosage of a medicine, and so they really have no need for a Pocket PC with its power and multimedia capabilities.

Features of Palm OS

While this book was being written, Palm OS version 4.1 was put on the market. Compared with previous versions, certain new options were introduced, such as a virtual file system, wireless connection to telephones, SMS, color for Web Clipping applications, enhanced display color rendering, etc. Few changes, however, were introduced into the basics of the operating system. The Palm concept remained the same: usability, mobility, solving a limited circle of tasks, but doing it all very well! Fig. 2.1 shows the initial screen appearance of a Palm device. Now the reader will be able to understand more easily the variety of pocket devices, having narrowed things down to two operating systems and their various versions (see also Figs. 2.4–2.6).

Fig. 2.1. Palm PDA

Below is brief description of the features of the Palm operating system. The core of the system was developed by Kadak, which sold the license to Palm

Chapter 2: Operating Systems of Pocket PCs and PDAs

Computing . One feature of the operating system is its strict adherence to a certain platform, type of processor, memory size, display, etc. Such hardware limitations, however, are the power behind this operating system. Thanks to its initial implementation on only one platform, the Palm pocket computer is much quicker than competitors' systems, and has the same processor power. The core of the Palm operating system supports multitasking, but the operating system itself can not make use of these functions, due to licensing restrictions. Therefore, only one application can be started at a time in the Palm operating system. The app;ication will be the operating system's main task, and only the interface of this application will be displayed. The first versions of Palm OS had 16 MHz Motorola processors, 128 KB RAM, and 512 KB ROM. The latest models still use the Motorola processors, but are much upgraded (Dragonball type, clock speed 33 MHz, RAM up to 8 MB, and ROM up to 4 MB).

All the software supplied by the developer (for Palm OS 4.1, Address Book, Date Book, Clock, To Do List, Memo Pad, Note Pad, Calculator, etc.) is integrated into the ROM just like the operating system. Therefore, upgrading or changing the operating system is possible only by changing the module. Additional applications copied to the device from a personal computer are loaded into the RAM, and are directly executed from there.

As for the screen display, the earlier versions of Palm OS supported only shades of gray. The latest versions are not much better. Even one of the newest devices — Palm i705 with OS 4.1 — is still monochrome. The best achievement is support of a display of 65,000 colors, which is still way behind the options of pocket computers with the Pocket PC operating system. The supported display resolution is 160 x 160.

Since version 3.5, Palm has supported sound reproduction in MIDI format.

A considerable influence upon the technology's development was exerted by the introduction of the Graffiti system of character entry in the earliest stages of Palm's development. Users, however, must learn how to enter the characters, but this is much easier than it is to make a pocket computer recognize the entered characters. Fig. 2.2 shows the Graffiti letters for the English alphabet, and Fig. 2.3 shows those for the Cyrillic one, for the sake of curiosity.

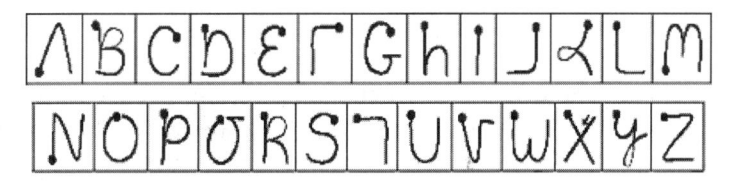

Fig. 2.2. Graffiti for the Latin alphabet

Part I: Pocket PC and PDA

А	Б	В	Г	Д	Е	Ё	Ж	З	И	Й
∧	6	ß	Γ	D	ε	ε∧	⌡	Z	U	U∧

К	Л	М	Н	О	П	Р	С	Т	У	Ф
∝	L	M	N	O	h	P	C	⌐	ɣ	O∧

Х	Ц	Ч	Ш	Щ	Ъ	Ы	Ь	Э	Ю	Я
X	V	C	W	S	I⁄	I∧	I	ε	σ	R

Fig. 2.3. Graffiti for the Cyrillic alphabet

Everything entered with the stylus is immediately displayed on the screen, and can be corrected if a mistake is made. The input area (the lower part of Fig. 2.1) is divided into two independent zones: the left one, where the letters are entered, and the right one, for numbers. For example, if you enter "0" into the left zone, it will be converted into the letter "O", and if you enter the same character in the right area, it will be taken as the numeral "0".

The idea of simultaneous use of the screen as the means of reading and entering information has been very successful, and the Palm's main competitor — Pocket PC — began developing alternative systems. As well as hand-written text (entered by drawing with the stylus on the screen), in some applications (e.g., Notepad), information can be entered using the characters on the keyboard display.

One of the advantages of the Palm operating system is its ability to interact and exchange information with a personal computer. For this purpose, the standard computer needs to have a special application installed that can perform a HotSync procedure (data exchange), and, from then on, everything is easy and reliable (the process is activated by pressing a button on the Palm device's cradle).

Simplicity and reliability are also features of the Palm OS devices when it comes to an Internet connection. Starting with the Palm VII model, the modem is inserted into the PDA, providing a connection with the Palm.Net company server. The modem can also be an accessory of another device. You can even connect to a cell phone via the infrared port or a cable. Note that, by using a cell phone (which, in turn, should have an integrated modem), you can set up a wireless Internet connection with any provider, including the one you use at home or in your office. The wireless Internet connection integrated, for example, into Palm VII, is possible only through the service provided by Palm for an extra monthly charge. Since the wireless Internet connection is limited in its speed and is rather expensive (the minimum charge for a service plan with a wireless Internet connection in the U.S. was $10 in 2002 to transfer just 50 KB of data monthly, and each subsequent byte cost 20 cents), the Palm company developed the special Web Clipping technology, which, first of all, allows the transfer of only the necessary text, and second, the compression. This considerably reduces the time of receiving the necessary information, but limits opportunities that companies participating in this technology have. However, there are more than 600 companies that already support Web Clipping, and they are listed on the Palm web site. In fact, the wireless Internet connection only became possible with the launch of Palm VII, which had 2 MB of writable Flash ROM, making it possible to upgrade the operating system.

Installing the appropriate applications and accessories can connect the Palm device to the 802.11b local wireless network, and work with it at a distance of up to 150–300 feet.

Features of Pocket PC

Microsoft's operating system for portable devices has also had an eventful existence. First of all, there were modifications of Windows CE (Compact Edition). The first devices (with Windows CE 1–2.11) were of two types. One was called PalmSize, because Palm devices had already entered the market, and this name stressed the size of the computer. Fig. 2.4 shows this device's start-up screen. This type of device became the basis for contemporary pocket computers that use the Pocket PC 2002 operating system. Another type of pocket computer is the Handheld. The main difference is in the size of the devices and, consequently, in the sizes of their screens (320 × 240, as opposed to 480 ×240);

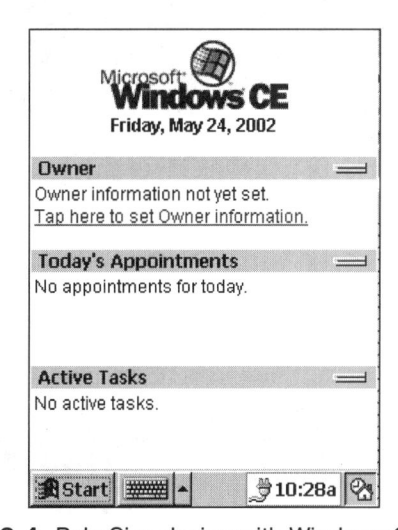

Fig. 2.4. PalmSize device with Windows CE

the latter models have an external keyboard, making them similar to small notebooks. Fig. 2.5 shows the display of a Handheld emulator with a range of applications from the special compact issue (Pocket Word, Pocket Access, etc.).

Fig. 2.5. Handheld computer with Windows 2.11

The latest (2002) pocket computers are equipped with the Pocket PC 2002 operating system (which, from here on, will be referred to as Windows CE where appropriate). Fig. 2.6 shows the original display of the Pocket PC operating system, which came to take the place of Windows CE.

Fig. 2.6. A computer with the Pocket PC operating system

When talking about a pocket computer with the Windows CE operating system, we mean a real computer, but of small size. The Pocket PC operating system is very similar to the desktop version. Indeed, a pocket computer may have many portable versions of the software usually used on a "big" PC: Word, Excel, Internet Explorer, etc., each of the applications featuring many options and settings. Of course, this does not simplify the usability of a Windows CE pocket computer, but it makes it almost as powerful as its desktop parther. This is the Windows CE philosophy: the more power and universality, the better.

Despite the possibility of upgrading any parther particular application at any time, upgrading the operating system was difficult, if not impossible. This is also applicable to Palm devices, as the operating system was integrated into the ROM chips. There is no hard disk in a pocket computer and, as a result, protecting the operating system from user errors (like system-file deletion, etc.), as well as the option of restoring the system to the developer's specifications, was provided for. It is impossible, however, to upgrade the system by writing other files to the ROM. Upgrading and even changing the operating system became possible only after rewritable ROM modules appeared.

The Windows CE display is saturated with colors, and features a high resolution; this is another obvious advantage over Palm OS. This enables efficient use of multimedia for which there are a multitude of portable applications. It is also possible to record (and reproduce) speech using pocket computers, i.e., to make sounds. From the programming point of view, the least attention in such devices should be paid to formatting or converting the image files for the applications; they will look just the same as on a regular PC.

The procedure for entering information is the same in a pocket computer as in Palm. It is done either on the display, or by pressing with the stylus on the corresponding character of the pop-up keyboard, or by using a character recognition application similar to Graffiti. In any case, when characters are entered, tips pop up, trying to guess the word being entered, which naturally accelerates the process. Moreover, when specific words or names are entered that were not in the system before, it saves them and can produce a corresponding tip later on.

To synchronize the data of the pocket computer with a PC, the ActiveSync application should be installed on the latter. Many users say that this is probably the weakest point in Windows CE. Sometimes the software can hardly, recognize the connected device and communicate with it.

As with Palm devices, pocket computers with Windows CE can connect to the Internet. One option is connecting to a wireless provider using a cell phone. Another variant is an attached wireless modem with an integrated antenna, or, lastly, you can use a standard modem connected to a telephone line.

The newest models of pocket PCs are provided with the latest OS, based on Windows CE — Pocket PC 2002. It differs a lot from both Windows CE and its predecessor, Pocket PC 2000. First, it works only with Intel processors of the StrongArm family — the most powerful ones in use today for pocket computers. Second, it supports Virtual Private Networks (VPN), has more reliable protection against unauthorized access, the option of remote server control, and the option of upgrading the operating system as new versions appear. Third, it has enhanced communication opportunities: a new file manager with access to system files has been introduced, the new Windows Media Player supports streaming audio and video, and the Internet pager MSN Instant Messenger is also now present.

At the same time, you still have to double click on the display in order to open a file or start an application. This is not always convenient when you have to do it with such a small display. Also, you can not print files: to do this, you have to copy them to a PC.

In this chapter, we described the two operating systems used in pocket computers. We are in no way trying to answer the question of which system is better. On the contrary, we have stressed the peculiarities of each, and it is up to the user to decide which goes best with his or her everyday tasks.

Chapter 3

Overview of Palm/Pocket PC Development Tools

Here, we give a brief description of the most popular programming tools for developing pocket-computer applications. The development environments are classified by both the language type and by their applicability to certain operating systems. We will give a detailed consideration of two popular Visual Basics, and justify using AppForge and eVB.

A Brief Overview of the Main Development Environments for Pocket Computers

Although the active history of pocket computers and PDAs stretches for just over eight years, there are a number of programming facilities that enable you to create applications for portable devices. Before describing these facilities, let's consider what kinds of applications for pocket computers can be created in general.

First of all, there are the standard applications that operate locally on pocket computers. Usually a Graphical User Interface (GUI) is created, and, possibly, a database (the latter is not obligatory). The codes of these applications are executed as a result of the user's actions, and are therefore called *event driven*. Such applications have the Palm Resource (PRC) extension in Palm devices and EXE in Pocket PC. Most applications require a set of special supporting files to provide for the operation of an application on a Palm or Pocket PCs. The set of such files (sometimes called virtual machines) depends on the developer's tool with which the application was created. This is not something new or extraordinary. This is how it works with any standard application created on Java or VB. For example, you cannot just copy an EXE file to the PC. You also have to copy a set of Dynamic Link Libraries (DLL) files as well.

Another type of application (applicable only for PDA with the Palm operating system) is Web Clipping, used specifically for work with the Internet. This technology was created with the purpose of saving expensive time on a wireless connection to the Internet, and accelerating data-block transfer. The essence of these applications is that, during a PDA's communication session with the Internet service provider, data transfer is performed through the intermediate proxy server Palm.Net, where all these data are compressed and only then go to the server or customer. The applications themselves (web sites, in a certain sense) are not loaded from the server, but are locally present on Palm. Creating such applications is analogous to creating common HTML files (of course, there are specific tags — see *Chapter 10*), with further compilation done using the free Web Clipping Application Builder utility. As a result, a file with the Palm Query Application (PQA) extension is created, and can be viewed using the Palm browser (Web Clipping Application Viewer).

The last type of application for pocket computers are the so-called conduits. Although these are applications for the pocket computers, they operate on PCs, and are used for data and application synchronization between the PC and the pocket computer. These applications can be created in any programming language, such as Visual Basic or C++. They are then entered into the application controlling the synchronization process (HotSync for Palm and ActiveSync for Windows CE) — the manager. AppForge provides the developer with a general conduit that can be changed if necessary, whereas the Palm Conduit Development Kit (CDK), which can be downloaded from the site **www.palmos.com/dev/tech/conduits**, enables the developer to make more profound changes in the conduit.

Let's now turn to an overview of the programming facilities that will enable the development applications for pocket computers. For convenience, below is a table (Table 3.1) classifying the tools by both the operating system in which they can be applied and the type of programming language on which they are based.

Table 3.1. A Classification of Programming Facilities

Name of application	Palm	Windows CE	Type of language
Palm SDK	Yes	No	C++
Code Warrior	Yes	No	C++

continues

Chapter 3: Overview of Palm/Pocket PC Development Tools 59

Table 3.1 Continued

Name of application	Palm	Windows CE	Type of language
Various PRC-Tools	Yes	No	C++
PocketC	Yes	Yes	C
VisualAge Micro Edition	Yes	No	Java
Waba	Yes	Yes	Java
CASL	Yes	Yes	Pascal
AppForge MobileVB	Yes	Yes	Visual Basic
NS Basic	Yes	Yes	Basic
Satellite Forms	Yes	Yes	Visual Basic/C
Pendragon Forms	Yes	No	no codes
PDA Toolbos	Yes	Yes	no codes
eMbedded Visual Basic	No	Yes	Visual Basic
eMbedded Visual C++	No	Yes	C++

Although this list is quite exhaustive, it probably does not contain some utilities or applications that are being developed or available in beta versions. However, it contains all programming facilities that currently allow the creation of more or less full-fledged applications for pocket computers based on Palm or Windows CE.

Let's consider the listed facilities and indicate the corresponding web sites of the developers, where you will be able to find more detailed information.

Palm SDK

(www.palmos.com/dev/tech/tools)

This is one of the first facilities used for creating applications for Palm PDAs. This software was developed by Palm, and intended for C/C++ programmers. Users need a compiler, which can be borrowed from Code Warrior or PRC Tools.

Code Warrior

(www.metrowerks.com)

This is also one of the "oldest" and most popular tools for developing applications for Palm, and has its own compiler. According to the developer's web site,

80% of all applications for Palm are developed with Code Warrior. Using this environment, full-fledged applications for Palm OS can be created, including wireless ones and those that use databases.

PRC Tools

This is a well-engineered programming facility, meant for C++ programmers, for Palm OS, and has a compiler. There are several companies developing this product. One of them is located in Norway (**www.falch.net**), and has a quite comprehensive Internet site. Another version of the programming environment is developed in Germany (**www.vfdide.com**). Finally, the very well-engineered environment PilotMag enables you to create forms for PalmPilot, and has a very convenient interface. You can download this and other applications created using PilotMag from the web site **www.members.tripod.com/pericak/**.

PocketC

(**www.orbworks.com**)

This developing environment is also meant for C programmers, but differs from the others in that you have the option of writing applications directly on the pocket computer using the text editor. PocketC makes it possible to create applications for both operating systems (Palm and Windows CE), as well as to develop applications on both a pocket computer and on a Windows-based PC, with the subsequent transfer of the executable file to the pocket computer.

VisualAge Micro Edition

This product was created by IBM and is based on a cut-down version of Java. It is used to develop applications for Palm OS. To make applications created for a pocket computer operational, a Java Virtual Mashine with a size of about 150 KB is also needed. The application supports only Palm OS, but the development can be done on both Windows and on Linux.

WABA

(**www.waba.com**)

WABA is an independent development environment for pocket-computer applications. It is a special language that is a cut-down version of Java, with its own virtual machine. Nevertheless, programmers can use Java tools to create WABA applications. Applications developed using this tool can be used on both Palm OS and Windows CE devices.

Compact Application Solution Language (CASL)

(www.caslsoft.com)

CASL stands out a bit from the competition. It is based on a language that resembles Pascal in its syntax. The software has a convenient interface that enables you to develop applications, including creating forms. It works on both Windows PCs and on Macintosh, provided the latter has VirtualPC installed. There are two versions of the software: standard (CASLide) and professional (CASLPro). The software (PRC files in particular) is compact, and does not require runtime files.

Satellite Forms

(www.pumatech.com)

Satellite Forms is one of the most successful Rapid Application Development environments (RADs), and makes it possible to create applications for Palm and for Pocket PC 2002. Although the main purpose of this environment is to create applications using databases, it can also create wireless applications. It is based on a language similar to Visual Basic, but there is also an SDK for C. The software has an improved development environment with a large number of options that allows the creation of serious applications. All this has a cost, of course — about $1,000.

Pendragon Forms

(www.pendragon-software.com)

This product is similar to the previous one, but supports only Palm, and can hardly boast the same universality. However, it is well suited for creating applications for data collection and data transfer between a PC and a pocket computer. The only problem is that, apart from the software, you also have to purchase runtime licenses, which make the product rather expensive.

PDA Toolbox

(www.pdatoolbox.com)

PDA Toolbox enables you to create applications with no code, and is mainly intended for creating applications with databases. Due to its simplicity and uniqueness, we will consider this product later in more detail. It truly allows users to learn to create applications for Palm OS in just a few minutes, so no programming experience is needed at all!

Nice and Smart Basic (NS Basic)

This language was originally intended for creating applications for the Newton platform, and it dates back to 1994. In 1998, versions supporting Palm OS and Windows CE appeared. Thus, the software is now available in three separate versions for each platform. Because of NS Basic's considerable similarity with Visual Basic and its slightly "underground" nature (Newton OS), this product will also be considered in more detail below, for it may certainly be of interest to some.

AppForge MobileVB

(www.appforge.com)

This relatively new product has become more popular thanks to two factors: its full compatibility with Visual Basic (it is actually an Add-in in VB) and its support of the two main pocket-computer platforms: Palm and Windows CE/Pocket PC. The second part of the book is dedicated to this product.

eMbedded Visual Basic

This product is developed by Microsoft, making it immediately of interest. Although it supports only Windows CE/Pocket PC, any VB programmer can immediately start working in it due to its external similarity to the familiar VB environment. Of course, eVB is a limited version of VB, as will be discussed in detail in *Part III*, which is dedicated to this product.

eMbedded Visual C++

This Microsoft product allows the development of the most complex applications for Windows CE/Pocket PC, including device drivers. With it, you can create DLL libraries and other components that can be activated from eMbedded Visual Basic.

Why Did We Choose AppForge MobileVB and eVB?

This question was basically answered in the previous section of the chapter. Here, we would like to add that our goal was to write a book about pocket PC programming primarily for VB programmers, or those interested in quick application development without low-level details. In addition, since 95% of the modern pocket PC fleet consists of devices with Palm OS and Windows CE, the software should by all means support both platforms. Although the first version of AppForge supported only Palm OS, the second version supports both. In itself, this already leaves many other developing tools lagging for behind. No other software, however, can match AppForge MobileVB for the power and variety of its functions. Of course, the AppForge virtual machine takes up a lot of space, and the applications operate somewhat slower than equivalent programs created, for example, with NS Basic, but AppForge is free from some of the other restrictions and inconveniences of NS Basic, and serves as great introduction to pocket PC programming. The product is moderately priced (about $500) and is sold for each operating system separately and also for both together.

At the same time, we could not leave out eVB, which, though a little weaker in power and options than AppForge MobileVB, is distributed for free, and does not even require the standard version of Visual Basic on the developer's computer. A VB programmer needs no time at all in order to master applications with this tool, since it is identical to the standard VB 6 (see *Chapter 12* for the differences and limitations of eVB).

Introduction to PDA Toolbox

PDA Toolbox's original and unique nature is due to the fact that it is available for any PDA user, who might have no experience in or knowledge of programming at all, to solve his or her specific programming tasks. Today, this is the simplest facility that allows the creation of full-fledged applications for Palm. Apart from its simplicity, and the fact that a created PRC file does not need any supporting files or virtual machines whatsoever, the product only costs about $25. The necessary widgets have integrated functions; you just need to select from the list. This makes code completely avoidable, and no code editor is provided in the software.

In light of this, we could not resist the temptation to say a few more words about this product.

The best way to understand PDA Toolbox within five pages is to create a simple application, which should give you an idea of the development environment and its features. The web site **www.pdatoolbox.com** contains some rather detailed educational material, and allows you to download a trial version of several MB. After the software is installed and started, the simple interface of the development environment appears, with the property window of the new project and a simple menu (Fig. 3.1).

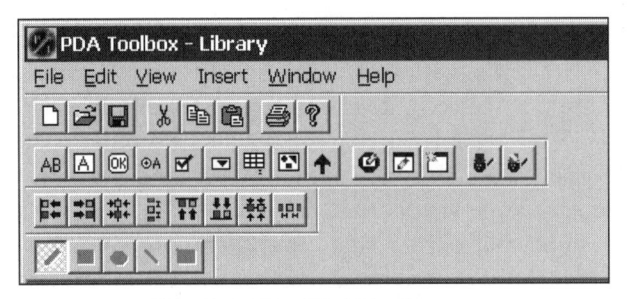

Fig. 3.1. The PDA Toolbox menu

The first line is standard, and serves for opening and saving projects, as well as performing some editing operations. The set of buttons on the left in the second line are the project widgets.

They are (from left to right):

- Label
- Field
- Command button
- Option selection radio button
- Checkbox
- A pop-up list with items that you can either determine during the process of development or select from the database
- A table widget, which allows several messages from the table to be displayed simultaneously
- The Digital Ink widget, which allows you to enter text with the stylus on the screen of the pocket computer
- Shift Indicator

The following three buttons are used to manipulate the project forms and their properties, the rightmost one being used to compile the project and create the PRC file.

The third line of buttons formats the widgets on the form. It may seem unnecessary to display the formatting functions in a separate line, but there is a reason for this. Small forms imitating the display size of the actual pocket computer prevent you from aligning the fields, labels, etc., by eye. The lowest line is used to create and edit the icons associated with the application being created.

Creating a New Project

Let's consider the procedure of creating an application used to store an inventory of a home library. On starting the procedure, a window containing its general properties will appear, into which the necessary information for identifying the future application should be entered (Fig. 3.2).

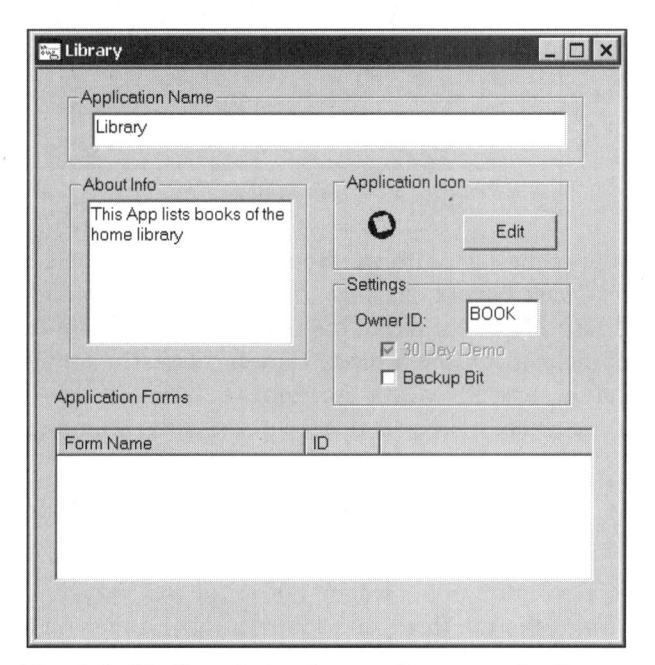

Fig. 3.2. Starting window for creating an application

Name the project "Library", and enter the information in the **About Info** field, which will be displayed in the special window **About...**. Also enter a unique program description (BOOK). Now save the project, and you will have the file Library.pfa. Press the **Edit** button to open a new window that will enable you to edit the icon. The lowest field will contain a list of forms as they are added.

Introducing a New Form into the Project

Add a blank form by clicking on the second button from the right in the second line of the menu (Fig. 3.1). A green square for the form will appear. Pressing the next button on the left will open the form properties window (Fig. 3.3).

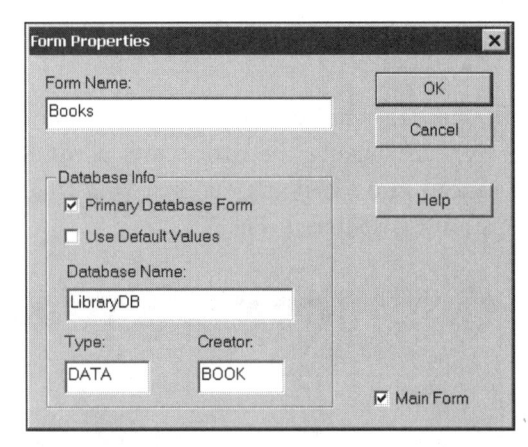

Fig. 3.3. The form properties window

Enter the name of the form (**Books**) in the upper field, and then check the **Primary Database Form** box, since this will be the main and only form connected with the database. Then indicate the name of the database (`LibraryDB`); it should differ from the name of the project. **Type** and **Creator** are necessary descriptors of any application for a PDA with the Palm operating system (see details in *Part 2*). If the database will be edited via this form, check the **Main Form** checkbox.

Adding Widgets to the Form

Clicking on the button in the second line of the toolbox (menu) will add the corresponding control to the form, and this control will then be dragged to the proper place. Each widget has a black dot in the bottom right corner (Fig. 3.4). You can change the size of the object by grabbing this dot with the cursor.

Add five labels to the form and five corresponding text boxes. Each text box added to the form automatically adds a field in the database table and is thenceforth connected with it. This is done using the text box properties window (Fig. 3.5). The first two upper fields (**Field ID** and **Field Type**) determine the name and type of the database field associated with the control. The other fields determine the position and size of the text box, as well as other characteristics.

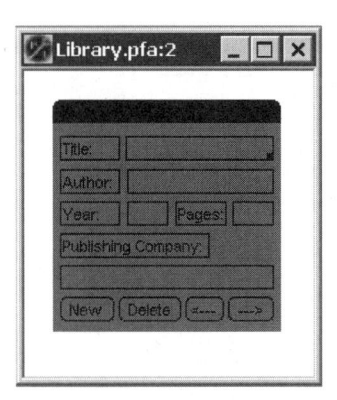

Chapter 3: Overview of Palm/Pocket PC Development Tools 67

Fig. 3.4. General view of the form being developed

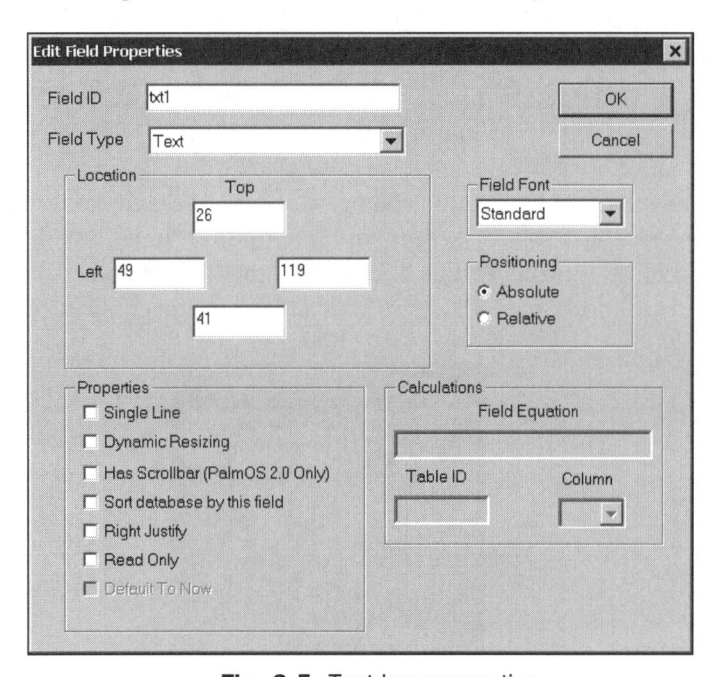

Fig. 3.5. Text box properties

You can use a formula to introduce the field values to the form, but this function is disabled in the trial version of the software.

While the text box control's properties determine the connection with the database, the button properties determine the operations on the records in the database. Each button possesses a set of functions that determine what happens when you press the button (Fig. 3.6).

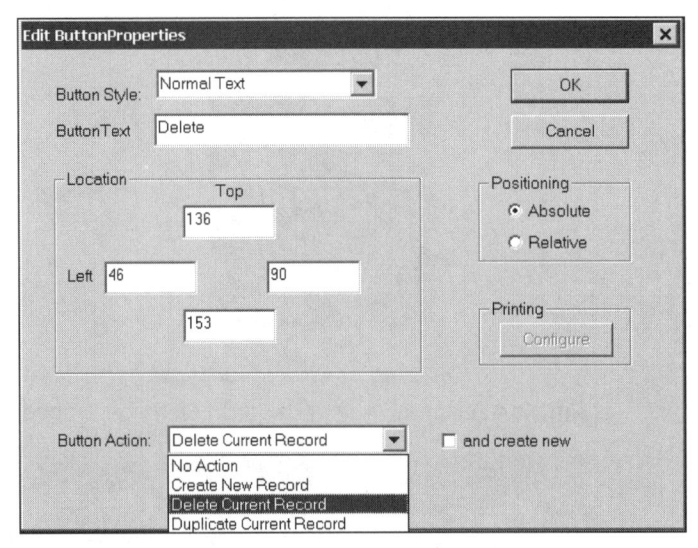

Fig. 3.6. Button properties

Such functions may include adding a record, deleting a record, moving to the next/previous/first record, etc. All you have to do is to indicate the corresponding button name in the **Button Text** field. Of course, the label and other controls have their own property windows, but they are obvious and we are not going to look at them here.

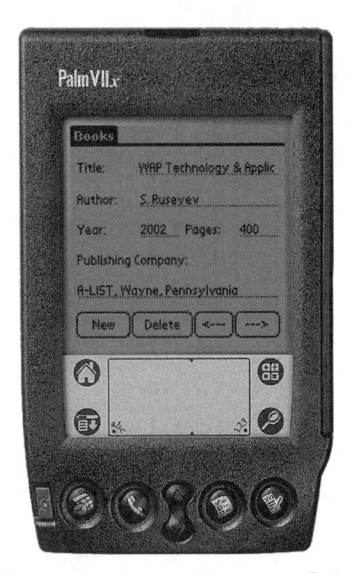

Fig. 3.7. An application working on a Palm emulator

Chapter 3: Overview of Palm/Pocket PC Development Tools 69

Having placed the controls as shown in Fig. 3.4 and selected the corresponding functions of the command buttons, we can create the executable file. To do this, save the project and click on the rightmost button in the second line of the menu. The file will have the extension PRC. Save it in an appropriate folder, from which it will later be sent to the real device during the synchronization session, or simply be dragged to the Palm OS emulator (see *Chapter 5*). Now that we've finished, you can see the result in Fig. 3.7.

Introduction to NS Basic

Using this product, you can create applications not only for the Palm and Windows CE operating systems, but also for the Newton OS. This is a rather complex development environment, similar to Visual Basic. (It is interesting that this product itself was written in VB.) The executable files created with it are notable for their small size and high speed of execution. Since it is very difficult to cover all possible tools in one book, we will not consider this language in detail, but it would be unjust to leave it out completely, since, after eVB and AppForge MobileVB, this is the tool that would be of most interest to a programmer who desires to master creating various applications for pocket computers quickly. The price of a version for one of the three platforms is about $150.

You can download the test version from **www.nsbasic.com**, the web site of NS Basic Corporation. It comes with a Palm OS emulator.

NS Basic possesses many convenient features that definitely resemble BASIC. It has the 13 controls described below, supports mathematical functions, and has many functions for working with databases. The executable file (PRC) can either contain the virtual machine within itself or exclude it. In the latter case, it becomes very compact. The drawback is a lack of tips (IntelliSense) on the properties and methods in the code editor, to which VB programmers have probably become used. There is no adequate debugging mechanism whatsoever. Another drawback is that objects (e.g., forms and modules) can not be saved as separate files: the whole project is saved as one file with the PRJ extension, and transferring forms or modules from one project to another is possible only by means of copying.

Development Environment

Let's take the Palm version of NS Basic as an example. The NS Basic development environment looks very much like Visual Basic's, and is shown in Fig. 3.8.

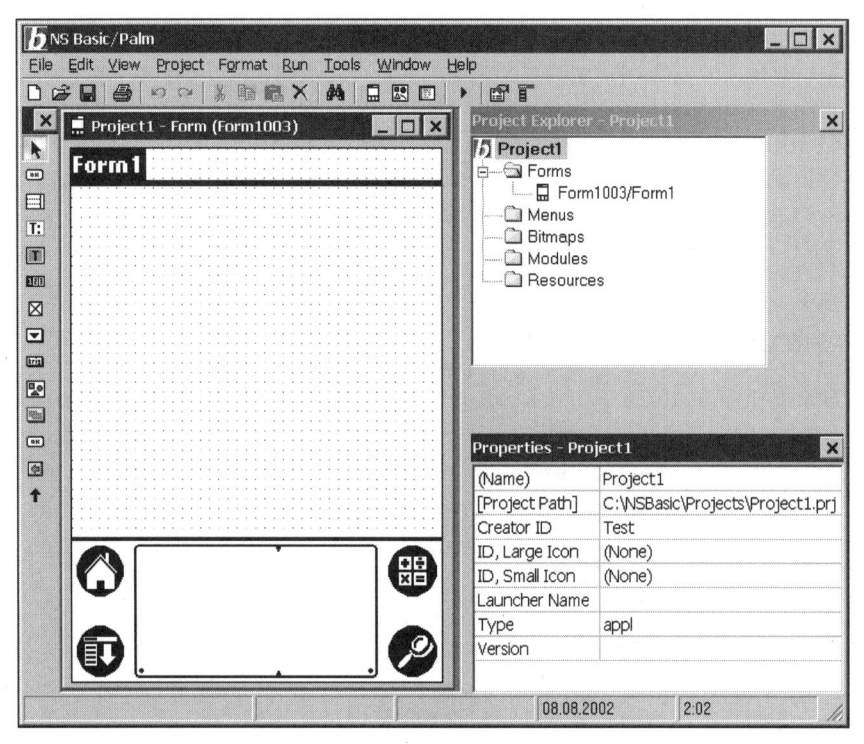

Fig. 3.8. General view of the NS Basic development environment

There are the following control elements (widgets) in the left part of the screen:

- Button
- List
- Label
- Field
- Option button (Push Button) — although it looks like a regular check box, there should always be at least two Push Buttons in the group
- Check box
- Pop-up Trigger (list)
- Selector Trigger — a special label activating a certain process when clicked
- Bitmap
- Gadget is a sensitive widget. It makes an invisible square area on the form sensitive to a click, which will execute the corresponding code
- Repeating Button repeats the event codes as long as the user holds the button pressed with the stylus

❏ Scroll Bar
❏ Shift Indicator

All NS Basic's widgets are based on Palm OS objects, even down to the internal designation of the objects, hence the strange "Form1003" in the name of the form. Apart from forms, the project may contain menus, bitmaps, and modules. NS Basic menus are separate objects created using the menu editor, almost like in Visual Basic. The menus then need to be identified with a particular form programmatically using the `MenuDraw` function and the name of the menu. In order to use the **Bitmap** control, you must enter a graphic file into the project, and then make its ID correspond to the **Resource ID** property of the bitmap control.

Development Environment Settings

The settings of both the project and the working area in NS Basic are very interesting. Select the **Options...** command from the **Tools** menu to open the window in which you can modify the properties of the project (Fig. 3.9). The next tab — **Editor** — can be used to specify colors and fonts for key words and other system requirements when the project is coded, as well as many other easily understandable settings.

The **Palm Screen** tab lets you make simple settings for the form's screen, such as fonts and switching on/off the grid on the form's surface. The **Compile/Download** tab is shown in Fig. 3.10.

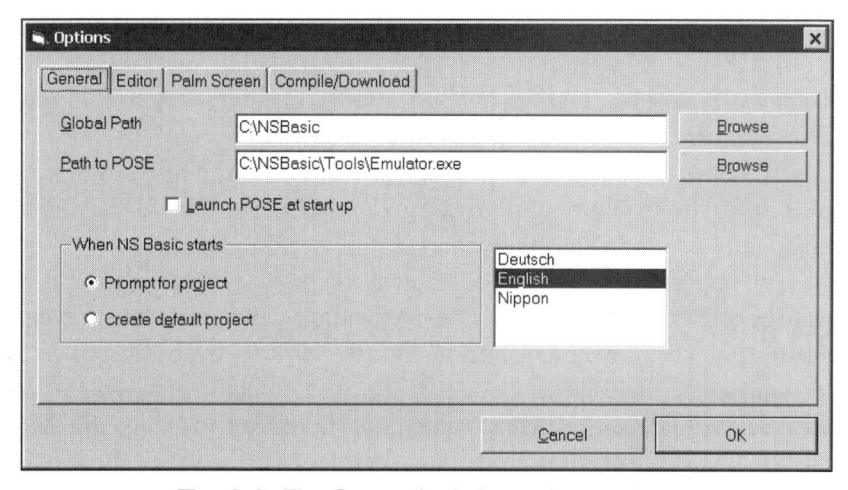

Fig. 3.9. The **General** tab for project settings

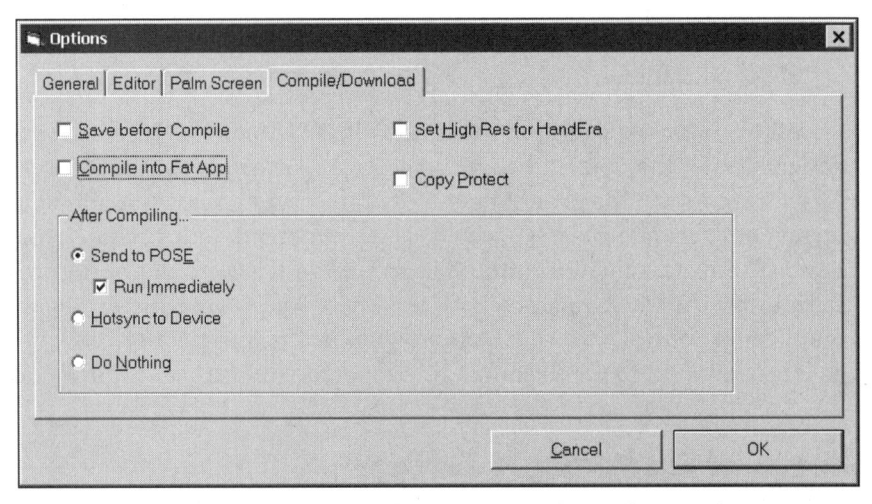

Fig. 3.10. The **Compile/Download** tab for project settings

The **Compile into Fat App** checkbox is simply the option of including runtime files in the executable PRC file. Of course, you only need one set of supporting files (runtime) in order to keep all the applications created on NS Basic working on the PDA. In the lower group of settings, indicate what to do with the compiled file. The settings shown in Fig. 3.10 enable you to open the emulator, which is convenient for testing the project.

Demo Example

To feel the real advantages of NS Basic, we'll consider a very simple application that shows on which day of the week a specified date falls.

Draw two labels, two fields, and one button on the form by selecting the controls from the toolbox and clicking on the form. The form will be as shown in Fig. 3.11.

The upper, txtDate field will contain the date, and the lower field — txtDay — will show the day of the week. Our application will have just one event, which will occur upon clicking the **OK** button. Double-click on the button to get into the editor, and enter the following code (Listing 3.1). Fig. 3.12 shows the editor against the background of the project. First, the necessary variables are declared. Then the PopupDate function is used, which displays a calendar on the screen (Fig. 3.13), and which passes an arbitrary source date as a parameter.

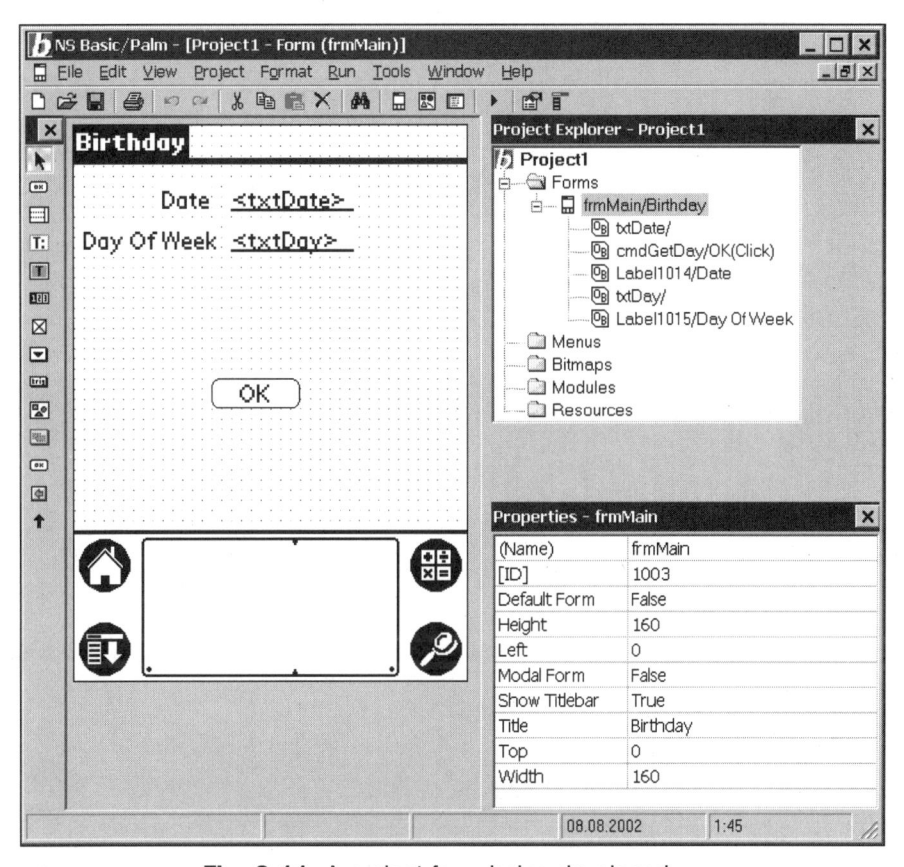

Chapter 3: Overview of Palm/Pocket PC Development Tools 73

Fig. 3.11. A project form being developed

Listing 3.1. The Application's Events

```
Sub object1006()
Dim dMyDate     as Date
Dim intResult   as Integer
Dim WeekDay     as String
'The variable contains the initial date, to be converted using
'the function ToDate from the text type to the Date type
dMyDate = ToDate("1998/07/16")
'function PopupDate shows Calendar
```

```
intResult = PopupDate(dMyDate,"Enter your birthday.")
If intResult = 0 Then
    MsgBox "Error"
    Exit Sub
End If
'The date value returned by PopupDate is stored in the variable
'dMyDate
'and assigned to the text property of the field txtDate
txtDate.text = Str(dMyDate)
'function DayOfWeek returns day of week number (1 - Sunday)
WeekDay = Str(DayOfWeek(dMyDate))
'converting the number of the day of the week into the name of the day
label1015.text = "It was:"
Select Case WeekDay
Case "1"
    txtDay.text = "Sunday"
Case "2"
    txtDay.text = "Monday"
Case "3"
    txtDay.text = "Tuesday"
Case "4"
    txtDay.text = "Wednesday"
Case "5"
    txtDay.text = "Thursday"
Case "6"
    txtDay.text = "Friday"
Case "7"
    txtDay.text = "Saturday"
End Select

End Sub
```

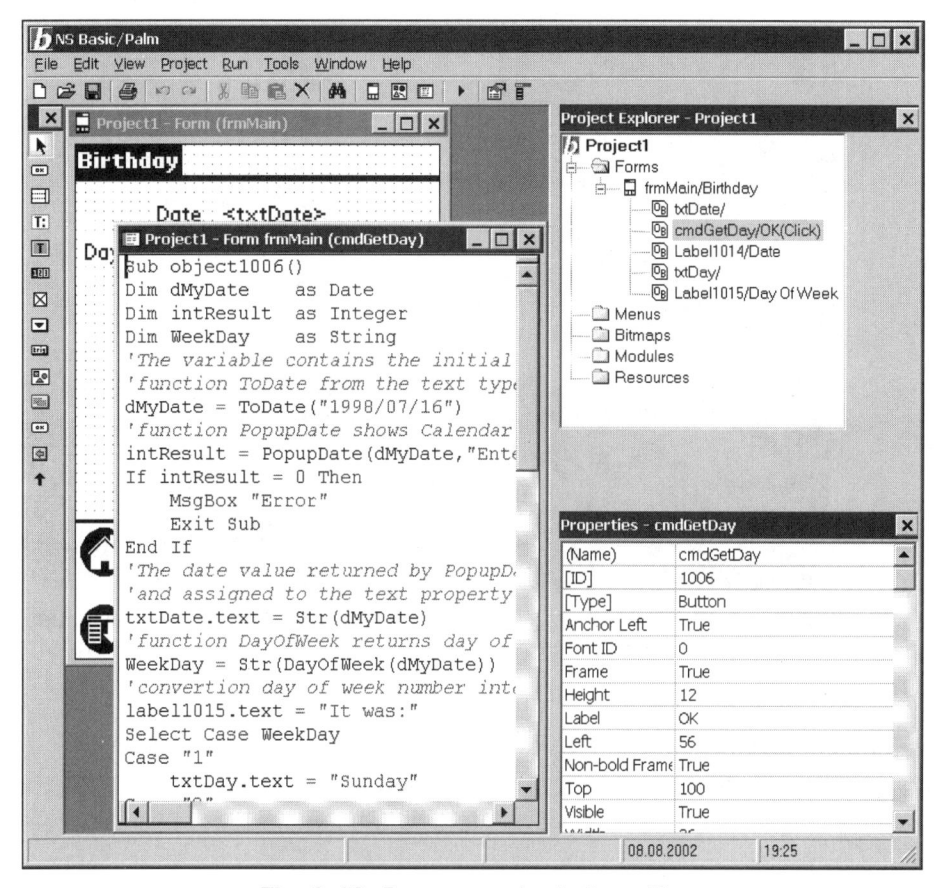

Chapter 3: Overview of Palm/Pocket PC Development Tools

Fig. 3.12. Program codes in the editor

When the user selects a date from the calendar by clicking on the screen, the `PopupDate` function returns it to the `dMyDate` variable, and it is displayed in the `txtDate` field on the screen.

The `DayOfWeek` function turns the date into the number of the day of the week, which is transformed into a text value by a simple algorithm (Fig. 3.14).

Figs. 3.13 and 3.14 were possible because we chose the options in Fig. 3.10. In a real-world situation, as soon as we are satisfied with the performance of the application we have created, it should be compiled and copied to a Palm device (in our case) during the synchronization process. Copying, however, will be automatic. It is important to save the PRC file in the right place on the PC, so that synchronization manager can find it. Also, if a "Fat" file is created, copying will be limited to one file.

76 Part I: Pocket PC and PDA

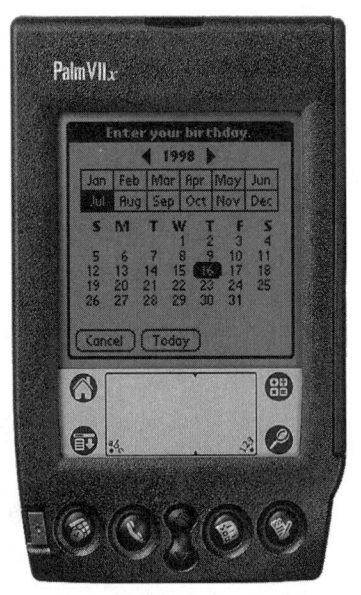

Fig. 3.13. The calendar on the emulator screen

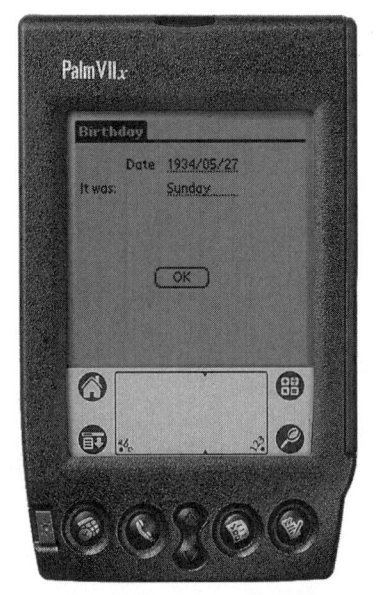

Fig. 3.14. The final screen of the application

This is the end of our introduction, and the following chapters will provide a fuller immersion into the world of programming portable computers.

Part II

Programming Palm OS with AppForge MobileVB

Chapter 4: Installing the AppForge MobileVB Development Environment

Chapter 5: Introduction to AppForge MobileVB

Chapter 6: Working with Ingots

Chapter 7: Databases in AppForge MobileVB

Chapter 8: Developing an Application with a Database

Chapter 9: Internet Programming

Chapter 10: Creating Web Clipping Applications

Chapter 4

Installing the AppForge MobileVB Development Environment

This chapter deals with the different versions of AppForge MobileVB, and system and PC requirements. It also looks at issues of integrating MobileVB with Visual Basic, as well as the general concept of pocket-computer applications created with MobileVB.

We already mentioned that AppForge MobileVB is a Rapid Application Development (RAD) software that allows the quick creation of applications for PDA and pocket computers. Most applications work on all Palm and Windows CE devices. The developers of AppForge keep improving their product: for example, the first version did not support Windows CE at all. The second version featured limited support of Windows CE: e.g., pocket computers with MIPS processors were not supported. Despite the restrictions that are still present, the third version (the most recent at the time of writing) is much more advanced than the first one.

In terms of user convenience, color displays appeared, as well as the option of programming the menu. From the programmer's point of view, the new version supports additional types of variables, new functions, MIPS processors, etc. The developers also added a range of useful controls.

The codes written for Palm require minimal treatment in order to convert them to Windows CE.

In this chapter, we will mainly consider the use of AppForge MobileVB for creating applications for Palm. First, this is because *Part III* will be dedicated to eVB software for creating applications for Windows CE only, and, second, because AppForge MobileVB was originally intended for creating applications for Palm, and currently supports this platform much better.

Versions of AppForge MobileVB 3

Currently, there are two versions of AppForge MobileVB: a simplified version (**AppForge MobileVB Lite 3.0.1 for Palm OS**) and a standard version.

The simplified (Lite) edition is much cheaper ($129), and is a great tool for a programmer who is just starting to write applications for Palm. This is an excellent means of mastering the concept of programming for PDA and pocket computers. Of course, this version is limited in comparison with the full one.

The standard edition ($899) has more controls and functions. Apart from the standard ActiveX included in the Lite edition, it includes AFClientSocket, AFINetHHTP, AFMovie, AFScanner, AFSignatureCapture, AFSlider, AFVscrollBar, and AFHScrollBar. Starting in *Chapter 6*, we will consider them in more detail. From here on, we will be discussing the standard version of the product.

The AppForge MobileVB Installation Procedure

Before you purchase the rather expensive MobileVB, it makes sense to try the free-test version first. This can be downloaded directly from AppForge's web site (**www.appforge.com**) after a simple registration via e-mail, which will be used to send you the registration key necessary to install the trial version. The key will allow you to create and compile applications. When it expires, the software will cease to open. The size of the file for the third version of MobileVB is 20 MB. Double-click on the file after it is loaded to start the installation process on the desktop. Fig. 4.1 illustrates the first step of the installation.

The next step will be the confirmation that the user has familiarized himself or herself with and agrees to the conditions of using MobileVB. Then a window to select a full or custom installation will appear. In the trial version, however, these options are identical. After clicking on the **Next** button and confirming the installation folder, the installation process will start. Then a window will appear reminding you that the booster (see below) must be loaded and installed on the pocket computer before applications created with AppForge will be able to work on it. The last window shown in Fig. 4.2 will offer the ReadMe file, which briefly describes the features of AppForge MobileVB 3.0.

Chapter 4: Installing the AppForge MobileVB Development Environment

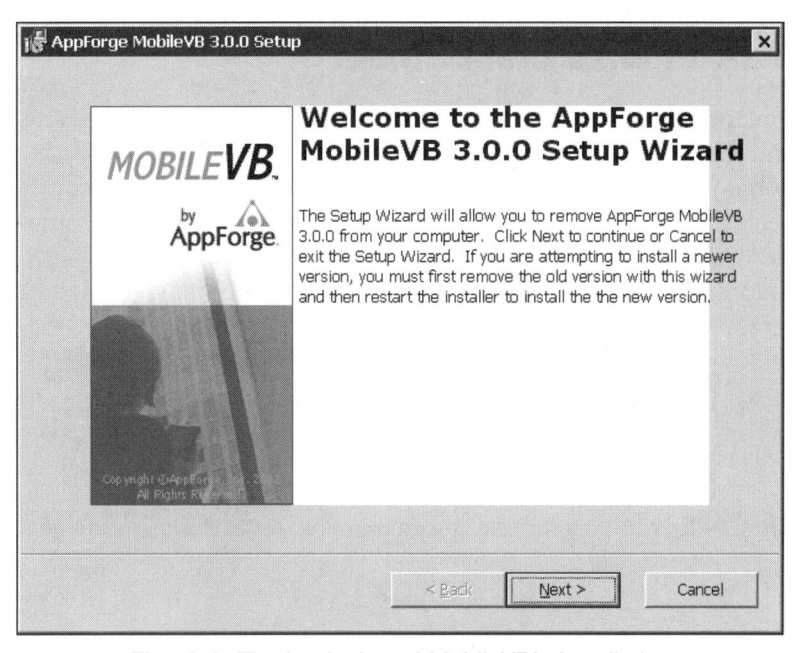

Fig. 4.1. The beginning of MobileVB's installation

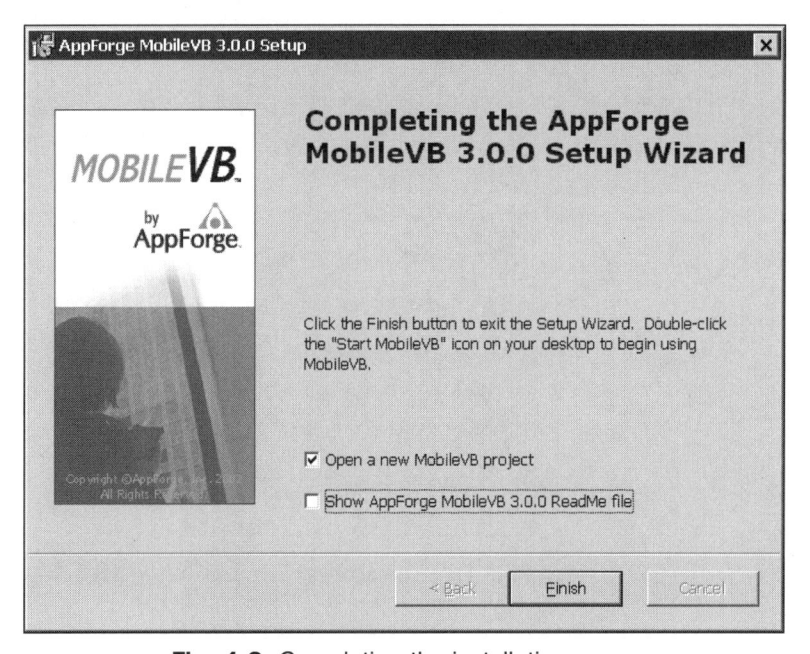

Fig. 4.2. Completing the installation

Integration with Visual Basic

AppForge MobileVB is not independent software, but needs to be integrated into the Visual Basic environment and exist there as an add-in. After MobileVB is installed, Visual Basic acquires an additional menu with commands specific to MobileVB, and a toolbox, with utilities that somewhat duplicate the menu (Fig. 4.3 and 4.4). In addition, the standard control panel of Visual Basic is supplemented with specific AppForge elements called *ingots* (Fig. 4.5).

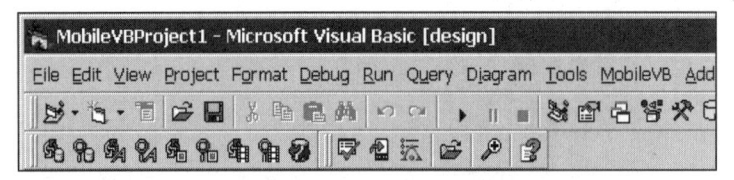

Fig. 4.3. The MobileVB toolbox in the Visual Basic environment

Fig. 4.4. The MobileVB menu

From this, it is obvious that, before installing AppForge, you must have Visual Basic version 6 installed.

Chapter 4: Installing the AppForge MobileVB Development Environment 83

Fig. 4.5. The ingots of AppForge are marked with an "i"

In addition, it is necessary to install version 4 or later of the Service Pack. AppForge can not be installed without Service Pack, and will quit installation, demanding that you update Visual Basic. You can download Service Pack version 4 or later from the Microsoft web site for free. The size of Service Pack version 5 is 133 MB, and the name of the file is vs6sp5.exe. At the time of writing, these files could be found at:

- http://msdn.microsoft.com/vstudio/downloads/updates/sp/vs6/sp4/default.asp (Service Pack 4)
- http://msdn.microsoft.com/vstudio/downloads/updates/sp/vs6/sp5/default.asp (Service Pack 5)

If all the above conditions are met, the installation of MobileVB will go easily and smoothly.

On the whole, the PC on which AppForge is to be installed should meet the following requirements: a processor with a clock rate exceeding 90 MHz, at least 20 MB of free space on the hard disk, and Windows 95 or later (including Windows NT).

We will see below that the concept of eMbedded Visual Basic is somewhat different. eVB is an independent product that externally recalls Visual Basic, but is very limited. Being a block (add-in) integrated into Visual Basic, AppForge MobileVB makes extensive use of the features of VB itself, while adding specific functions.

Compatibility with Visual Basic

As an add-in to Visual Basic, MobileVB naturally supports many functions of Visual Basic that work on the portable device in exactly the same way as on the PC. Strictly speaking, MobileVB is not quite an add-in. MobileVB has its own compiler and its own set of specific functions. The differences in the functions are only evident when the specific character of portable computers or PDA is considered, or rather when we consider their limited nature compared with desktop computers. AppForge was developed keeping in mind that mobile devices have a limited memory, slower processors, and a small screen. This imposed certain limitations upon the functions and libraries used in the software, which also makes the programmer take into account the conditions mentioned above, and not overload the applications with forms, global variables, etc. In the next few chapters, we will consider in more detail the features of Visual Basic that are not supported. This is often related to the inefficiency of a particular object of Visual Basic as applied to mobile devices. For example, MobileVB does not support variables of the `variant` type. This is mostly because they take up too much space, and should be replaced with a concrete type.

Booster

In order for an application created on AppForge MobileVB to work on a portable device, the device needs to have a set of supporting files (in one sense, a virtual machine). Such an approach is typical for many programming facilities, e.g., for Java or Visual Basic. A virtual machine is simply a set of files supporting the work of the application on a specific or different platforms. In this case, the set of these files is called the booster. It can be easily installed on the portable computer or PDA directly from VB using the menu command **Install Booster to Device**, and then selecting the type of mobile device — Palm or Windows CE. (Of course, the portable computer should be connected to the PC via a cable or the IF port.) The current version of AppForge MobileVB provides boosters for Palm, Pocket PC (with SH3, MIPS, and ARM processors), and Nokia Series 80 (the Symbian OS). The company's web site provides free boosters for only Palm and Nokia, which can be

Chapter 4: Installing the AppForge MobileVB Development Environment 85

downloaded and installed on the user's mobile device. Users have to purchase the booster for Windows CE. The booster consists of three components: AFCore, pCOM, and ByteStreamVM. AFCore contains the services necessary to work with the control elements of AppForge, called "ingots." pCOM is used to control all the components of an application created on AppForge. Finally, ByteStreamVM is the compiler (interpreter). The files for pocket computers with Windows CE have the DLL extension, and those for the Palm operating system use PRC. Both the ingots and the various libraries that support AppForge MobileVB are understood as components. The booster can be downloaded from the company's web site (**www.appforge.com/booster**). Fig. 4.6 illustrates a fragment of the process of installing the booster files on the PC (for later transfer to Palm).

Fig. 4.6. The AppForge booster-installation screen

Ingots

All AppForge MobileVB ingots can be divided into four groups: basic, professional, communicational, and multimedia. If basic ingots are used in the project, then the BasicIngots.prc file should be installed on Palm, and the BasicIngots.dll file on Pocket PC. Correspondingly, the files where other ingots are implemented should be transferred to the pocket computer/PDA if they are needed. Of course, just as when working with Visual Basic, there is no need to find all the files and then transfer them to the pocket computer. Just reference them and include them. References to the ingots used are made in the same way as in Visual Basic: select the **Components** command from the **Project** menu (**Project | Components**) and check the boxes opposite the necessary ingots. All AppForge ingots have the AppForge prefix before their names.

Libraries

AppForge possesses an extensive set of its own functions for work with various objects. For example, the AppForge PDB Library contains a set of functions for working with databases, and the AppForge Numeric Library contains functions for generating random numbers. These functions will be described in detail in *Chapter 6*. The other libraries contain functions facilitating interaction with the Palm device. Just as with the ingots, if functions from a certain library are used, then that library needs to be included in the standard manner. The library file itself should be installed on Palm, which is done automatically if this library is included. Then, in the process of creating the installation package, this file will be installed in the file directory for later transfer to Palm during the next HotSync procedure. Fig. 4.7 shows the inclusion of the libraries in the MobileVB project.

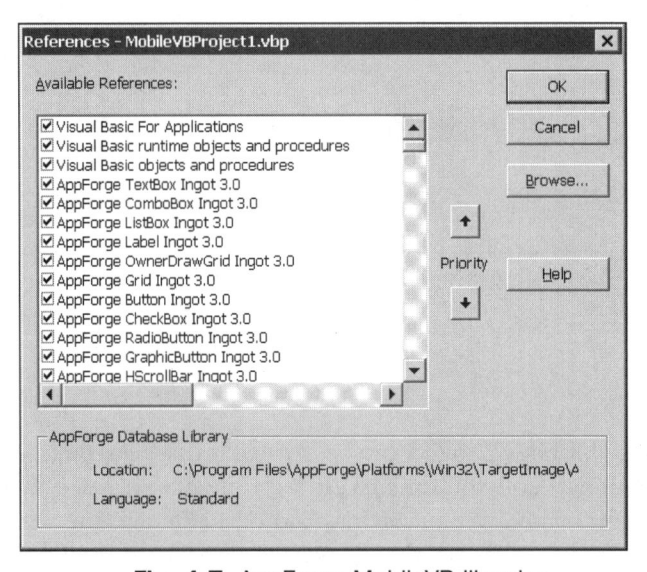

Fig. 4.7. AppForge MobileVB libraries

Testing

In order to develop and test applications created using MobileVB, the programmer need not necessarily have his or her own pocket computer. Select **Run** from the Visual Basic menu, and the application will be started directly in the development environment. The application is then debugged as if it were a standard application written in Visual Basic. But no matter how well the application works within the AppForge MobileVB development environment, it should be tested on a real device, or at least on a universal emulator. How to acquire and use an emulator is described in *Chapter 5*.

Porting a Ready Application to a Pocket Computer

When the application is ready to be copied to the mobile device, just select the **Deploy to Device** menu and the type of the device: Palm, Pocket PC, or Nokia. The application will be compiled and ported to the device, which should be connected to the PC. The connection session of the pocket computer with the PC is called ActiveSync and HotSync for Palm. The synchronization process with Pocket PC is automatic. To execute it, connect the pocket computer to the PC via a cable or the IF port, and synchronization will begin. For a Palm, synchronization needs to be initialized. Fig. 4.8 shows a synchronization session with a pocket computer. The pocket computer will display the synchronization status.

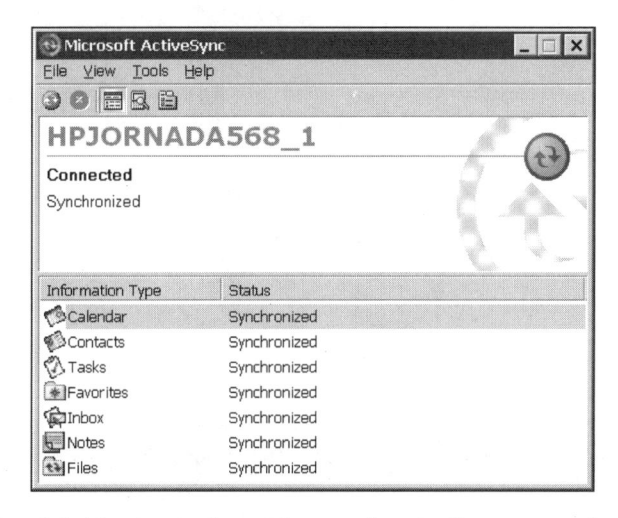

Fig. 4.8. The beginning of the synchronization process between the PC and the pocket computer

You also have the option of porting ready-to-use files not directly to the end device, but into a folder on the desktop. You may need to do this if an application is completed but needs extra testing (e.g., on the emulator) before being ported to the real device. You should always remember that a poorly debugged application may cause various (and serious) errors in your pocket computer's performance.

Project Settings

Using the MobileVB menu, the user can set or change certain parameters. Select **Settings** from the MobileVB menu to open the dialog box and select the icon for the future application. If you click on the **Dependencies** element, then in the right part you can include additional files in the project, which can be databases or drawings. When scanning the files, MobileVB can determine the additional files used, but only when they are applied via the properties of the ingots. When a file is applied only in the codes (e.g., the database file, PDB), it should be entered manually using the dialog box described here.

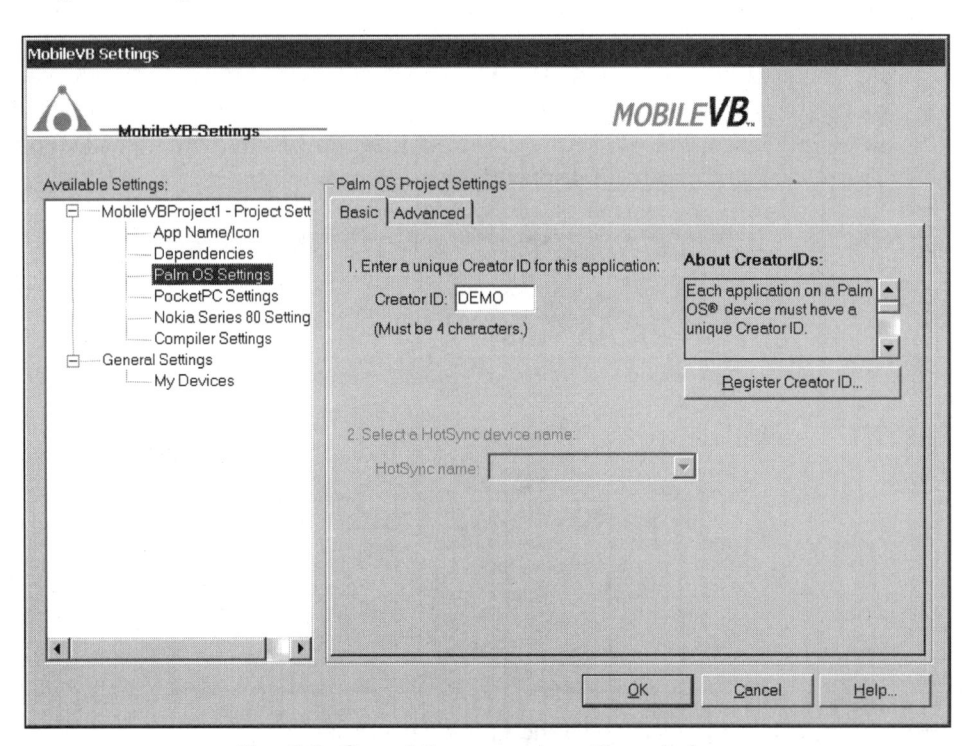

Fig. 4.9. One of the property-setting windows

Each application created for Palm should have its own unique descriptor, which should consist of 4 characters (Latin letters and figures). Two applications with the same descriptor cannot work on the same device. Therefore, AppForge recommends developers to register their descriptors if they plan to create commercial applications. Registering a new Creator ID and searching for available ones is done at **http://dev.palmos.com/creatorid/**. Fig. 4.9 shows one of the options of setting the project properties. The other (e.g., installing dependent files) will be considered in detail in the following chapters.

For a mini computer with the Windows CE operating system, you can specify the name of the developer (identifier) and indicate the folder on the portable computer in which the future application is to be installed.

Additional Features

Apart from special utilities for working with files that we will consider in *Chapter 5*, AppForge MobileVB has special tools that simplify creating the application. Since the portable device has a small display, the standard size of the form on which the ingots are placed is also small. If there are many ingots, the details are hardly discernable. Here the option of enlarging the view of the area, which is integrated into MobileVB, comes in handy. To do this, use the **Zoom Window** command from the **MobileVB** menu.

Application Compatibility for Palm OS and Windows CE

When starting to create an application on AppForge MobileVB, as a rule it is first necessary to select the operating system for which the application is intended. This is done upon opening the new MobileVB project (see *Chapter 6*). Of course, if the application is complex, it would be nice to have the option of making it work with another operating system as well. Unfortunately, there is no universal and integrated method in MobileVB for doing so. The formal reason for this is that the library of integrated functions (Palm OS Extended Functions Library) for Palm OS does not work with Windows CE, since the two platforms are completely different. We could suggest just using functions and ingots that are supported by both platforms, but such an approach would water down the options of the application.

The best solution is to create two different visual interfaces (for Palm OS and Windows CE) with the same code. First the completed application for Palm OS is created, and then a new project for Pocket PC is opened. The modules, codes, and ingots from the Palm form are copied to the blank form of a Pocket PC project. Then the code is added (copied) into the new form from the original one. Such an approach has the advantage that each version of the application can be more accurately adapted for the particular type of portable device. On the other hand, supporting and synchronizing two projects of the same type may not be very convenient.

Even if you try to avoid functions and ingots that do not work on another platform when creating a Palm project, it is still necessary to adapt the size of the form to the display size of the pocket computer, which exceeds that of the Palm device. Therefore, it makes sense to note another solution found on the AppForge web site: creating additional codes that regulate the size of the original form and the ingots on it, and also changes their relative positions while observing the proportions and fitting the form to the new size. It is also recommended that you create the source application for the Palm platform. When determining the type of portable device using the values Screen.Width (or Screen.Height), you should perform the procedure of relatively repositioning the ingots (or not if the application works on the Palm device). Taking into account that the Windows CE operating system is more powerful and quicker than Palm, these codes are recommended for use when the application works on Pocket PC, and not on Palm, since, in this case, the codes work faster.

Databases in AppForge MobileVB

We will consider databases in detail in *Chapters 7* and *8*, but now we will just say a few words about them. The databases in MobileVB are binary files with the PDB extension (Palm DataBase), each equivalent to one table. Such a file can be created in code, or, using the **Database Converter** utility, one of the MS Access tables can be converted. A special part of the file, known as the schema, stores the information on the whole file structure. A database thus created allows for simplified and convenient record manipulation.

When discussing databases for pocket computers, we must include synchronizing the data stored on the pocket computer with a database on the desktop. MobileVB lets you create special utilities responsible for the transfer of data. Such applications are called conduits, and are discussed in detail in *Chapter 7*.

Chapter 5

Introduction to AppForge MobileVB

Here we give an easy example how to create, compile and copy an application onto a pocket computer. We also describe the limitations of AppForge MobileVB, its main utilities, and Palm emulator (POSE).

Creating a New Project

Let's move on to creating a real application, and consider all the stages of its "life", from the creation of the interface and codes to copying to the actual portable device. Let's start by creating a very simple application — "Hello World!" — to get a feel for the specifics of and get a taste for programming for portable devices.

Open the development environment by selecting the **Start/Programs/ AppForge MobileVB** command from the **Start** menu. Opening a new **MobileVB** project is accompanied by an offer to select a platform (Fig. 5.1). We select Palm OS, although this is not crucial.

The principal issue here is compiling for a particular operating system and processor. When opened, **MobileVB** will add a blank form, which should be saved in some folder. (If you fail to do this, then when you try to place the ingot on the form, a warning will appear telling you to save the project first.) Then assign a unique descriptor to the project. This can, however, be done during compilation. To do this, select the **MobileVB Settings** command from the **MobileVB** menu. In the window that appears (see *Chapter 4*) enter a set of 4 symbols in the **Creator ID** field.

Fig. 5.1. Selecting the project platform

Place the **AFLabel1** label on the form and select **Alignment** and the font (**FontName**) Times New Roman 18 for its properties. Now put the command button on the form with the default name — **AFButton1** (Fig. 5.2).

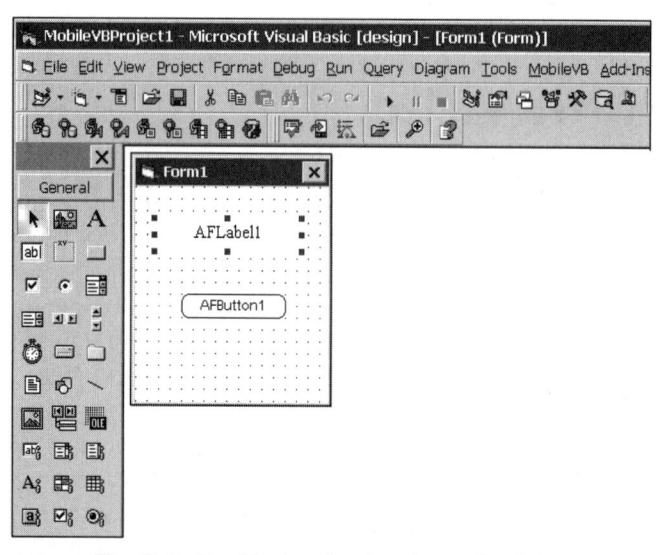

Fig. 5.2. Positioning the ingots on the form

Double-clicking on the button leads us to the AFButton1_Click() event field. Write the following code:

```
AFLabel1.Caption = "Hello World!"
```

We know from VB that since **Caption** is the default property of the ingot, it can be omitted. In MobileVB, this would cause an error during compilation. All properties must be specified!

Debugging and Testing the Application

First of all, note that it is very easy to change the size of the form; it is done in the same way as in Visual Basic. The original size of the form, however, corresponds to the display size of the pocket computer/PDA, and it is better not to change it. In more serious cases than the one described here, you may need to change the size of the form. In such situations, it is better to elongate the form than to widen it, since it is more convenient to move the form up and down on the screen than it is to move it from right to left.

Testing the application is done in the same way as in VB. After the breakpoint is set, for example, on the `Form_Load` event, you can move along the project by steps using the <F8> key.

So, we can easily start the application by pressing the <F5> key or the **Start** button on the **Visual Basic** toolbar. Clicking on the **AFButton1** command button leads to the expected result. Here is what the application looks like while running in Visual Basic (Fig. 5.3).

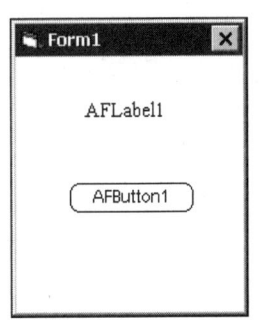

Fig. 5.3. Application execution

Compilation

When we are fully satisfied with the application's performance, we can start to think about copying it to the PDA. But first we must ensure that there are no errors or conflicts related to the fact that MobileVB may not support the type of variables used, or certain fonts or functions. Select the **Compile and Validate** option from the **MobileVB** menu and let MobileVB find possible problems. As a result, we get a warning about an error (Fig. 5.4). It turns out that we used the Times New Roman font for our label, and it is not supported by AppForge in its initial form. It should be modified into a format understandable for AppForge.

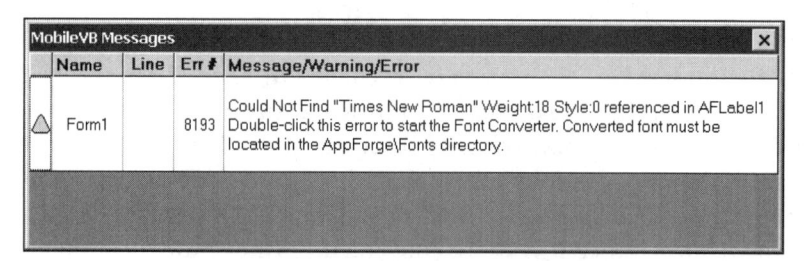

Fig. 5.4. The error-description window

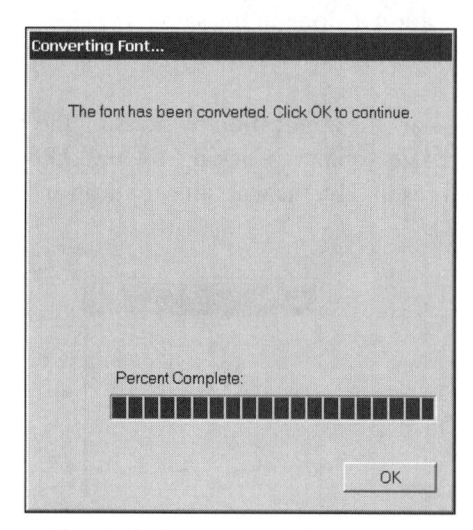

Fig. 5.5. A successful font conversion

Now it is time to encounter some additional intelligent abilities of AppForge MobileVB. Instead of thinking about which fonts are supported, how a problem can be corrected, and where an error should be looked for, just double-click on the warning window in the error message area in order to open the font converter window, which is described in detail below. Press the **Select** button to select the new font in the window that appears (Times New Roman in our case). Finally, after several seconds of converting and creating the new font file, we get a message telling us that the font conversion has been successful (Fig. 5.5). Repeated compilation of the project does not result in an error message. Nevertheless, it should be noted that,

Chapter 5: Introduction to AppForge MobileVB   95

even if the application works perfectly in the development area, it does not mean that it will work without a hitch on the portable device. It is still prudent to test the application on the real device or on an emulator, which will enable you to move on to the next stage — copying the application to a real device.

Copying the Application to the Pocket Computer

After the application has been successfully compiled, you can start porting it to the pocket computer. To copy an application to a Windows CE device, you need to perform the following steps:

1. Install the ActiveSync application on the desktop if this has not already been done (the application is supplied together with the device).
2. Connect the pocket computer to the desktop PC via the serial, USB, or IR port.
3. Set the activated ActiveSync connection (it is usually activated by itself as soon as the pocket computer is connected to the desktop).
4. Install the virtual AppForge machine (booster) on the pocket computer.

After the above steps are performed, select the **Deploy To Device** command from the **MobileVB** menu, and then the **Pocket PC** command. AppForge may ask whether or not it is necessary to compile the program again. Answer "yes", especially if there have been changes introduced into the project since the last compilation. Confirm the save. The process of creating the CAB file will be repeated (but we now know that there will be no errors!), and it will be ported to the pocket computer in the folder selected in the **MobileVB Settings** menu (see *Chapter 4*). You can see the application right after it is installed on the device[*]. Fig. 5.6 shows the appearance of the application on the pocket computer.

Here, some clarification is necessary. AppForge MobileVB actually supports three processors: ARM, MIPS, and SH3, meaning that you can create three different CAB files: MobileVBProject1.ARM.CAB, MobileVBProject1.MIPS.CAB, and MobileVBProject1.SH3.CAB.

---

[*] The pocket computer must, however, have the AppForge virtual-machine files — the booster — installed.

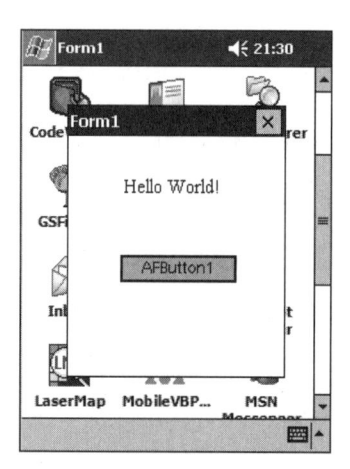

Fig. 5.6. The Hello World! application on the pocket computer

To install the application on a Palm device, first make sure that:

1. Palm has the HotSync Manager application installed.
2. Palm's HotSync Manager is open.
3. The AppForge virtual machine (the booster version for Palm) is installed on the Palm device.

Select the **Deploy to Device** command from the **MobileVB** menu, and then select the Palm OS option. Questions similar to those covered above about the project recompilation will appear, which should be answered positively. If no Creator ID was introduced into the project settings (the **MobileVB Settings** submenu of the **MobileVB** menu), it should be introduced now. Also, select the HotSync name that corresponds to the device being synchronized. **HotSync Name** is the value that appears in the upper right part of the Palm display when the HotSync Manager is activated on it. Now place the Palm device into its cradle and press the **HotSync** button. If there is no button, open the HotSync application on the Palm display, and the application will be copied to the device.

You can also save the compiled application on the desktop and send it to Palm in the next synchronization session, but, for now, **MobileVB** will just compile the application, convert it to a file of the Palm format (with the PRC extension), and install it in either the Palm Install folder or wherever the developer wants (the MobileVBProject1.prc file). With each HotSync session, Palm checks the installation folder to see if any new applications are available, and copies them if necessary. Fig. 5.7 shows the appearance of the same application on a Palm PDA.

Chapter 5: Introduction to AppForge MobileVB

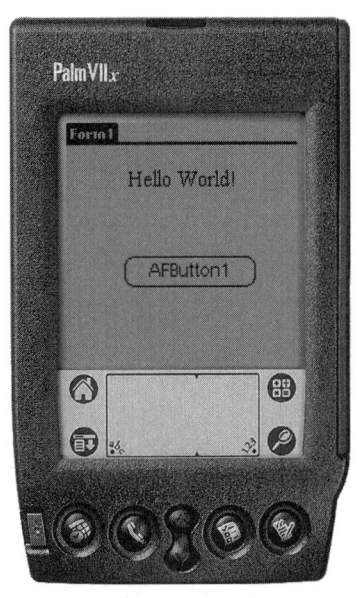

Fig. 5.7. The Hello World! application on a Palm PDA

The Limitations of the AppForge MobileVB Developing Environment

For all its universality and convenience, **MobileVB** has a range of drawbacks that complicate, or rather limit, working with it. From our point of view, the main limitation does not so much concern the functions used in VB (neither their number nor their abilities), but more the impossibility of using the same interface and codes for Palm and Windows PC simultaneously. Unfortunately, after creating an application for Palm, it is tricky to convert it for a Windows CE pocket device, which will be discussed in the following chapters. Such universality, however, is truly difficult, since the two operating systems are absolutely different. We could accomplish this by simply limiting the set of functions, the ingot performance, etc.

The main problem that the programmer will encounter when trying to convert an application created for one operating system for use in another will be the different behavior of the ingots. For example, in Pocket PC form, overlap is admissible, whereas in Palm you first need to hide one form and then show the other. Taking this into account, you should select the programming style that will best enable you to obtain maximum universality for your application. Since, on the whole, Palm is weaker than Windows CE, it imposes more limitations. Hence, if an application is planned for both platforms, it is best to start with Palm.

There are objective reasons, though, why **MobileVB** theoretically should not (rather than can not) support all features of full-fledged VB. **MobileVB** was developed to create applications especially for handheld devices, which are considerably more limited than PCs, and these limitations are therefore reflected in the development environment, with the purpose of protecting the developer from errors and, if possible, of minimizing the drawbacks of pocket computers.

- *Limited RAM.* You should try to write applications using a minimum of RAM in order to achieve greater efficiency and speed.
- *Self-contained power supply.* The batteries usually work for 8–10 hours, so a power-consuming application that often reads information from the RAM (or writes it) reduces the lifetime of the batteries.
- *Slow processor speed.* A range of functions were eliminated (especially those of a mathematical character that require intensive use of the processor). Ingots were also limited in the number of properties and methods.
- *Lower-resolution display.*
- *Absence of a hard disk*, with RAM used instead.

Also keep in mind that, if a standard function is supported in Visual Basic, it is often supported only in a limited version in AppForge MobileVB. We can take the often-used **MsgBox** function as an example. In VB, it has 5 arguments (text, icon, heading, the connection with help information, and the `reference` number). The three last arguments do not exist in **MobileVB**. There is no sense in listing either non-supported functions or limited ones in the book. This information is described in detail either in the help for the development environment or in clear error messages that appear during compilation.

You should also be aware of another obvious limitation: **MobileVB** does not support API functions. API functions are integrated into the operating system (in our case, Windows). Nevertheless, Windows CE possesses a range of useful API functions — so many that a separate book could be dedicated to them.

The following popular features of Visual Basic are also not supported: loops with `For Each..Next` or `With..End With`, the **Optional** parameter, pop-up forms, dynamic arrays, and certain other features about which you can get more information from **MobileVB**'s Help menu or from the company's web site. Note, however, that each new version of the application supports many more functions and features of VB useful within the framework of tasks to be perofrmed by **MobileVB**.

Utilities

Although **MobileVB** does not support many VB functions or limits those available, **MobileVB** has its own integrated libraries that have functions specially intended for work on portable devices. These libraries are briefly described in *Chapter 4*. *Chapter 7* deals with some of them in more detail.

Apart from additional libraries, **MobileVB** possesses special utilities that serve to convert standard video and photo files, fonts, etc. into special formats supported by **MobileVB** and that work most efficiently on mini-computers. There are five corresponding converters and viewers:

- Database converter
- Font converter
- Graphic-file converter
- Movie converter
- Project converter

Let's look at each of them in more detail. The last converter is used to convert a project created in previous versions of AppForge (up to version 1.2.1, inclusive) into the current version. This may be necessary as the second and the third versions support more functions and features.

We have already briefly considered the font converter previously in this chapter. The Font Converter is used to convert the common font (True Type Font (TTF)) into the analogous version for mobile devices. First, select the font from the list using the **Select** button (Fig. 5.8). Then click on the **Convert** button to perform the conversion. The converted font is saved as a file with unique name with the CMF extension by default in the Font folder in the AppForge folder. Of course, you could select another folder, but when you have to assign the font to a label or another ingot, you may then spend a lot of time searching for the required files. Once you have converted the font and saved it in the format supported by

MobileVB, you can use it in another project. There is also the Font Viewer utility. You can view a font's properties (style, size, number of characters, height of the elements) by selecting the CMF file from the menu. Selecting the area below an individual character (letter) enables you to see its width, Unicode.

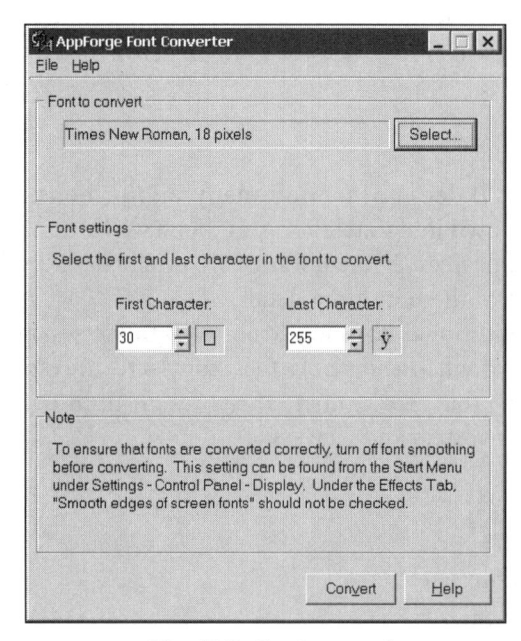

Fig. 5.8. Font converter

Another useful utility is the Graphic Converter. Its purpose is to convert BMP files into the AppForge RGX format, which is supported by both Palm and Pocket PC. The color is lost in this conversion. Generally speaking, BMP files saved in 16-bit format can be used directly, but converting them considerably reduces their size (by up to 30 times!). Using this utility is somewhat like using the previous one. First, the graphic file is selected from the **File** menu or by clicking on the **Select** button, and then conversion takes place after clicking on the **Convert** button. The converter is shown in Fig. 5.9.

When the selected image has colors that are not available on the end portable device, then you can imitate the missing colors with those closest to them. To do this, check the **Dither Image** checkbox. Actually, the colors are lost when the files are converted. Thus, leaving the box unchecked leads to even better image quality.

The Movie Converter converts AVI files into the AppForge RVM video format, which also levels off the colors, but reduces the size of the original file.

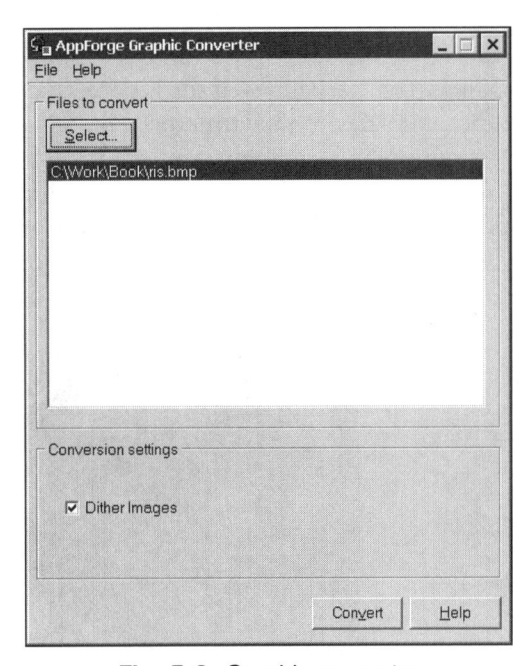

Fig. 5.9. Graphic converter

Finally, the Database Converter is used to convert an MS Access database into a binary file with the Palm DataBase (PDB) extension. One table from Access is converted into one PDB file each time. This is considered in more detail in *Chapter 7*, which is dedicated to databases in MobileVB.

Palm Emulator

As will be repeated below, no matter how well an application is debugged and tested in MobileVB, when it is copied and tested on the real device, there are certain performance differences, and it is possible that errors will occur. This is simply because there are many versions of Palm and pocket computers, each with different physical characteristics. The difference is in the display size and the processor speed, and, mainly, in the versions of the Palm operating system. Therefore, testing the application on the real device is necessary, rather than simply desirable. It is quite difficult, however, to have the whole set of Palm devices, and not very many programmers can boast of this.

Fortunately, the Palm company has aided the developers with a real device emulator (Fig. 5.10). Its versions can work both in a Windows environment, Mac OS and Unix. From here on, we will call the emulator Palm Operating

System Emulator ("POSE"), and refer to its Windows version. POSE can be downloaded for free from the Palm web site (at the time of writing, the address was **http://www.palmos.com/dev/tools/emulator/**). POSE is actually a software copy of the real device on your PC screen. On it, you can test all the applications just as you would on a real PDA. POSE not only provides a substitute for about a dozen real pocket computers, but considerably accelerates the process of testing, debugging, and testing again, saving you the trouble of copying the ready-to-use application onto the real device.

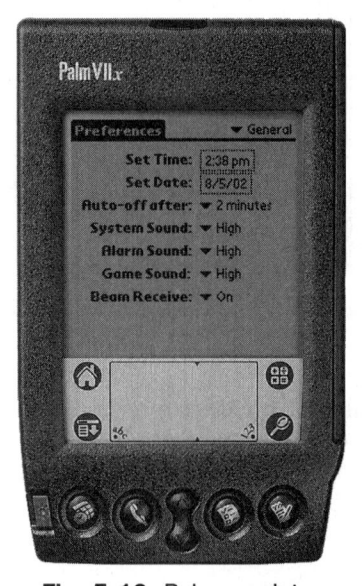

Fig. 5.10. Palm emulator

You can see in Fig. 5.10, and you will see further on, that POSE supports the following features:

- Copies exactly the appearance of the real device, including the Graffiti area
- Imitates text entry both from the desktop PC keyboard and using the mouse in the Graffiti area
- An on/off button
- Command shortcut buttons for selecting the application, menu, calculator, and search
- Up and down scrolling buttons
- The **About Palm...** button

- An option to save the display as a BMP file
- An option to change the memory size
- Other features that will be discussed below

Obtaining an Emulator

A POSE, however, is not much use without ROM files (ROM Image Files). These contain codes specific for the particular Palm model: Palm III, Palm V, Palm VII and their variants, as well as PalmPilot. The ROM files make up the operating system for the emulator, and the emulator is itself an analog of the computer without the operating system. You should download these files from the Palm web site, or, using the emulator, you can get the ROM file from your own Palm during HotSync. To get the ROM files from the company web site, you must first agree to certain conditions and become a member of the Palm OS Developer Program. You will be asked to answer some questions on the web site, and, after a couple of days, the company will inform you of its decision. If they accept you, you will be provided with a password that allows you to download certain files. Unfortunately, developers must sign the agreement using not virtual mail, but snail mail, which can be a problem for those outside the United States. The size of the ROM files is 1–2 MB, depending on the version. In this book we will mostly refer to the version for Palm VII, since this is one of the latest versions, and the only one that supports wireless connection simulation (see *Chapter 10*). To obtain the ROM files of other devices, such as Handspring, Handera, Symbol, etc., visit the web sites of the respective manufacturers. Due to the complexity of the ROM files that you will receive from the manufacturers, we will tell you in more detail how to load a ROM file from a particular Palm device. To load a ROM file from Palm to a desktop, you should:

1. Connect Palm to the desktop PC.
2. Install ROM Transfer.prc on your Palm device. You can find this application in the root directory of your emulator. You can either use Palm Install Tool for this, or simply drag the file from the folder into the emulator (you will find more details on this method of installation later in this chapter).
3. Start the emulator.
4. In the window that opens (Fig. 5.11), select the **Download a ROM image from a Palm OS device** option. If this window fails to appear, click with the right mouse button on the emulator and select **New** from the menu (Fig. 5.13).
5. Follow the simple instructions and set the type of the connection speed, the port number, etc.

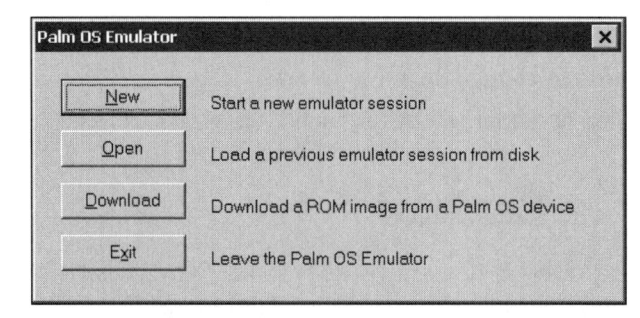

Fig. 5.11. The ROM file loading from Palm for the emulator

After the ROM file is installed, your emulator will become a copy of your real Palm device.

Note that some ROM files on the Palm web site also feature debugging options, whereas the ROM downloaded from the real device lacks such an option.

Installing the ROM File

After the ROM file is downloaded from the device or the web site to the desktop PC, you can start installing it on the Palm emulator. There are several ways of doing this. The simplest is to double-click on the ROM file to be installed. As a result, a window similar to the one shown in Fig. 5.12 will appear.

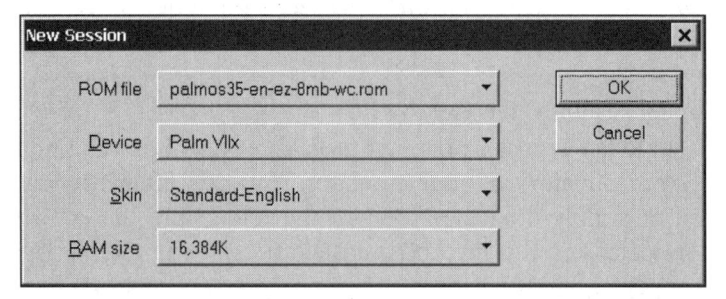

Fig. 5.12. Installing the ROM file on the emulator

The upper pop-up line will allow you to select the ROM file (if there are several of them), the **Device** line will automatically show the Palm model corresponding to the selected ROM file, and the lower line will help you select the memory size. Click

Chapter 5: Introduction to AppForge MobileVB

OK to complete the ROM file installation on POSE. Another way to install the ROM file is through the pop-up menu. Clicking on the emulator with the right mouse button brings up the menu shown in Fig. 5.13.

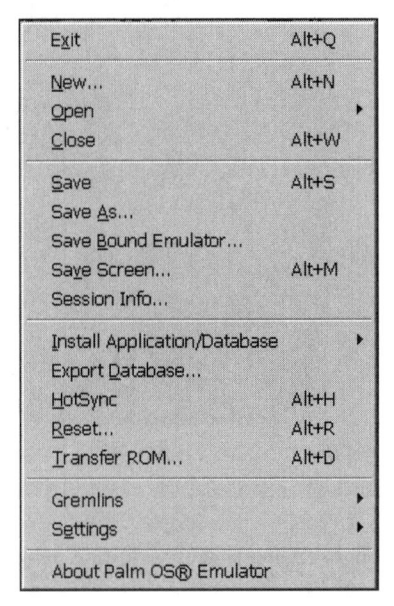

Fig. 5.13. The emulator pop-up menu

If you select **New** from this menu, you will return to the window shown in Fig. 5.12.

Installing the Booster

We mentioned above that the booster is needed to make applications created on MobileVB work on Palm (or Windows CE). Therefore, you need to install the booster as well. The simplest way of installing the booster on the emulator is to open the C:\Program Files\AppForge\Platforms\PalmOS\TargetImage folder and drag all the files it contains to the emulator. After the last file is dragged to POSE, you will see the booster icon in the panel (see Fig. 5.14, the upper right corner). Now you can install and test applications created on AppForge MobileVB.

Fig. 5.14. The booster on the Palm's application panel

Installing the Application on the Emulator

We have already partially considered installing the application on POSE, when we dragged the booster to it. Any application is a file with the PRC extension, and, possibly, a set of accompanying files, such as databases with the PDB extension, or graphics. All we need to do is to drag and drop them on the emulator in order to install and subsequently use them. You can also use the pop-up menu (see Fig. 5.13). Select the **Install Application/Database/Other** command to open the standard dialog window that asks you to select the file to be installed. This procedure is necessary for all the files included in the application.

Gremlins

We have already considered several important commands of the emulator pop-up menu (see Fig. 5.13). The **Gremlins** command is of special interest. Gremlins is a utility inherited from Macintosh. Gremlins is a series of pseudo-randomly generated data-entry events on the Palm device. It tries to exhaust all the options that a human being can not implement within the limited testing time. If an error is detected by Gremlins, the series of events leading to it can be reproduced, which helps you immensely in the process of testing and debugging. The Gremlins options can be set from a special window (Fig. 5.15).

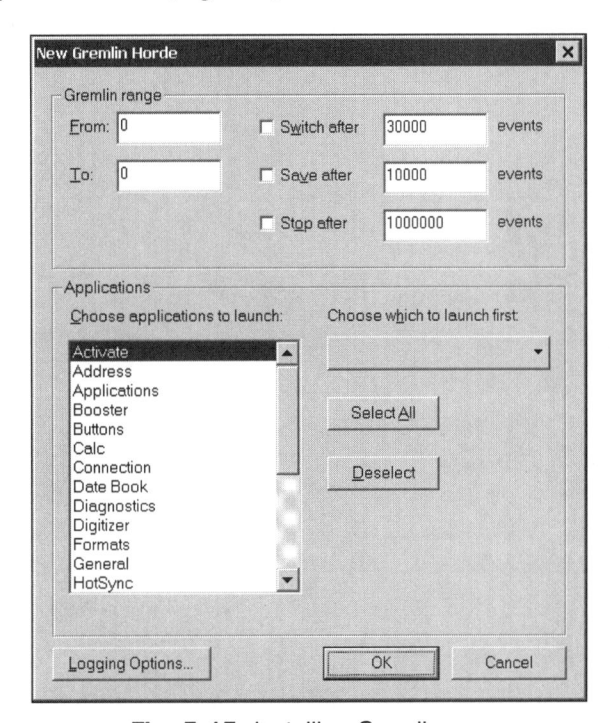

Fig. 5.15. Installing Gremlins

This window enables you to enter source values from 0 to 999, specify the required number of times a series should be tested, and select the application for testing. You can also specify many more parameters from the window opened by the **Logging Options** command button.

Settings allows you to set a number of parameters that simplify testing. The emulator is well-documented. Here we have just given you a small excursion around this very useful utility, which will be referred to very often later.

▶ Note

Although the Palm company supports and improves the emulator, it is not its developer. The original emulator, which used to be called CoPilot, was created by Greg Hewgill and a number of other developers.

Chapter 6

Working with Ingots

The main accomplishment of the AppForge developers is that they have managed to create compact, efficient ingots. All of them possess fewer properties and methods than their standard analogs in Visual Basic. First of all, this is dictated by the limitations of the pocket computer/PDA processor, the limited memory size, and its self-contained power supply. But they also work within a Windows environment. The AppForge MobileVB ingots are located in the lower part of the control panel, and marked with a yellow letter "i" (see Fig. 4.5 (in *Chapter 4*)). Almost every element has an analog in VB, but if you try to use an ingot from VB, you will get an error message. Ingots are easily added to the project as standard ActiveX components. To do this, select **Components** from the **Project** menu and select the necessary ingot from the window that appears (Fig. 6.1).

The names of all the components in which we are interested are preceded by the word AppForge.

After the ingot is selected in the **Components** window, it appears on the toolbar. The ingots are applied to the form of the project in absolutely the same way as in Visual Basic. Before starting to describe developing the first application, it is worth saying a few words about the available ingots. Table 6.1 below lists the main AppForge MobileVB ingots supported by the third version.

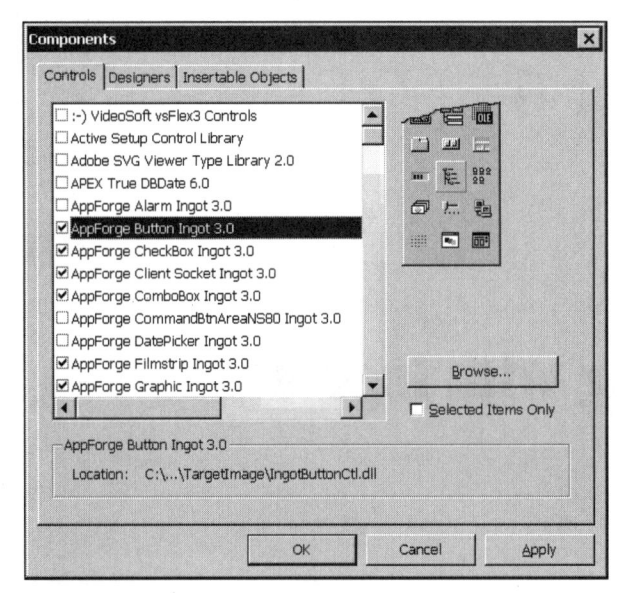

Part II: Programming Palm OS with Appforge MobileVB

Fig. 6.1. Selecting ingots for an AppForge MobileVB project

Table 6.1. A List of the Project Objects (Except for the Form)

Name of element	Description
AFButton	Same as command button
AFCheckBox	Checkbox
AFClientSocket	Communication ingot
AFComboBox	ComboBox
AFFilmstrip	Displays a series of images
AFGraphic	Static graphic image
AFGraphicButton	Command button with image
AFGrid	Grid
AFHScrollBar	Horizontal scrollbar
AFVScrollBar	Vertical scrollbar
AFINetHTTP	HTTP ingot
AFLabel	Label
AFListBox	ListBox

continues

Table 6.1 Continued

Name of element	Description
AFMovie	Video file is played
AFRadioButton	Option button
AFScanner	Invisible ingot. Used for reading commercial codes
AFSerial	Communication ingot
AFShape	Applies geometrical figures to the form
AFSignatureCapture	For entering text via the display. Saves the text in a variable of the String type
AFSlider	Ingot for scrolling photo files
AFTextBox	TextBox
AFTimer	Manages the code via a specific time interval
AFTone	Creates tones

Detailed descriptions of the methods, properties, and events of the above ingots are in the instructions supplied with AppForge MobileVB. In this and later chapters, we will demonstrate some of them with concrete examples. The most specific and unusual ingots will be considered later in this chapter. As stated in the introduction, our task is to bring out the simplicity and pleasure of programming for pocket computers and PDAs. This book is not a manual, and our approach is by all means subjective. Due to the limits of this book, or to our own personal interests, some aspects will unfortunately not be covered. To demonstrate some ingots, let's consider a simplified game.

Project Description

The purpose of our project will be to create a form of blackjack to work on Palm. The player can take up to 4 cards from the deck, and then the computer, acting as the dealer, can do the same. A comparison of points determines the winner. For the algorithms below, we will assume that any number of points over 21 means a loss. In order to encourage the player, the dealer will take off her clothes as the player wins, or put them back on as the dealer wins. We are not going to go into the particulars of the files prepared for this purpose, but are rather going to discuss the format of these files.

The Project's Graphic Files

The **MobileVB Help** menu declares that the software supports both BMP and JPEG files. We managed to place the JPG file into the graphic ingot during the process of developing the application. But attempts to specify the `Picture` property "on the fly" (during the application's execution) always ended in an error message. As a result, we had to create all the necessary files as BMP files. Since none of the graphic ingots of our project has an associated file, it is worth remembering that before the project is compiled, we have to indicate all the graphic files that we want to use. There are four of them: 4 cards of different suits, and, say, a series of 6 files with the image of the dealer. The size of the graphic ingot and the size of the image needn't be the same. The ingot cuts the file if the the image exceeds its size. In order for the **MobileVB** project to be able to find all the graphic files, they should be placed in the same folder as the project.

Creating the Project Interface

First, let's make the graphic files with the images of the cards and the dealer. Do not rush to duplicate every card of the deck, though. The resources of the pocket computer (especially Palm) are rather limited both in terms of RAM and operating speed. We will simply imitate each card in order to save space. Create 4 files with the image of the card suit in each. Since Palm supports the widely used BMP format, save the files in this format. Here, we have only two options: color or monochrome. As yet, AppForge does not support the other, more colorful BMP formats. However, you can create a file with any color spectrum in BMP and then use the AppForge utility to convert this file into RGX: the image will become monochrome, but the file will be considerably reduced in size. Therefore, deciding on the file format mainly depends on the type of device for which the application is created.

Now open the new **MobileVB** project, select Palm as the operating system of the future application, and have the new blank form to begin with. Place five graphic ingots on the form (`AFGraphic`) (see Fig. 6.2): one as the image of the dealer, and the other four as the card images. These four will represent the collection of the ingots (`imgCard()`) with the indices from 0 to 3. Above these graphic objects, apply the set of labels with indices from 0 to 3. These labels will serve to identify the value of the card (from 6 to Ace). Here, the **Zoom** function selected from the **MobileVB/Zoom Window** menu is another useful utility. Fig. 6.2 shows the lower part of the form enlarged using the **Zoom** window.

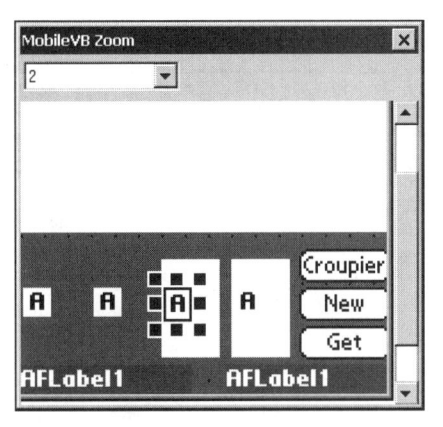

Fig. 6.2. The label is right above the graphic object

Here, we have deliberately highlighted the border of one of the labels (third from the left) and highlighted in white the area in the graphic objects used to imitate the cards. The card image itself turned out to be smaller than the area we selected for the card, and has rounded corners as well. To avoid absurdity, we selected a **BackColor** property of the form, labels, and graphic elements of the same color — green. Let's also add two labels to the form to show the player's and dealer's points, one label at the top of the form to identify the winner, and three command buttons: **Croupier** — the dealer's game, **New** — start a new game, and **Get** — the player gets another card.

The general view of the form is shown in Fig. 6.3.

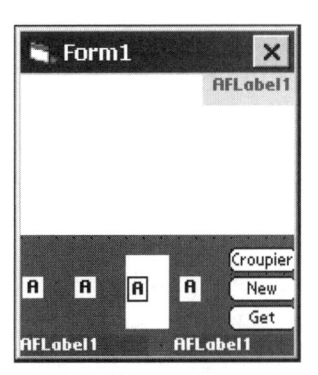

Fig. 6.3. Form in the design view

Let's sum up all the project ingots in Table 6.2.

Table 6.2. A List of the Project Objects (Except for the Form)

Ingot	Name	Purpose	Note
AFButton	CmdDealer	Show dealer's cards	
AFButton	CmdNew	Start new game	
AFButton	CmdGet	Show player's card	
AFGraphic	imgDealer	Dealer's image	
AFGraphic	ImgCard(i)	Card suit image	Set of 4 ingots
AFLabel	LblCard(i)	Shows the card value	Set of 4 ingots
AFLabel	lblMyScore	Player's score	
AFLabel	LblDealerScore	Dealer's score	
AFLabel	LblWin	Shows the winner	

Before turning to the codes, clear the Caption properties of all labels, so that there are no system messages that have anything to do with the project while the form is loading. Also, specify the BackColor property of the LblCard(i) labels as green, so that they merge with the field background.

When the application is started, the player must first draw cards from the deck. So we'll start the application with the cmdGet_Click event. First of all, we have to count the cards drawn. If four cards have already been taken, all we can do is inform the player that the limit has been reached, even if he or she still has very few points. Store the number of the drawn card in the iCardNumber variable, which is declared on the module level, i.e., it remembers its previous value when the cmdGet_Click procedure is called.

Then, inform the intValue local variable of the card's value. We assume that there are 36 cards in play, where the Jack, Queen, and King are valued as 2, 3, and 4, respectively, and Ace is 11. Use the RandomLong function from the AppForge MobileVB library to generate the card value randomly. This function returns a long number from zero to a value less than the one indicated in the argument by one. This card value will be taken into account when the player's score is counted in the lTotalMyScore variable. Finally, we call the SetCardValue procedure which shows the card on the display.

This procedure is represented in Listing 6.1.

Listing 6.1. The `cmdGet_Click` procedure

```
Private Sub cmdGet_Click()
Dim intValue As Integer
' - module level variable counts open cards
iCardNumber = iCardNumber + 1
' - ignore the procedure if number of cards > 4
If iCardNumber > 4 Then
    ' - MsgBox in MobileVB can not have more then 2 arguments
    MsgBox "Sorry! No more cards allowed!", vbCritical
    Exit Sub
End If
' - setting a random value between 2 and 11
' - (function RandomLong return values between 0 and 9)
intValue = 2 + RandomLong(10)
' - player point count
iTotalMyScore = iTotalMyScore + intValue
' - display points on the screen
lblMyScore.Caption = "My Score: " & iTotalMyScore
' - function for displaying cards
Call SetCardValue(intValue, iCardNumber)
End Sub
```

Note that the `RandomLong()` function requires initialization. The initialization of the function consists of specifying the first source value. If the first specified value is the same for different series, then the sequence of numbers in the series will also be the same. Initialization is done using another library (MobileVB) function, `SeedRandomLong`, which, in turn, requires an argument. Just call this function once, for example, when the application is loaded. You can use any random whole value as an argument. We will use another **MobileVB** function as an argument — `TimerMS` — which returns a whole number based on the current time.

Thus, the initialization of the `RandomLong()` function looks like `SeedRandomLong TimerMS`, and is located in the `Form_Load` event.

Let's consider in more detail what is going on in the SetCardValue procedure. As is evident from Listing 6.1, there are two arguments assigned to this function. One indicates the value of the card (from 2 to 11), and the other indicates its number (from 0 to 3). If the first parameter has a value from 6 to 10, then the lblCard(i) label should have this numerical value. With other values of the parameter, the label will show the first letter of the card's name. The second part of the procedure specifies the value of the suit of the card. Here, we again use the random number generator from 1 to 4, and load the corresponding file in the graphic ingot. The full SetCardValue procedure is shown in Listing 6.2.

Listing 6.2. The SetCardValue procedure

```
Public Sub SetCardValue(intCardValue As Integer, _
                        intCardNumber As Integer)
Dim intSuit As Integer

Select Case intCardValue
Case 11   ' - Ace
    lblCard(intCardNumber - 1).Caption = "A"
    ' - changing the label background color to white
    lblCard(intCardNumber - 1).BackColor = &HFFFFFF
Case 2   ' - Jack
    lblCard(intCardNumber - 1).Caption = "J"
    lblCard(intCardNumber - 1).BackColor = &HFFFFFF
Case 3   ' - Queen
    lblCard(intCardNumber - 1).Caption = "Q"
    lblCard(intCardNumber - 1).BackColor = &HFFFFFF
Case 4   ' - King
    lblCard(intCardNumber - 1).Caption = "K"
    lblCard(intCardNumber - 1).BackColor = &HFFFFFF
Case Else   ' - number card
    lblCard(intCardNumber - 1).Caption = CStr(intCardValue)
    lblCard(intCardNumber - 1).BackColor = &HFFFFFF
End Select

' - generating 1 of 4 suits
intSuit = 1 + RandomLong(4)
Select Case intSuit
Case 1
    imgCard(intCardNumber - 1).Picture = "diamonds.bmp"
Case 2
    imgCard(intCardNumber - 1).Picture = "hearts.bmp"
```

```
Case 3
    imgCard(intCardNumber - 1).Picture = "spades.bmp"
Case 4
    imgCard(intCardNumber - 1).Picture = "clubs.bmp"
End Select

End Sub
```

Actually, our method of random card generation is imperfect. The probability that a card will repeat itself (which will never happen when playing with a real deck) is not so low — about 16%. Our task is rather to demonstrate the specific programming techniques than to go into the details of developing a real game. The interested reader will always find the right algorithm or a way to improve the existing one.

> **A mathematical digression for a methodical reader**
>
> Let's calculate the probability that, out of four randomly generated cards, at least one pair will be the same. Our method of random card generation imitates a situation in which the player takes cards one by one from 4 decks in front of him or her. After the player has taken a card from the first deck, the probability that the second card will be different is 35/36. The probability that the third card will be different than both of the previous two is 34/36, and the probability that the last card will be different from all three of those is 33/36. Therefore, the probability that at least one pair of identical cards will appear is equal to $1 - (35 \times 34 \times 33)/(36 \times 36 \times 36) = 0.158$.

After the player is satisfied with the points gained, he or she should click on the **cmdDealer** button to let the dealer take her turn. In the `cmdDealer_Click` procedure, the first thing to be done is to clear all the cards and make them ready to be filled again. The `Caption` property of each label should become blank. The `Picture` property of each graphic object bearing the suit of the card should also be blank, and the color of the label values of the cards should be returned to green, to avoid white spots. Then let the procedure generate the necessary number of cards. As soon as the value of the next card makes the total value of points exceed 21, we leave the cycle and stop at the previous one, since an excess of points always means a loss. The `cmdDealer_Click` procedure is shown in Listing 6.3.

Listing 6.3. Generating the dealer's cards

```
Private Sub cmdDealer_Click()
' - variable for the dealer's points
Dim iScore As Integer
Dim k As Integer
Dim iCardValue As Integer

' - clearing controls to accept new values
For k = 0 To 3
  lblCard(k).Caption = ""
  lblCard(k).BackColor = &H8000&
  imgCard(k).Picture = ""
Next k

k = 1
' - setting the first card's value
iCardValue = 2 + RandomLong(10)
iScore = iCardValue
Do While iScore < 22
    ' - the function for displaying the card
    Call SetCardValue(iCardValue, k)
    ' -- setting the card value in the cycle
    iCardValue = 2 + RandomLong(10)
    ' -- displaying the dealer's score
    lblDealerScore.Caption = "Her Score: " & iScore

    iScore = iScore + iCardValue

    k = k + 1

    If k > 4 Then Exit Do

Loop
' -- the dealer's score before the last card will be passed to the procedure
Call DealerAction(iScore - iCardValue)

End Sub
```

Chapter 6: Working with Ingots

The `DealerAction` procedure is simply the code of rules that determines the winner. In addition, the procedure displays information on who is the winner, and depending on it, we load a top-down or bottom-up file with the image of the dealer. The procedure is shown in Listing 6.4.

Listing 6.4. Provedure for determining the winner

```
Public Sub DealerAction(iDealerScore As Integer)
' -- invisible label over the picture of the dealer
lblWin.Visible = True

' -- the player won
If iTotalMyScore <= 21 And iDealerScore > 21 Then
    ' -- assuming we have 6 files with pictures of the dealer:
    ' 1.bmp,..., 6.bmp
    If intClothesNumber = 6 Then
        intClothesNumber = 6
    Else
        intClothesNumber = intClothesNumber + 1
    End If
    imgDealer.Picture = CStr(intClothesNumber) & ".bmp"
    lblWin.Caption = "You won!"
End If

If iTotalMyScore <= 21 And iDealerScore <= 21 And _
   (iTotalMyScore - iDealerScore > 0) Then
    If intClothesNumber = 6 Then
        intClothesNumber = 6
    Else
        intClothesNumber = intClothesNumber + 1
    End If
    imgDealer.Picture = CStr(intClothesNumber) & ".bmp"
    lblWin.Caption = "You won!"
End If

' - the dealer won
If iTotalMyScore > 21 Then
    If intClothesNumber = 1 Then
        intClothesNumber = 1
```

```
        Else
            intClothesNumber = intClothesNumber - 1
        End If
        imgDealer.Picture = CStr(intClothesNumber) & ".bmp"
        lblWin.Caption = "I won!"
End If

If iTotalMyScore <= 21 And iDealerScore <= 21 And _
    (iTotalMyScore - iDealerScore < 0) Then
        If intClothesNumber = 1 Then
            intClothesNumber = 1
        Else
            intClothesNumber = intClothesNumber - 1
        End If
        imgDealer.Picture = CStr(intClothesNumber) & ".bmp"
        lblWin.Caption = "I won!"
End If
' - to prevent errors
If intClothesNumber < 1 Then intClothesNumber = 1
If intClothesNumber > 6 Then intClothesNumber = 6

End Sub
```

There is one last procedure we have not yet considered: `cmdNew_Click`, which resets all ingots before a new game is started (Listing 6.5).

Listing 6.5. Procedure for starting a new game

```
Private Sub cmdNew_Click()
Dim i As Integer
' - card number starts with 0
iCardNumber = 0
' - hide label so as not to mask the image
lblWin.Visible = False
' - clear score labels
lblMyScore.Caption = ""
lblKrupieScore.Caption = ""

iTotalMyScore = 0
```

```
For i = 0 To 3
  lblCard(i).Caption = ""
  ' - reset the green background for labels
  lblCard(i).BackColor = &H8000&
  imgCard(i).Picture = ""
Next i

End Sub
```

The ready-to-use application looks as shown in Fig. 6.4.

Fig. 6.4. The ready-to-use application during execution

Now that the application is completed, you need to compile it and copy it to Palm. Before we do this, we should make sure that all external files we used in the application (e.g., pictures) are included in the project as dependent. For this purpose, select the **MobileVB Settings** command from the **MobileVB** menu. As a result, we will have the window shown in Fig. 6.5, where all the necessary files are added using the **Add** button. Now select the **Compile and Validate** command from the same menu to compile the project. First, a check of the ingots to check that they are properly used will take place (Fig. 6.6).

Then, a special window with error messages (if there are any) should appear. Double-clicking on the line with the revealed error usually moves the cursor to the error. If there are no errors or messages, you can move on to copying the application to the pocket computer (with the **Deploy to Device** command). If we are talking about copying the application to a Pocket PC, then the CAB file would first be created (Fig. 6.7), which would be copied and installed on the device during synchronization of the device. Note that, in general, when the application is to be installed on a Pocket PC and not on a Palm, then the device should be connected to the PC when the **Deploy to Device** command is called.

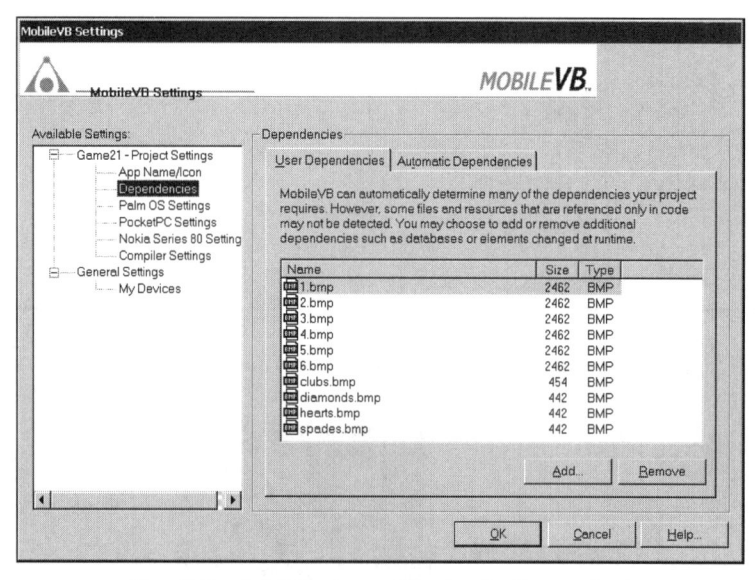

Fig. 6.5. Adding dependencies to the project

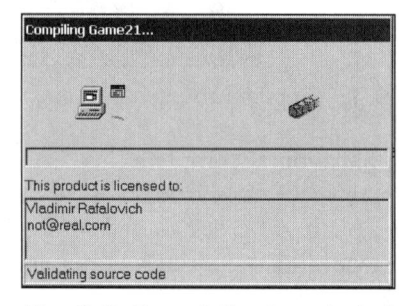

Fig. 6.6. Compilation has started

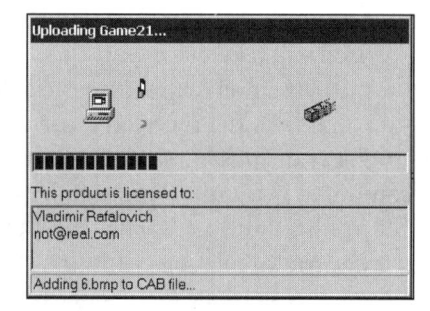

Fig. 6.7. Creating a CAB file for copying the application to a pocket computer

Chapter 6: Working with Ingots 123

On a Palm, a binary file with the extension PRC will be created, which will be copied to the Palm during its next synchronization with the desktop PC. The file can be dragged to the emulator for testing.

Fig. 6.8 shows a view of our application in the general application window of Palm.

Fig. 6.9 shows a fragment of the game on a monochrome emulator.

Fig. 6.8. The "Game 21" application after installation on the emulator

Fig. 6.9. The developed application on the emulator

Now let's consider some specific ingots that differ from the standard ones available in Visual Basic.

The *AFMovie* Ingot

This ingot enables you to play video files on a handheld device. To do this, the AVI file should first be converted into an RMV file (a special AppForge format) using the **Movie Converter** utility. In this version of AppForge (version 3), sound is not supported.

This ingot should be transferred to the form. In the development stage, it will be transparent. Use `FileName` to select the required RMV file. The file is started using `Play` and stopped using `Stop`. Set the `LoopMovie` property to `True` to loop the playback of the file. Note that, if the video file is set using the `FileName` property during the project's development, this file will be automatically included in the project during its compilation. If the property is used programmatically in codes, then the set of the necessary files should be included in the project.

The *AFFilmstrip* Ingot

This ingot is very much like the previous one, but instead of playing one video file, it plays a series of separate files (frames) loaded into the ingot in a certain sequence (which can be reset during the development process). After the ingot is projected to the form (Fig. 6.10), you can select sets of separate files, change their sequence, or delete unnecessary files, using the Frames property. Using the AnimationStyle property, set the play mode: single, loop, or bounce. This file is also started using Play, and stopped using Stop. The image size of the file need not necessarily be the same as that of the ingot, since the display size of the ingot is regulated by width and height independently of the size of the files.

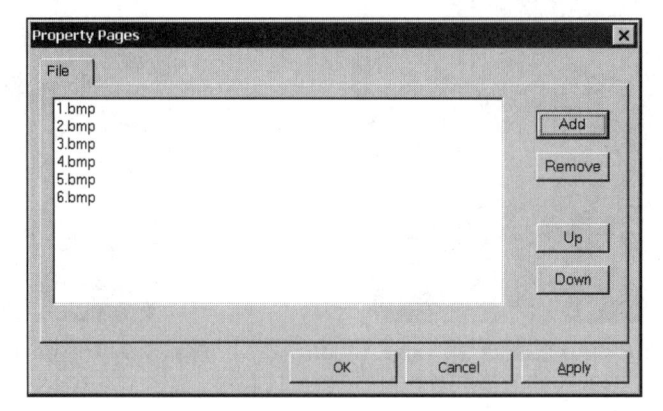

Fig. 6.10. The Frame property window, enabling you to manipulate files

The *AFSignatureCapture* Ingot

This is the most unusual, but definitely not the most useless ingot in the entire set of AppForge MobileVB tools. We know that practically all information (except for the synchronization processes) is entered into the pocket computer or PDA via the screen. This ingot is adjusted in such a way so that it provides the user with the option of entering the information via the display using handwritten text. To illustrate the performance of this ingot, let's create a new project. Apply two ingots of the AFSignatureCapture type to the form (with the names Signature1 and Signature2, respectively), two command buttons: cmdCopy and cmdPaste, and two labels. The first button will copy the image from Signature1 into the variable of the module level (strText). The second button will transfer the contents of this variable to the Signature2 ingot. The codes are indicated in Listing 6.6, and the result is seen in Fig. 6.11.

Listing 6.6. The procedure of copying the contents of the `Signature` ingot

```
Private Sub cmdCopy_Click()
strText = Signature1.SignatureData
End Sub

Private Sub cmdPaste_Click()
Signature2.SignatureData = strText
End Sub
```

Fig. 6.11. Saving and copying the image

The attempt to transfer the contents of the usual text field to `AFSignatureCapture` failed, since the nature of the contents of the text variable contents is not text.

Chapter 7

Databases in AppForge MobileVB

A considerable number of the applications developed for mobile devices involve the use of databases. In fact, the first PDA (which appeared a little earlier than pocket computers) was the address book. Therefore, we can say that even the first handheld device dealt with databases. Much time has passed since then, and the databases for pocket computers have been improved and developed further. The main hindrance to creating a sound mechanism for a database-control system is the relatively small size of the memory of a pocket computer or PDA, and databases tend to occupy more and more space as information is accumulated. The development of a database mechanism for pocket computers/PDA was done in parallel with the synchronization of the database with such a mechanism on the PCs. First of all, synchronization is needed in order to copy the information accumulated on the mobile device to the PC, and second, to transfer data from the PC to the pocket computer/PDA, since manual entry of large volumes of data on a pocket computer is too laborious. The first process is necessary if the mobile device is used to gather information on various physical localizations, and gathering and centralizing of the information will be needed later on, say, in a single corporate database. The second situation occurs when the user purchases a portable device and already has a considerable database with addresses, telephones, etc., which needs to be quickly transferred to his or her portable device from the desktop. Now, let's consider in more detail what the database used in MobileVB is. What is a database? First of all, it is a collection of one or more tables united by a common subject. Each table contains a set of fields, and each record contains the data for each field (or at least one, called the *primary key*). Each field in each specific table is unique, and the number of records can be unlimited. A database in Palm has the same structure, and that's why the option to convert an MS Access database into a Palm database appears. Conversion is possible with the use of the Database Converter utility, which was briefly discussed in *Chapter 5*. Strictly speaking, the Palm database is a binary file with the PDB extension. This file can contain only one table from MS Access. Therefore, one Access database can be transformed into several Palm files. Each type of data in Access is transformed to the corresponding type in Palm. Table 7.1 shows the types of Access data and their equivalents in Palm.

Table 7.1. Transformation of Data Types

Data type in Access	Data type in Palm
Text	String
Memo	String
Number, Field Size = Byte	Byte
Number, Field Size = Integer	Integer
Number, Field Size = Long Integer	Long
Number, Field Size = Single	Single
Number, Field Size = Double	Double
Number, Field Size = ReplicationID	Not supported
Number, Field Size = Decimal	Not supported
Date/Time	Date
Currency	Currency
AutoNumber	Long
Yes/No	Boolean

The Database Converter Utility

AppForge developed its own database standard and provided the application with a special utility to convert a table from Access into a PDB file. Fig. 7.1 shows the utility's general appearence.

How the converter works is obvious. Press the **Select** button to choose the necessary MS Access base, and then select the table to be converted from the drop-down list.

Chapter 7: Databases in AppForge MobileVB 129

After a successful conversion, the PDB file that results by default has the name of the table being converted.

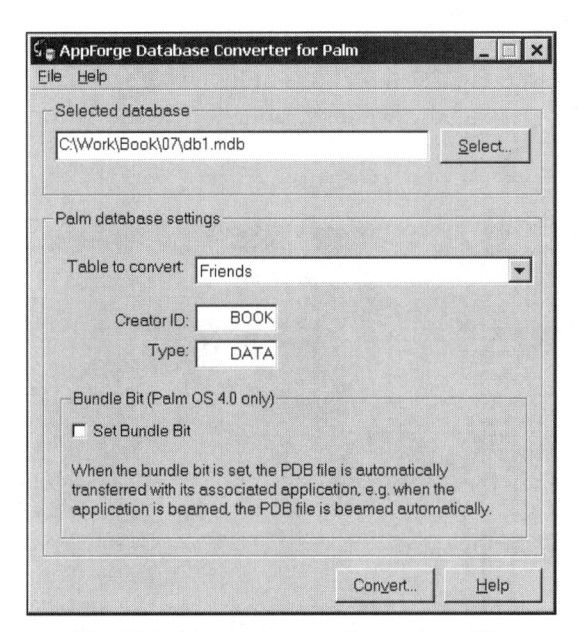

Fig. 7.1. The Database Converter utility

In order to distinguish the databases, you need to enter two unique identifiers during the conversion: **Creator ID** and **Type**. They are entered by the developer. **Creator ID** is the same value that is entered when the project properties are specified (see *Chapters 4* and *5*). This is necessary so that the database is associated with a certain application and is deleted from the PDA as soon as the application is deleted. In addition, as we will see below, **Creator ID** is needed in order for the special synchronization application (the conduit) to know which database is to be updated. Nevertheless, it is not necessary for the PDB file and its corresponding application to have the same identifier. We will see in Listing 7.2 that the actual connection between the application and the database is performed via the PDBOpen function, which has no Creator ID in its parameters. In most cases, the Type identifier should be selected as DATA. Even if the application makes use of two or more files, all of them should have the same Creator ID and Type.

It should be mentioned that if the source table had a primary key, then in the final file the converter will create an analogous field used by the library functions of AppForge MobileVB for working with the records of the table. In addition, the converter will create a system message called **Schema**. It contains information on each field in the table: the field name, type of data, and number of the field. This information can be examined using another utility: Database Viewer. Fig. 7.2 shows this utility, where the table itself, named **Friends**, is in the lower part of the window, and its schema is found in the upper part of the window.

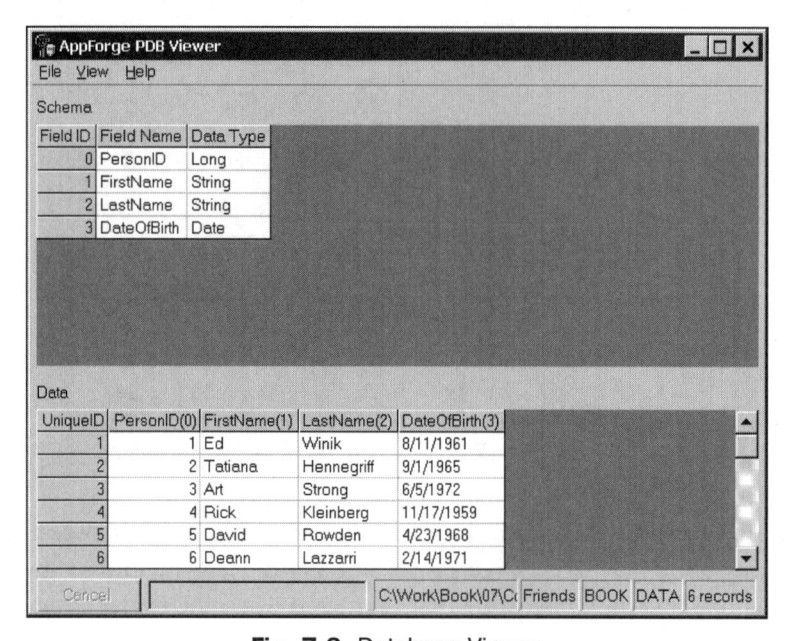

Fig. 7.2. Database Viewer

You can see that during the conversion, the **UniqueID** field was added to the table. In our case, it duplicates the **PersonID** field, which is the the primary key in the Access database. When new records are added to the table being converted (or when old records are deleted from the table), it is the **UniqueID** field that will be the primary key, whereas the values of the **PersonID** field are to be checked and accurately supported by the developer.

When the table conversion is finished, Database Converter will ask if you would like to create a special project module, which will contain the basic procedures for working with the newly created file.

Now let's consider these functions in more detail.

Functions of the Module Created During Conversion

The module created by the converter is a real Visual Basic module, and therefore can be easily added to any project in the usual way.

The module consists of the following parts: declaration of variables, the `OpenFriendsDatabase`, `ReadFriendsRecord`, and `WriteFriendsRecord` functions, and the `CloseFriendsDatabase` procedure. The word `Friends` contained in each name is generated by the converter and corresponds to the name of the Friends.pdb file (or to the table in Access).

The variable declaration area is shown and explained in Listing 7.1.

Listing 7.1. Variable declaration

```
Option Explicit
'   - Use these constants for the CreatorID and TypeID
Public Const Friends_CreatorID As Long = &H54455354
Public Const Friends_TypeID As Long = &H44415441
'   - Use this global to store the database handle
Public dbFriends As Long
'   - Use this enumeration to get access to the converted database Fields
Public Enum tFriendsDatabaseFields
        PersonID_Field = 0
        FirstName_Field = 1
        LastName_Field = 2
        DateOfBirth_Field = 3
End Enum

Public Type tFriendsRecord
        PersonID As Long
        FirstName As String
        LastName As String
        DateOfBirth As Date
End Type
```

The `dbFriends` variable will be used in the application for database identification, the size of the listed `tFriendsDatabaseFields` type obviously depends on the number of fields in the database, and the user's type of data `tFriendsRecord` enables you to store the records from the database.

The next logical step is to open the database to start work with it. This is done with the `OpenFriendsDatabase` function, whose contents are shown in Listing 7.2. First, the environment (conditional compilation) where the application operates is determined: is this a development stage, or it is already being executed on Palm? The file is opened using the integrated `PDBOpen` function. This function returns zero if an error occurs while opening the database. The first argument of the `PDBOpen` function indicates what method the database is searched by. In this case it is by the file name. Other variants are by `Type` and by `Creator ID`. The **Help** menu of AppForge MobileVB contains a detailed description of other arguments, which in our case have the default values.

Listing 7.2. The function opening the database

```
Public Function OpenFriendsDatabase() As Boolean
  ' - Open the database
  #If APPFORGE Then
    dbFriends = PDBOpen(Byfilename, "Friends", 0, 0, 0, 0, _
                       afModeReadWrite)
  #Else
    dbFriends = PDBOpen(Byfilename, App.Path & "\Friends", _
                       0, 0, 0, 0,  & afModeReadWrite)
  #End If

  If dbFriends <> 0 Then
    ' - We have successfully opened the database
    OpenFriendsDatabase = True
  Else
    ' - We have failed to open the database
    OpenFriendsDatabase = False
    #If APPFORGE Then
      MsgBox "Could not open database — Friends", vbExclamation
    #Else
      MsgBox "Could not open database — " + App.Path + _
             "\Friends.pdb" + & _
              vbCrLf  & vbCrLf & _
             "Potential causes are:" + vbCrLf + _
             "1. Database file does not   & _
             exist" +  vbCrLf + _
             "2. The database path in the PDBOpen call is & _
             incorrect", vbExclamation
```

```
    #End If
  End If

End Function
```

The function opposite to the one described above closes the database: `CloseFriendsDatabase()`. It also uses the library function `PDBClose`, and is shown in Listing 7.3

Listing 7.3. The function closing the database

```
Public Sub CloseFriendsDatabase()
  ' - Close the database
  PDBClose dbFriends
  dbFriends = 0
End Sub
```

Two more MobileVB functions are those for reading and updating records. The `ReadFriendsRecord()` function is shown in Listing 7.4. This function reads the records and returns the result to the `MyRecord` variable of the `tFriendsRecord` user type, declared at the beginning of the module (see Listing 7.1). The value of each field of the record is recorded in each element of the structural variable `tFriendsRecord`. The function itself returns `True` if the operation was successful, and `False` if there was an error.

Listing 7.4. Reading a record from a database

```
Public Function ReadFriendsRecord(MyRecord As tFriendsRecord) As Boolean
  ReadFriendsRecord = PDBReadRecord(dbFriends, VarPtr(MyRecord))
End Function
```

The function for recording data from a variable into the database is shown in Listing 7.5. The function acquires the value of the user's variable, and each field of the current record of the database is changed according to the new values.

Listing 7.5. Creating a record in the database

```
Public Function WriteFriendsRecord(MyRecord As tFriendsRecord) As Boolean
  WriteFriendsRecord = PDBWriteRecord(dbFriends, VarPtr(MyRecord))
End Function
```

The Universal Conduit

A discussion about databases would be incomplete without mentioning how to synchronize the data between the PC and the Palm. It is just this data synchronization during the connection session between the devices (HotSync) for which conduits are intended. Therefore, a conduit is an application that moves the data between databases on different computers. Conduit is not an AppForge product, but a notion that exists in the world of pocket computers. The conduit is controlled by HotSync Manager, another application responsible for the operation of the desktop PC with the pocket computer during the connection session. HotSync Manager has a list of all conduits, each of them being responsible for a particular synchronization process, such as data transfer from Access on the PC to the corresponding file on the pocket computer. As a result, having connected two computers (via a cable or the IR port), HotSync Manager consecutively executes the task of each conduit. When the operation of the last conduit is complete, the session is complete. Obviously, the conduit is a rather intelligent application with the following functions:

- Opening and closing the databases on the PC and pocket computer
- Determining the procedures to be performed: load data from the pocket computer/PDA to the PC, vice versa, or perform both procedures
- Determining the records modified on one of the computers, updating them, and, if necessary, deleting old records or adding new ones
- Converting data from one type into another if the filed types in both databases are different

Now let's consider in more detail the data-synchronization process. Each Palm PDA has its own unique identifier (Palm ID). This is why HotSync Manager distinguishes each Palm individually, and during synchronization checks the data update for the particular Palm. Data synchronization can be done by one of two methods: SlowSync (slow synchronization) and FastSync (fast synchronization). The method should be selected taking into consideration optimization and minimization of the run time. In SlowSync, the conduit compares each record on Palm with each record on the PC. In FastSync, only the records marked as updated are compared. HotSync Manager saves the ID number of the PC that was connected to the pocket computer/PDA last time on the pocket computer. If the Palm is connected to the same PC in the current session, then FastSync is performed. If HotSync Manager detects that it is another PC, then SlowSync takes place.

Chapter 7: Databases in AppForge MobileVB 135

The conduit can be written completely in Visual Basic and third-party applications. For example, there is the Palm Conduit Development Kit (CDK), which you can download from the Palm web site (**www.palm.com**). This tool enables you to create conduits in both C++ and VB. AppForge, however, has provided a universal conduit to move data between any database-management system (via ODBC) and PDB files. Now we'll take a look at working with the universal conduit in more detail.

There are two options of specifying the properties of the conduit — graphically and using the UCConfigCmd.exe utility. We are going to consider a graphic case and a situation in which the new data from Access on the PC is to be added into a table on Palm. Open **Universal Conduit** from the MobileVB start menu (Fig. 7.3).

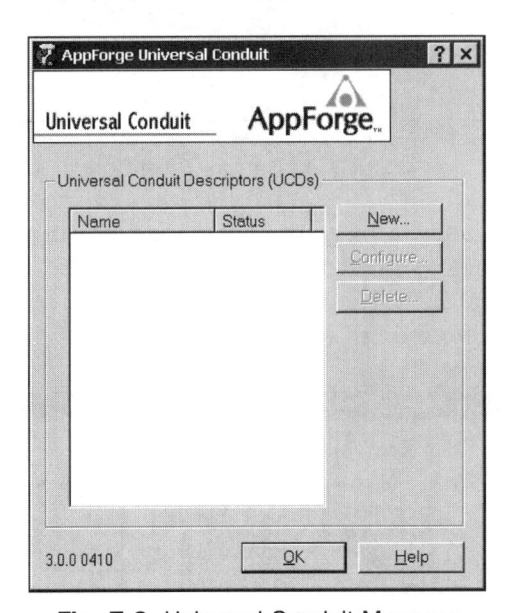

Fig. 7.3. Universal Conduit Manager

We now have to create the new conduit. To do this, click on the **New** button and go to the second step. Remember that in order to create a conduit (Fig. 7.4), you must:

- ❒ Create ODBC DSN for the database.
- ❒ Indicate, when needed, Creator ID for the application created on AppForge.
- ❒ Indicate for each table the field with the unique value for use in synchronization.

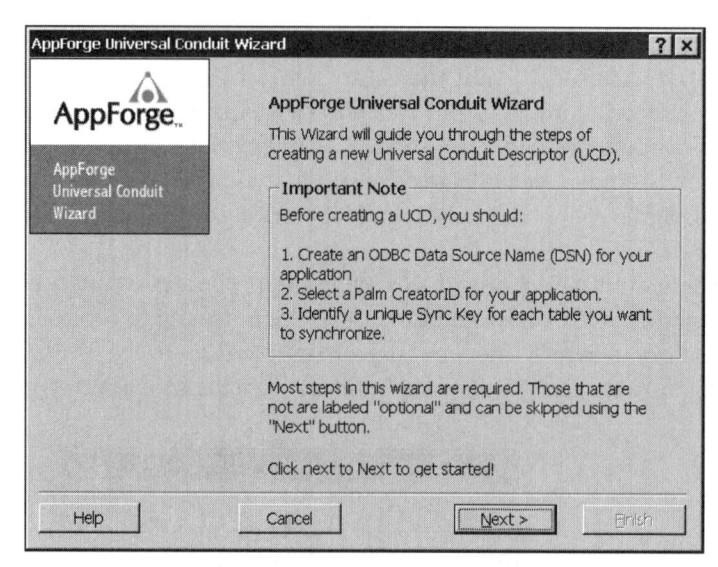

136 Programming Palm OS with Appforge MobileVB

Fig. 7.4. The Universal Conduit wizard

The next window asks you to enter the name of the conduit and Creator ID (Fig. 7.5). The name should make some kind of sense, since it will appear in the list of conduits (Fig. 7.3). The Creator ID should correspond to the PDB file with which you want to establish synchronization.

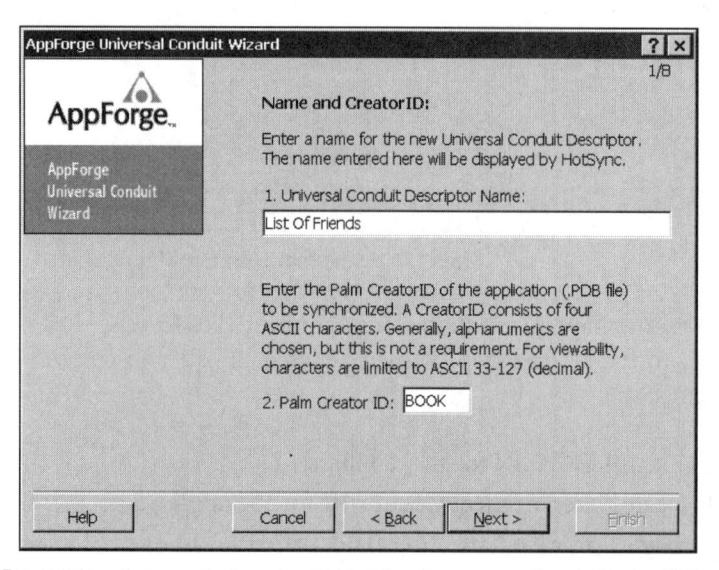

Fig. 7.5. Describing the conduit and establishing its connection with the Palm database

Chapter 7: Databases in AppForge MobileVB   137

The next step will be determining the database on the PC. To do this, select the required DSN from the list (Fig. 7.6). With MS Access, there is no need to create a DSN. After selecting MS Access Database from the list, a dialog window will appear, and the wizard will ask you to select the specific database.

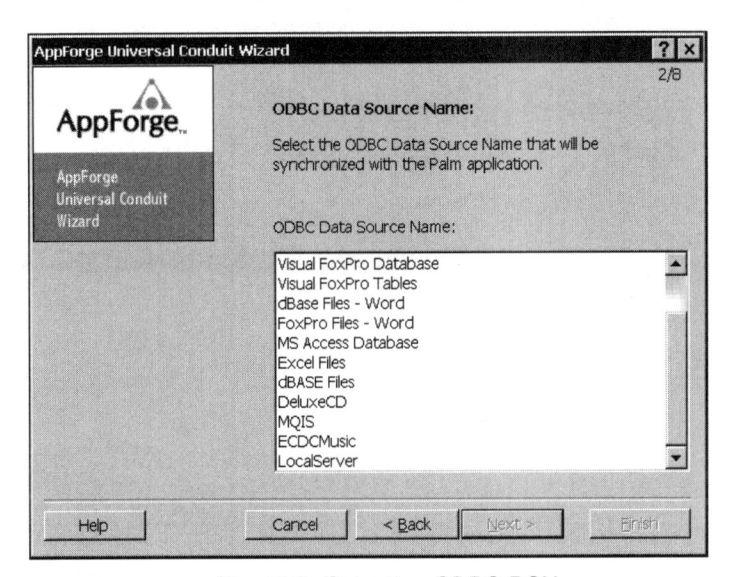

Fig. 7.6. Selecting ODBC DSN

After it is selected, we will see the list of all tables contained in the selected database displayed — Fig. 7.7. Select the required tables (in our case just one) and go to the screen for choosing the conduit type (Fig. 7.8).

If we select several tables, then the same steps need to be repeated for each table. The following types of synchronization are possible in the universal conduit:

- No synchronization (**Do Nothing**).
- Synchronize the tables between themselves. The changes in one table are recorded into the other, or vice versa. If the record was updated on both Palm and on the desktop computer, then the information from Palm is moved to the desktop (**Two-way**).
- The new records from the table on the desktop PC are added to the table on the Palm (**PC appends to Palm**).
- The new records from the Palm table are added to the database on the desktop PC (**Palm appends to PC**).

❐ The data of the Palm table are replaced by the data from the desktop PC (**PC replaces Palm**).
❐ The data of the PC table are replaced by the data from Palm (**Palm replaces PC**).

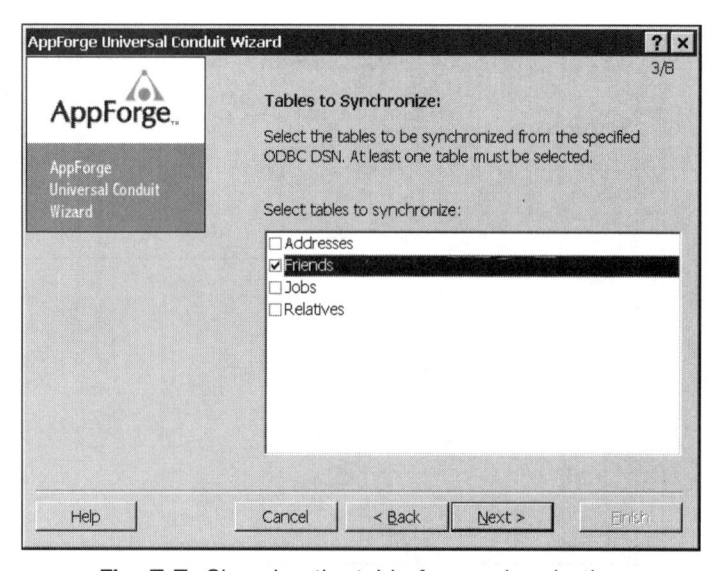

Fig. 7.7. Choosing the table for synchronization

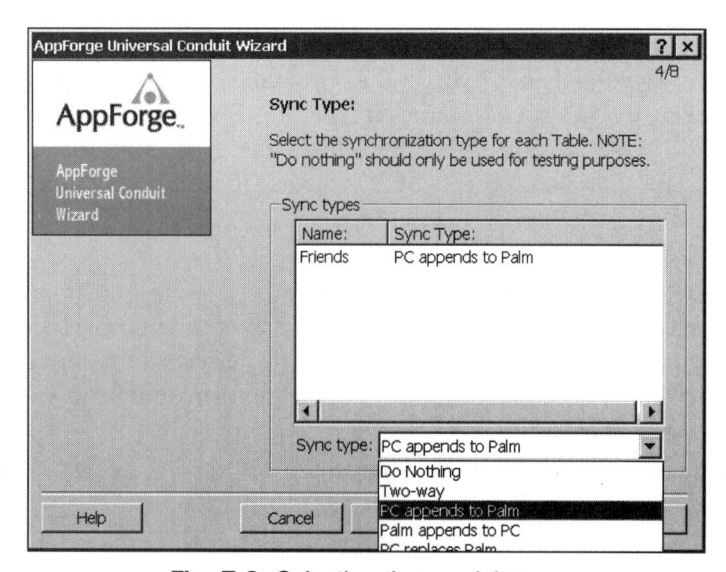

Fig. 7.8. Selecting the conduit type

Select **PC appends to Palm** and go to the next step (Fig. 7.9). Here we will perform item 3, indicated in Fig. 7.9 — setting the unique field by which the synchronization will be performed. Obviously, in our case this is the **PersonID** field, containing unique data for both tables.

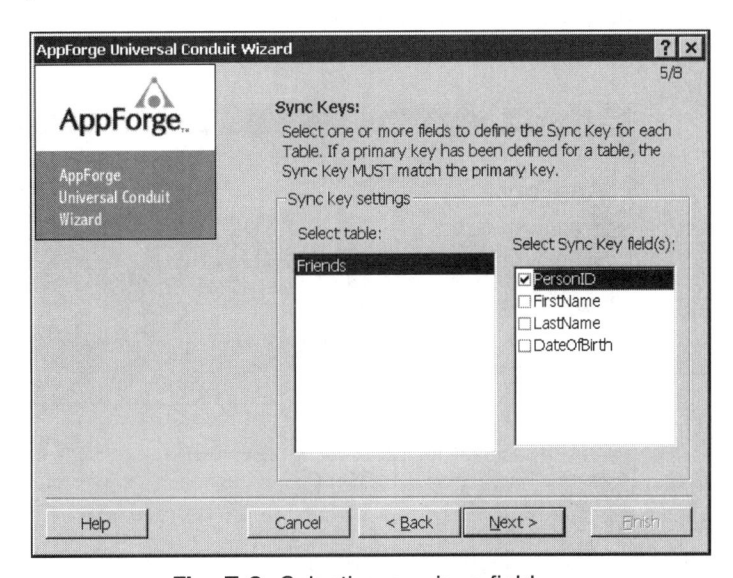

Fig. 7.9. Selecting a unique field

The next step (which is not shown) can be skipped, since it simply asks if you would like to create a Visual Basic module to work with the table records on Palm. We looked at this module when the "Friends" table was converted from MS Access into a Palm file. The last display shows the main settings of our conduit (Fig. 7.10). The **Finish** button completes the creation of the conduit that will add new records from Access on the PC into the friends.pdb file on Palm.

The left part of the display shows that you can select additional options for installing the conduit from the **Universal Conduit Manager** window (Fig. 7.3).

There is another problem, though, that needs to be solved in a programmatic way. If the **PersonID** field in MS Access used the **AutoNumber** function, the corresponding field in the friends.pdb file will not have this option, since Palm does not support it. To solve this problem, avoid creating the fields with **AutoNumber**, and instead create a procedure that generates identification numbers in a similar way for the Access and Palm databases. Nevertheless, the following general situation is possible. Suppose that after the new PDB file was created from the MS Access table, both tables had 8 records (as in Fig. 7.2). Then suppose that 5 records were added to the Friends table from the Access database. Then, **PersonID** for the new records will be: 9, 10, ..., 13. Let's also suppose that 3 other records were added directly into the Palm table via an application. Then say that we increased the **PersonID** value by 1. It is clear, however, that during synchronization, Palm adds just 2 records, notwithstanding that the contents of the other three records may be different in both databases.

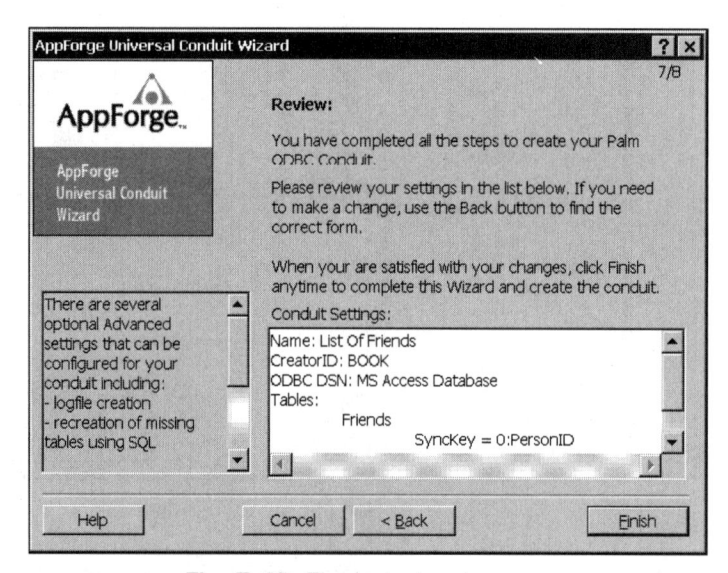

Fig. 7.10. The last wizard screen

To avoid such situations, you should either have an intermediate table into which the data will be entered only during the synchronization, and which will be compared with the main table, or perform synchronization by the person's last name.

As mentioned above, the conduit is executed by an instruction of the HotSync Manager, which in turn is initialized when Palm is connected. It is also worth mentioning here that the universal conduit is, as yet, not intended for use with databases on the Pocket PC — only with Palm PDA.

Chapter 8

Developing an Application with a Database

In the '70s and '80s, my grandfather received a pension of $1,200 a month, and he knew that he could afford to spend no more than $40 per day. Every evening before dinner, he sat down at the table to write down his daily expenses and summed them up. If the expense exceeded $40, he knew that the budget of the next day would be cut down. If the expense was less than $40, then I — the witness of his calculations — could figure on some candies. The most difficult thing for my grandfather was to recall all his daily expenses. As soon as he finished summing them up my grandma would recall something else, and the result was recalculated. Suppose my grandpa had a Palm! He could not only have entered his expenses right in the store and then summed them up in the evening, but also systematized his monthly purchases by type, sorted them out into categories, and had information on what category of expenses (food, clothes, utilities) took up the most money and which one cost the least, etc. The shrewd reader has already found in this story a target for our next project, with the database being its core.

The database whose prototype we will create on MS Access will have 2 tables: **Expense** and **Category**.

There will be five fields in the **Expense** table: **ID** (integer), **ExpenseName** (text), **Cost** (currency), **CategoryType** (integer), and **Date** (date/time). The **ID** field acts like the primary key. This will not be an auto number, however, since the user will enter his or her expenses via the Palm, and we have already noted that Palm has no similar function, and that the **ID** should be created separately.

There will be two fields in the **Category** table: **Category** (text) and **ID** (integer). In our example we do not provide an update of this table with new categories, but rather leave it for the reader as an independent warm-up. Of course, the reader could devise a better design for the database, but in our example we are not going to demonstrate database programming, just show a way to use AppForge's library functions for manipulating databases. The PDB files are not relational databases, and it is the programmer's task to support the data integrity.

Use the method described in *Chapter 7* to convert both tables into the Expense.pdb and Category.pdb files. To do this, enter two parameters in the **Database Converter** utility. The first is `CreatorID`, which can be any 4-letter word. You should remember that the same word must be used for the **CreatorID** project. Select the word "DATA" as the `Type` parameter, since, as a rule, it is used to identify databases. Note that this set of parameters should be used for both of our databases. During the conversion of each table, **Database Converter** will ask if you would like to create a base module featuring some functions for working with the database. We considered this module in detail in *Chapter 7*. As a result, we will have two analogous modules: `modCategoryDatabase` and `modExpenseDatabase`. It is also important to mention that the name of the database for Palm is case sensitive, so it is important to write the file name correctly in the codes. Renaming the PDB file after is it created is also not permitted. This is because the original file name is written inside, and so an attempt to open it in AppForge MobileVB would fail if the file was renamed. Open the new MobileVB project and add these two modules to it. Using the **References** command in the **Project** menu, add two libraries to the project (if they aren't there already): AppForge PDB Functions and AppForge Numeric Functions. The ingots to be used are: `AFGrid`, `AFButton`, `AFTextBox`, `AFComboBox`, and `AFLabel`.

Name the blank form we already have in the project frmMain. Add the `AFGrid` ingot named `grdExpense` to it. It will be used to display expenses on the screen. We will need five columns in `grdExpense`, one for each of the fields of the Expense.pdb database. Correspondingly, specify the `Col` property value — 5. Set the corresponding properties of the ingot so that it is centered in the form. Now let's decide what functions we will need to manipulate the records. First of all, we should have the option of adding a new record, editing an existing one, and deleting an erroneous one. Therefore, add three buttons: **cmdAdd**, **cmdEdit**, and **cmdDelete**. Now it would be nice to have the option of sorting the expenses by quantity, date, category, etc. Create an array of buttons `cmdSort(i)` to sort the corresponding fields of the table. This method may not be the most aesthetically pleasing, but it will show us how the fields are to be sorted. Finally, it would be good to have something like a report of the current day's expenses, or those of some other

Chapter 8: Developing an Application with a Database 143

date, entered in the special `txtCriteria` field. This button will be called **cmdReport**. For a nicer appearance, set the `Appearance` property to 3D. As a result, after some cosmetic manipulations, we have the form in the development stage, as shown in Fig. 8.1.

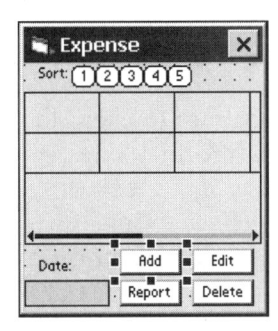

Fig. 8.1. The main form of the project

Displaying Records

It makes sense to display records on the screen while the `frmMain` form is loading. To do this, place the call of the `ResetGrid` and `FillGrid` functions into the `frmMain_Load` event. The first function clears the `grdExpense` ingot and sets the size of its fields, whereas the second function fills it with data. We have selected these procedures as separate blocks, since we will refer to them again. Listing 8.1 shows the contents of the first procedure.

Listing 8.1. The `ResetGrid` procedure

```
Private Sub ResetGrid()
' - Clear Grid control
Me.grdExpense.Rows = 0
' - Set column names
Me.grdExpense.AddItem "ID" & vbTab & "Expense" & vbTab & "Cost" & _
vbTab & "Cat." & vbTab & "Date"
' - Set column width and row height
Me.grdExpense.ColWidth(0) = 15
Me.grdExpense.ColWidth(1) = 40
Me.grdExpense.ColWidth(2) = 25
Me.grdExpense.ColWidth(3) = 35
```

```
Me.grdExpense.ColWidth(4) = 55
Me.grdExpense.RowHeight(0) = 15
' - MobileVB function to make the first record current
Call PDBMoveFirst(dbExpenses)

End Sub
```

Of course, it would be nice to check the database for the records in it before we move the cursor to the first one. We can see that as the descriptor of the Expense.pdb database, the `PDBMoveFirst` function uses the global variable `dbExpense`, which was defined in the `modExpensesDatabase` module at the opening of the database (see details in *Chapter 7*). The `FillGrid` function is presented in Listing 8.2.

Listing 8.2. Filling the Table ingot with data

```
Private Sub FillGrid()
' - variable having the structure of the Expense table
' - and containing the current record
Dim recExpense As tExpensesRecord
' - variable having the structure of the Category table
' - and containing the current record
Dim recCategory As tCategoryRecord
Dim strCategory As String
' - Reading records from Expense.pdb in cycle
Do While Not PDBEOF(dbExpenses)
     ' - the function reads the record and returns True if success.
     ' - The record's data is stored in the recExpense variable.
     ' - The function is defined in the modExpensesDatabase module
     If ReadExpensesRecord(recExpense) Then
        ' - library function for searching by field value. Used
        ' - to search by CategoryType in the Category.pdb table
        PDBFindRecordByField dbCategory, 1, recExpense.CategoryType
' - If successful - stores the Category field from the
' - record
        ' - in the variable
        If ReadCategoryRecord(recCategory) = True Then
           strCategory = recCategory.Category
        End If
```

```
        ' - Filling grdExpense with records
        Me.grdExpense.AddItem recExpense.ID & vbTab & _
 recExpense.ExpenseName & _
 vbTab & recExpense.Cost & vbTab & strCategory & vbTab & _
 recExpense.Date
      End If
      Call PDBMoveNext(dbExpenses)
Loop

End Sub
```

As a result of the procedures described in Listings 8.1 and 8.2, the form filled with the data will appear on the display of the PDA. Now let's consider how working with records is implemented in MobileVb.

Deleting Records

To delete a record, we must first identify it. In our case the only field that differentiates the records from each other is the **ID** field in the **Expense** table, displayed in the zero field of the `grdExpense` ingot. Therefore, the user should first select a record in the ingot, by pressing with the stylus on the leftmost (zero) field. The selected record will be highlighted as you choose: the whole row or just the selected cell (Fig. 8.2). For this purpose, specify one of the four values of the `SelectionType` property: `None`, `Cell`, `Row`, or `Col`. Now, we need to locate the record identifier (ID) value in the global variable. To do this, create a simple algorithm in the `grdExpense_SelectCell` procedure with the purpose of writing the ID of the selected row into the `g_lRecordID` variable (Listing 8.3a). This variable will be necessary when editing the record.

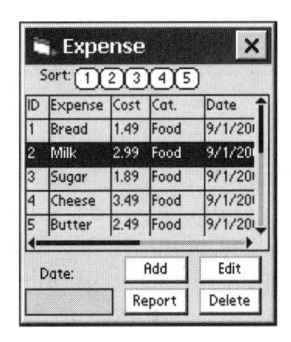

Fig. 8.2. Selecting the row

Listing 8.3a. The grdExpense_SelectCell procedure ("with error")

```
Private Sub grdExpense_SelectCell()
' - if the record was selected with a click on the first column -
' - store the value in the global variable of type Long
If Me.grdExpense.Col = 0 Then
    g_lRecordID = Me.grdExpense.Text
Else
    ' - if not, show the message box
    MsgBox "Please select a row using the first column!", vbCritical
End If

End Sub
```

Now place the code of Listing 8.4 in the Click event of the cmdDelete button.

Listing 8.4. The procedure for deleting records

```
Private Sub cmdDelete_Click()

        PDBFindRecordByField dbExpenses, 0, g_lRecordID
        PDBDeleteRecord dbExpenses

        Call ResetGrid

        Call FillGrid
End Sub
```

The PDBFindRecordByField library function finds the selected record in the database by the value of the first field, assigned to the function as the third parameter. The second parameter is the number of the field, and the first one is the database descriptor. The point of this function is to make the selected record current, and thus mark it for further manipulation.

The next PDBDeleteRecord function deletes the current record by default. The last two functions update the display.

Sorting Data

Now let's consider how the data are sorted. There is only one function that is directly intended for data sorting: `PDBSetSortFields`, with parameters that determine the database and the number of the field by which the sorting should be done. Write the following procedure in the `cmdSort_Click` event (Listing 8.5) using the `cmdSort(i)` button array for sorting.

Listing 8.5. The sorting procedure

```
Private Sub cmdSort_Click(Index As Integer)
   Call ResetGrid
   PDBSetSortFields dbExpenses, Index
   Call FillGrid
End Sub
```

The most important part of this simple procedure is the order of the functions with which we are already acquainted. The call of the `ResetGrid` function clears the `grdExpense` ingot from the data. Then the data are sorted in the virtual memory, and only then should you fill `grdExpense` with the data. Of course, the more reasonable data-sorting solution would be clicking on the corresponding column of `grdExpense`, but we wanted to separate the functions by different procedures in order not to jam the codes and to demonstrate the simple logic of using the functions of the MobileVB PDB Functions library.

Adding a New Record

Creating a new item in your expenses is a more laborious task than deleting a record. Logically, this process consists of 4 steps:

- Moving to the last record of the database and determining its ID
- Opening a new form for entering the new record
- Creating the next ID value for the new record
- Recording the new row in the database

Let's consider all the procedures and functions involved in this process. The first step, which consists of determining the ID of the last record, is done by pressing the `cmdAdd` button. The procedure is shown in Listing 8.6.

Listing 8.6. The procedure for adding a new record

```
Private Sub cmdAdd_Click()
  ' -  variable for storing the last record of the database
  Dim recExpenses As tExpensesRecord
  ' -  set global variable g_bEdit to false - we are adding,
  ' -  not editing
  g_bEdit = False
  ' -  moving to the last record in the database
  PDBMoveLast (dbExpenses)
  ' -  storing the last record ID in the variable
  If ReadExpensesRecord(recExpenses) Then
    g_lLastID = recExpenses.ID
  End If
  Me.Hide
  frmEdit.Show
End Sub
```

The comments clearly describe the process. There can not be two forms on Palm. You should hide the current form first, and then show the other one. We should mention that in practice, the `Unload (form)` function does not unload the form from the memory, but only hides it. As a result, all the loaded forms remain in the memory while the application is working. Therefore, it is obvious that using many forms on the pocket computer can't be done, since this would slow down the performance.

The second form of our project is `frmEdit`, shown in Fig. 8.3. It has three text fields: `txtExpense`, `txtCost`, and `txtDate`, and also contains the `cmbCategory` drop-down list for entering information. Here also is the `cmdSave` button to save the form, close it, and return to the first one.

Fig. 8.3. The form for entering new data

Chapter 8: Developing an Application with a Database 149

The next step is to open the second form and fill the drop-down list with the available categories of expenses, and insert the current date. The procedure responsible for this should not be entered in the `Form_Load` event, but rather in the `Form_Activate` one, because the form is loaded in the Palm memory only once, when it is called for the first time. For repeated calls, the `Load` is not used, and so the codes are to be placed in the `Activate` event (Listing 8.7).

Listing 8.7. The form activation procedure

```
Private Sub Form_Activate()
' - variable containing the record from the dbCategory database
Dim recCategory As tCategoryRecord
' - variable containing the record from the dbExpense database
Dim recExpense As tExpensesRecord

' - clear the combobox
cmbCategory.Clear
PDBMoveFirst dbCategory
' - fill the combobox
Do While Not PDBEOF(dbCategory)
    If ReadCategoryRecord(recCategory) Then
        cmbCategory.AddItem recCategory.Category
    End If
    ' - moving to the next record of the Category table
    Call PDBMoveNext(dbCategory)
Loop

' - in Edit mode - filling controls with values from the record
If g_bEdit Then
  PDBFindRecordByField dbExpenses, 0, g_lRecordID
    If ReadExpensesRecord(recExpense) Then
        txtExpense.Text = recExpense.ExpenseName
        txtCost.Text = recExpense.Cost
        txtDate.Text = recExpense.Date
        Me.cmdCategory.Text = GetCategory(recExpense.CategoryType)
    End If
Else     ' - clear controls for the new record
        txtExpense.Text = ""
        txtCost.Text = ""
```

```
            txtDate.Text = ""
            txtDate.Text = Date
        End If

End Sub
```

The codes are self-explanatory, but let us again consider the logic of their execution. First, the variables that will contain records from each database are declared. Then scan the `dbCategory` table in the loop, record the data in the declared variable, and fill in the drop-down list using only the names of the categories. For a new record, the `recExpense` variable is not used.

Now, when the form is open, enter the data in the text fields and select the expense category. In addition, add the identification field value (ID), which is invisible in the text fields.

When this is done, save the newly created record and close the form. All these procedures are performed by clicking on the `cmdSave` button (Listing 8.8). First, record the new data in the `recExpense` variable. The text for the expenses is taken directly from the `txtExpense` textbox. The `data` and `cost` fields should be preliminarily converted into the `Date` and `Currency` types in order to correspond to the data in the database. We calculate the value of the `ID` field by adding 1 to the last record's ID value stored in the global variable.

Listing 8.8. Saving changes in the database

```
Private Sub cmdSave_Click()
  Dim recExpense As tExpensesRecord
  On Error GoTo Err
  ' - storing data from the form in the record variable
  recExpense.ExpenseName = Me.txtExpense.Text
  recExpense.Cost = CCur(txtCost.Text)
  recExpense.Date = CDate(txtDate.Text)
  recExpense.CategoryType = GetCategoryID(Me.cmdCategory.Text)

  If g_bEdit = False Then
    ' - creating a new ID for the new record
    recExpense.ID = g_lLastID + 1
    PDBCreateRecordBySchema dbExpenses
  Else
    ' - using the current ID in the Edit mode
```

Chapter 8: Developing an Application with a Database   151

```
    recExpense.ID = g_lRecordID
    PDBEditRecord dbExpenses
  End If
  PDBWriteRecord dbExpenses, VarPtr(recExpense)
  PDBUpdateRecord dbExpenses

  Me.Hide
  frmMain.Show

  Exit Sub
Err:
  MsgBox Err.Description
End Sub
```

The last lines of Listing 8.8 hide the `frmEdit` form and show `frmMain`.

There are three functions that directly participate in recording the data to the database: `PDBCreateRecordBySchema`, `PDBWriteRecord`, and `PDBUpdateRecord`. The first function creates the new record in the database according to a certain schema. The second function splits the `recExpense` variable into separate fields and records it in the database, and the third function confirms the record in case there happen to be changes made in it. To use the first function, the database must contain a so-called "schema". This is a system record in the database file that contains certain parameters, such as the number of fields, their data types, etc. (see the details in *Chapter 7*). Since we created our files using the Database Converter, schemas were created in each file. Only the first function (`PDBCreateRecordBySchema`) is necessary when a new record is created, whereas the other two functions should be used both when creating a new record and when modifying existing records.

The only field we can not enter in `dbExpense` directly from the form is the `Category` field, since in `dbExpense` we have only the category identifier, and not its description. Of course, this is one of the habits of working with relational databases. But in this case, it helps us to demonstrate how to work simultaneously with two data files. Create the self-evident `GetCategoryID` function to make the description of the category correspond to its ID (Listing 8.9).

Listing 8.9. The `GetCategoryID` function

```
Private Function GetCategoryID(Category As String) As Integer
  Select Case Category
```

```
    Case "Food"
        GetCategoryID = 1
    Case "Clothes"
        GetCategoryID = 2
    Case "Electricity"
        GetCategoryID = 3
    Case "Medicine"
        GetCategoryID = 4
    Case "Apartment"
        GetCategoryID = 5
    Case "Transportation"
        GetCategoryID = 6
    Case "Other"
        GetCategoryID = 7
    End Select
End Function
```

Editing a Record

Record-editing procedures were briefly considered in the previous section. By pressing the `cmdEdit` button, we hide the `frmMain` form and show the `frmEdit` form. We also set the value of the `g_bEdit` global variable to `True`. Then, when the `frmEdit` form is activated (Listing 8.7), knowing the value of the ID of the selected record, we find it using the `PDBFindRecordByField` function, save its value in the local variable, and record the values in the ingots. Since the variable returns not the category description but its ID, then, using the `GetCategory` function, which is the opposite of and analogous to the `GetCategoryID` function (Listing 8.9), we obtain the name of the category.

When the change is saved (Listing 8.8) the `PDBEditRecord` function is used instead of the `PDBCreateRecordBySchema` function.

Creating a Report

Now let's move on to creating a special utility that will allow us to view the expenses by category for certain dates. If the application was created in VB, then the best solution would be to create the additional form with the controls accurately positioned for better report readability. We, however, would like to abstain from creating an unnecessary form, since after loading into the memory, it will remain

Chapter 8: Developing an Application with a Database 153

there until the end of the application's performance, and will occupy some of the PDA's resources. Therefore, we will display the result of the report via MsgBox. First of all, create a text box (txtCriteria), where the arbitrary date of the report will be entered (Fig. 8.1). The codes for the report will be placed in the Click event of the cmdReport button (Listing 8.10).

Listing 8.10. The procedure for creating a report

```
Private Sub cmdReport_Click()
  ' - variables for records
  Dim recExpense As tExpensesRecord
  Dim recCategory As tCategoryRecord

  Dim strCategory As String
  ' - The array for storing categories (1..7)
  Dim sExpenseByCategory(7) As Single '
  ' - Variable for calculating the day's total  Dim sTotal As Single
  Dim i As Integer

  ' - if a date is not entered - exit sub
  If txtCriteria.Text = "" Then
    txtCriteria.SetFocus
    Exit Sub
  End If
  ' - clear grid to show filtered data
  Call ResetGrid
  ' - looking up dbExpense records  Do While Not PDBEOF(dbExpenses)
    If ReadExpensesRecord(recExpense) Then
      ' - selecting records by a criteria - the date entered
      If recExpense.Date = CDate(Me.txtCriteria.Text) Then
        ' - serching for a category name by the ID
        PDBFindRecordByField dbCategory, 1, recExpense.CategoryType
        If ReadCategoryRecord(recCategory) = True Then
          strCategory = recCategory.Category
        End If
        ' - filling in the grid according to the selected record
        Me.grdExpense.AddItem recExpense.ID & vbTab & _
```

```
                              recExpense.ExpenseName & _
                          vbTab & recExpense.Cost & vbTab & _
                          strCategory & vbTab & recExpense.Date
        "Transportation" & vbTab & sExpenseByCategory(6) & vbCr & _
        "Other" & vbT        ' - calculating the sum per category
        sExpenseByCategory(recExpense.CategoryType) = & _
        sExpenseByCategory(recExpense.CategoryType)     +     recEx-
pense.Cost
      End If
   End If
   ' - moving to the next record
   Call PDBMoveNext(dbExpenses)
   Loop
   ' - calculating the day's total
   sTotal = 0
   For i = 1 To 7
     sTotal = sTotal + sExpenseByCategory(i)
   Next i

   ' - The report in the message box
   MsgBox "Food   " & vbTab & sExpenseByCategory(1) & vbCr & _
          "Clothes" & vbTab & sExpenseByCategory(2) & vbCr & _
          "Electricity" & vbTab & sExpenseByCategory(3) & vbCr & _
          "Medicine" & vbTab & sExpenseByCategory(4) & vbCr & _
          "Apt." & vbTab & sExpenseByCategory(5) & vbCr & _
ab & sExpenseByCategory(7)
          "TOTAL:" & vbTab & sTotal
End Sub
```

The logic of this procedure is simple. First of all, check if the date for which the report is to be generated has been entered. Then clear the grdExpense ingot, scan all the records of the table, selecting those with a suitable date, and enter them on the display (grid). In doing this, we calculate the expenses by category, sorting them according to the corresponding elements of the sExpenseByCategory array. At the end of the procedure, sum up the expenses in all categories to obtain the total expenses for the selected date, and show the report as MsgBox (Fig. 8.4).

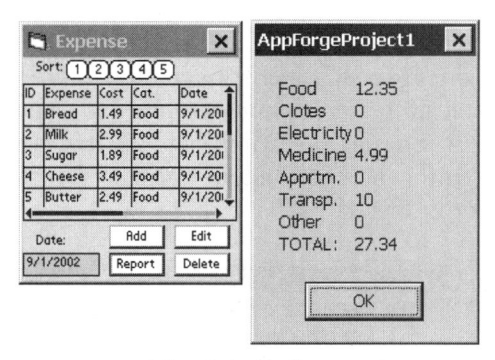

Chapter 8: Developing an Application with a Database   155

Fig. 8.4. Daily report

Compiling the Application

Now we can start to compile the application. Prior to this, however, we need to include all the files with which the application works into the project. If this is not done, the necessary files will not be copied to the Palm. We have not used pictures in this project, but only two database files. These files were not automatically detected by the project, since they were called only in the codes. Include these files into the project (select the **MobileVB Settings** submenu from the **MobileVB** menu) as shown in Fig. 8.5.

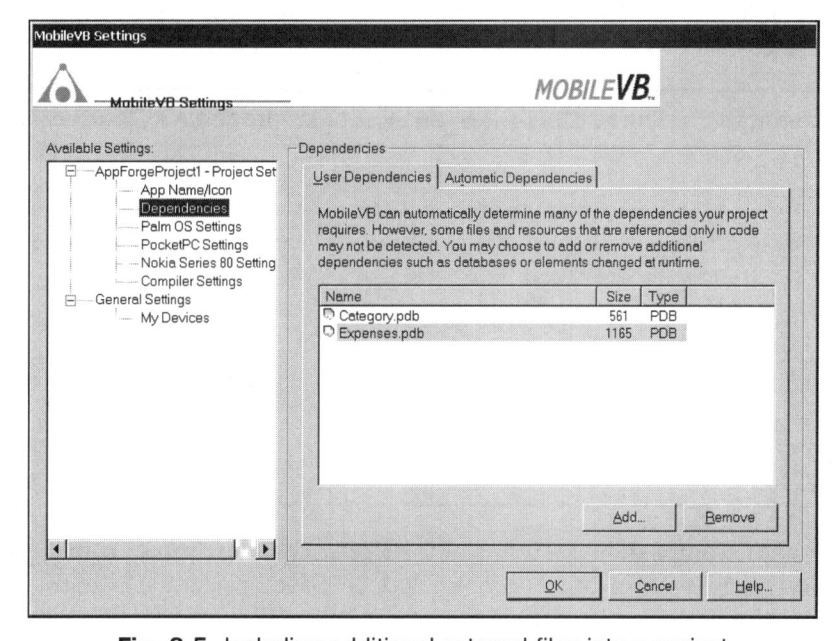

Fig. 8.5. Including additional external files into a project

Now select the **Compile and Validate** submenu from the **MobileVB** menu and start the compilation process, which pretty much comes down to checking the codes, but does not lead to the creation of a new file. When the process is over, we will have just the error message shown in Fig. 8.6. It says that converting a variable of the `String` type into one of the `Long` type may be not safe, and a method of eliminating the error is offered.

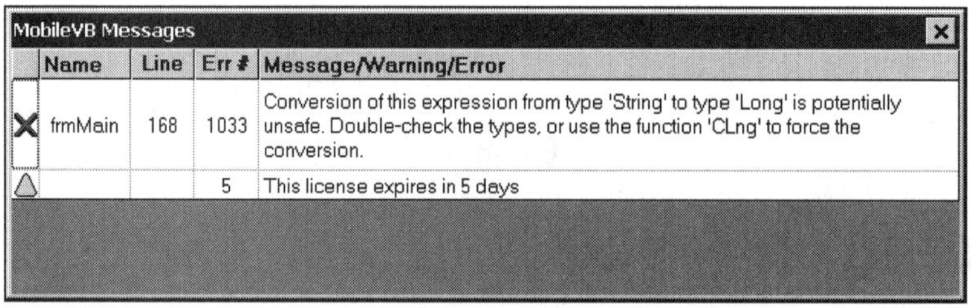

Fig. 8.6. The error message after the application is compiled

If you double-click on the "X" in the left part of the error message line, the application will automatically open the problematic procedure. This is, of course, very convenient. It turns out that it is the procedure described in Listing 8.3a. Indeed, we have not taken into account the fact that in the left part, the global variable has the `Long` type, and the `String` type is returned from the right part. The correct procedure is written in Listing 8.3b.

Listing 8.3b. The `grdExpense_SelectCell` procedure ("correct")

```
Private Sub grdExpense_SelectCell()
  ' -- if record was selected with a click on the first column,
  ' -- store the value in the global variable of the Long type
  If Me.grdExpense.Col = 0 Then
  g_lRecordID = CLng(Me.grdExpense.Text)
  Else
    ' -- if not, show a message box
    MsgBox "Please, select a row from the first column!", vbCritical
  End If
    End Sub
```

The compilation process is now successful, and we can start to create the installation package. For this purpose, select the **Save Project Package...** submenu from the **MobileVB** menu, and then select the **Palm OS** command. We will then be asked to select the folder to which the newly created files will be copied. Unexpectedly,

Chapter 8: Developing an Application with a Database 157

we get a window not with error messages (Fig. 8.7), but with warnings that some ingots positioned at the very top of both forms should be slightly moved down, since otherwise they would cover up certain system messages on the display.

Name	Line	Err #	Message/Warning/Error
frmEdit		3000	Ingot AFLabel1 on form frmEdit will overlap the Caption Tab on PalmOS devices. Property "Top" should be at least 15.
frmEdit		3000	Ingot AFLabel2 on form frmEdit will overlap the Caption Tab on PalmOS devices. Property "Top" should be at least 15.
frmMain		3000	Ingot cmdSort on form frmMain will overlap the Caption Tab on PalmOS devices. Property "Top" should be at least 15.

Fig. 8.7. Warnings window

Generally speaking, this message can be ignored, which is justified by the files created in the indicated folder. Nevertheless, it is best to correct the ingots by moving them slightly down. After this, the files can be re-created, and at the next synchronization session they will be successfully copied to the Palm. Currently, we find three files in the selected folder: Expense.prc, Expenses.pdb, and Category.pdb. All of them will be copied to the handheld device, and now we have the additional option of testing our application by dragging these files to the emulator (Fig. 8.8).

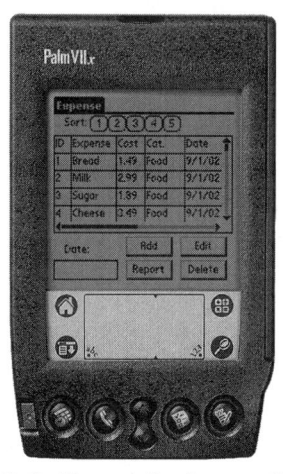

Fig. 8.8. The application on the emulator

Remember, however, that the successful compilation of an application in the AppForge MobileVB development environment does not provide a 100% guarantee that it will successfully perform on the mobile device. Much depends not only on the processor type, but on the model of your Palm. Therefore, testing the application on the device or on the emulator is a necessary step. The more complex the application, the higher the probability that it will give you a possibly unpleasant surprise.

Chapter 9

Internet Programming

Many contemporary pocket computers or PDA have no independent means of connecting to the Internet. This is, however, a matter of time, and not a long time either. Connecting a handheld device to the Internet is possible via an additional modem connected externally to the device, and then via a cable to a line jack, or with the use of a cell phone that serves to dial the provider's phone number. Nevertheless, it is exactly the demand for an independent connection to the Internet that will be the main incentive for purchasing mobile computers. This, in turn, will stimulate the creation of special web sites that take into account the specific character of mobile devices. The main and important feature of the pocket computer/PDA as concerns the Internet is its small display, where no regular web page can be viewed. The low speed of the Internet connection is another essential limitation that cannot be ignored. A relatively weak processor and a small virtual memory will also have an effect on the features of the design of web sites intended to be browsed on pocket computers. For example, we will have to forget about viewing images, and be content mainly with text. Such limitations tend to make the Internet for pocket computers/PDA more of a business phenomenon than one related to entertainment.

Project Description

In this section, we will consider a typical example of Internet programming using AppForge MobileVB. The core of the project is the following: having connected to the Internet and opened our application, the user can read news from certain web sites, selecting various articles. Similarly, it is possible to provide the user with the option of finding out the weather in any place of the world, stock prices and sales volume, and flight schedules, etc. Before we started the project, we had to spend some time looking for specific news site without many pictures and that had no script languages integrated in its HTML or ASP files. In fact, we will end up having to create a primitive browser that will detect readable text by scanning the HTML pages received from the server, and removing the tags from them. We found a suitable site: **mobile.go.com/pocketpc/AG_ABCNewsStory?category=int&i=1**. Having analyzed it, we found that if you specify an integer value of the variable `i`, it is possible to open the HTML files with news stories that are systematically updated on the site. For example, **http://mobile.go.com/pocketpc/AG_ABCNewsStory?category=int&i=2** will show the second article.

Before we turn to developing the application, note that the above "acrobatics" are the result of the lack of a browser ingot in MobileVB. The availability of such a browser would not only simplify our task, but also considerably expand our possibilities.

Creating the User Interface

Like a human being with both a soul and body, any application has both an external interface and codes. The visual interface is something like the body of the application, and the codes are its soul. The interface is dead without the codes. Without discussing which component is the primary one, we think it most logical to begin with the construction of the "body."

Start the new MobileVB project from Visual Basic. Select the required platform (Palm), and have a blank form. Name the project InternetProject, and call the form `frmNews`. First, remove all of the AppForge MobileVB ingots from the project, leaving only the most necessary — `AFTextBox`, `AFLabel`, and `AFButton` — and include `AFINetHTTP` if we do not have it on the toolbar.

The `AFINetHTTP` ingot is the most important one. It will execute the connection with the Internet using HTTP and HTTPS. However, the majority of the functions it uses are integrated into Palm INet Library — the function library developed for Palm VII and the Palm.Net service. If the particular Palm PDA does not contain this library, then this ingot will not be able to provide a connection to the Internet. This means that this ingot and the application will not work on a Pocket PC, since they are suitable only for Palm OS.

Place the ingots on the form as shown in Fig. 9.1 — the text box for the article number (`txtArticleNumber`) at the top, with the label beside it. The news screen will be placed below. Select a text box as the news screen, which will be named `txtBrowser`. Enlarge it to the maximum, without moving the borders of the form. Specify `MultiLine` to `True` in the property window, which enables us to place a large volume of information there. For a full text view, set the `ScrollBars` property to the value `2-Vertical`. This will permit you to automatically scroll the text vertically.

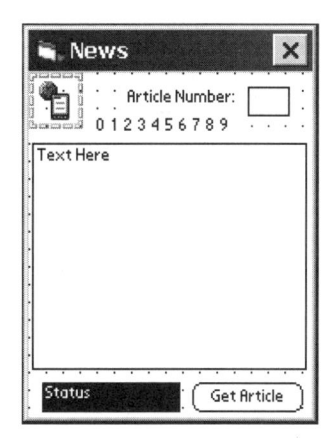

Fig. 9.1. An application form for a Palm in the development stage

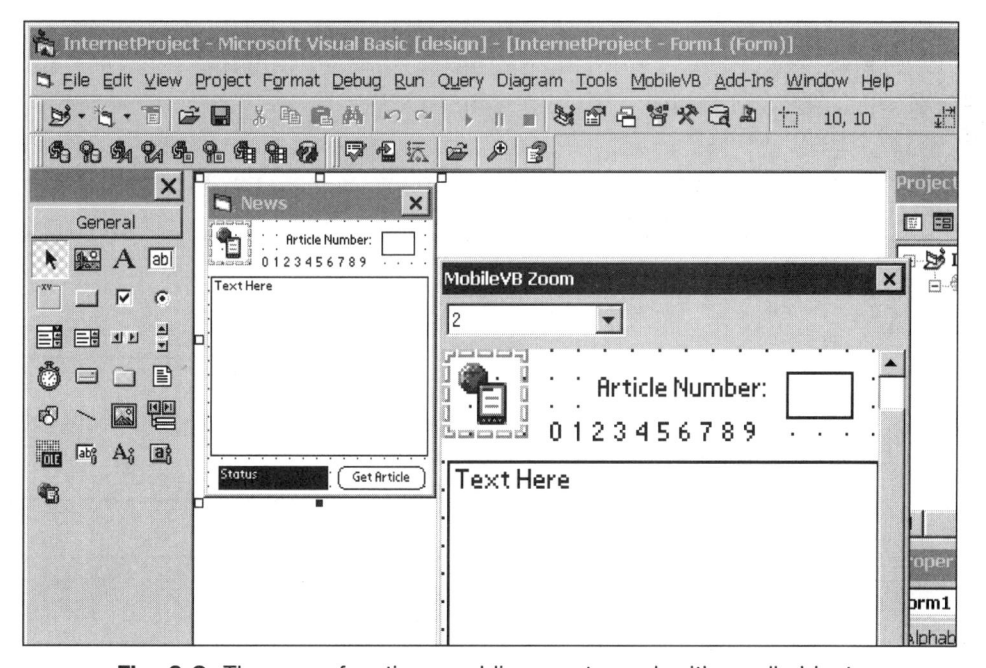

Fig. 9.2. The zoom function, enabling you to work with small objects

Leave the rest of the properties as they are. Locate the **Get Article** (`cmdGet`) button under `txtBrowser`. Place the `lblStatus` label beside it, which will inform the user about the connection status with the web site. We could end the interface construction here, but we are dealing with a handheld device in which it is inconvenient to enter text, so it is best to try escape this or have an alternative way. So, place 10 labels numbered 0 to 9 (`lblNumber(i)`) above the browser. Clicking on such a label will enter the corresponding number in the article text box. This will considerably simplify data entry. However, if the user wants to read article 23, then he or she will have to enter the figures. Placing such small objects on a small form takes too much time and labor, so here the zooming function integrated in MobileVB may be of use. Select the **Zoom Window** command from the MobileVB menu in order to be able to discern small details of the project (Fig. 9.2). Finally, add the `AFINetHTTP` ingot named `ctlInternet`. This is actually the end of the application interface construction, and we can now turn to the codes.

Creating the Code

We will write codes according to the logic of the application. After the form is loaded, the user should select the number of the article. He or she can enter a number in the `txtArticleNumber` textbox or click with the stylus on a numbered label. Then, when the `Click` event happens, the code in the set of labels will look as shown in Listing 9.1.

Listing 9.1. The `lblNumber_Click` procedure

```
Private Sub lblNumber_Click(Index As Integer)
   txtArticleNumber.Text = Index
End Sub
```

The user should then press the **Get Article** button. Listing 9.2 shows the self-explanatory code.

Listing 9.2. Connection to the site

```
Private Sub cmdGet_Click()
    ' - The URL property defines the site address,
    ' - where the i parameter is the textbox value
    ctlInternet.URL = "http://mobile.go.com/" & _
```

```
                    "pocketpc/AG_ABCNewsStory?category=int&i=" & _
                    txtArticleNumber.Text
    ' - the Execute method is used to actually connect to the site
    ctlInternet.Execute
End Sub
```

Since the status of connection with the web site will change, the StateChanged event will take place. This event has an integrated parameter of the Long type, which determines the current status of the ctlInternet ingot. We want these changing states to be displayed on the lblStatus label. Obviously, there is no reason to display numbers there. Load the project objects browser to translate the numeric values of the connection state into understandable words. To do this, select the **Object Browser** command from the **View** menu. In the left part of the browser window that opens, find the AFINetHTTP class and the AFInetHTTPStatusConstants line under it. After clicking on it with the mouse button, in the right part of the display, you will have a list of constants corresponding to the particular status. On the lower panel of the browser, you can read the numeric value of the constant and its meaning (which is clear from the names of the constants, see Fig. 9.3).

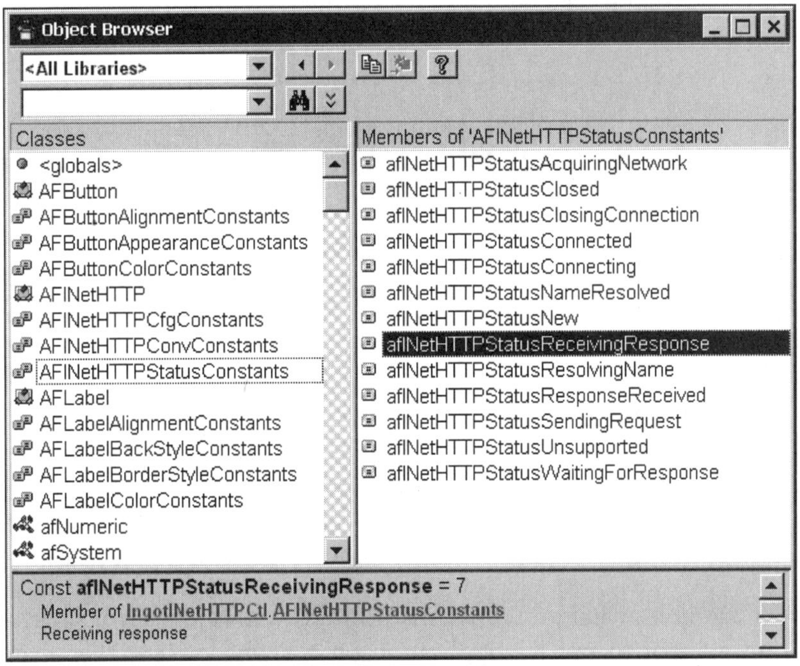

Fig. 9.3. Determining the integrated constants using the Object Browser

Now it is possible to write the entire procedure for the lInternet_StateChanged event (Listing 9.3).

Listing 9.3. The procedure for tracing the web site connection status

```
Private Sub ctlInternet_StateChanged(ByVal newState As Long)
' - use the object browser to get constant values
Select Case newState
    Case 0
        Me.lblStatus.Caption = "Connection just opened"
    Case 1
        Me.lblStatus.Caption = "Looking up host address"
    Case 2
        Me.lblStatus.Caption = "Found host address"
    Case 3
        Me.lblStatus.Caption = "Connection to host"
    Case 4
        Me.lblStatus.Caption = "Connected to host"
    Case 5
        Me.lblStatus.Caption = "Sending request"
    Case 6
        Me.lblStatus.Caption = "Waiting for response"
    Case 7
        Me.lblStatus.Caption = "Receiving response"
    Case 8
        Me.lblStatus.Caption = "Response received"
    Case 9
        Me.lblStatus.Caption = "Closing connection"
    Case 10
        Me.lblStatus.Caption = "Closed"
    Case 11
        Me.lblStatus.Caption = "Network unreachable"

End Select

End Sub
```

Case 11 may indicate problems with the AFINetHTTP ingot's performance, such as an attempt to use the application on a Palm device earlier than version VII, which does not have the necessary library. In the process of changing the connection status with the host, an error may occur. If this happens, the `ctlInternet_Error` event starts, in which only one line is located:

```
Me.lblStatus.Caption = Me.ctlInternet.SystemError
```

If the connection with the web site is OK, then after case 8 ("Response received"), the `ctlInternet_ReceivedData` event occurs, in which the information should be received, processed, and entered in the text field. This procedure is simple, and is presented in Listing 9.4.

Listing 9.4. The ingot receiving data

```
Private Sub ctlInternet_ReceivedData(ByVal totalSize As Long)

If totalSize <> 0 Then
   ' - if not zero - data received
   ' - the GetChunk method transfers data from the server to the variable
   txtBrowser.Text = Remove(ctlInternet.GetChunk(15000))
End If
End Sub
```

The `Remove()` function used in the `ctlInternet_ReceivedData` procedure clears tags from the information received in HTML format. We want to get actual text and transfer it to the `txtBrowser` field. To do this, any text in angle brackets (< >) and the brackets themselves need to be eliminated from the text. The `Remove()` function is shown in Listing 9.5.

Listing 9.5. The function for deleting the angle brackets (< >) and the text within them

```
Public Function Remove(strData As String) As String
   Dim strNew As String
   Dim strOld As String
   ' - any tag is defined by 2 brackets: opening and closing
   Dim lFirst As Long
   Dim lLast As Long

   strOld = strData

Here:
   lFirst = InStr(1, strOld, "<")
```

```
      If lFirst > 0 Then
        lLast = InStr(1, strOld, ">")
        strNew = Mid(strOld, 1, lFirst - 1) & Mid(strOld, lLast + 1)
        strOld = strNew
        GoTo Here
      Else
        Remove = strOld
      End If
End Function
```

This is the end of the application's development. We mentioned above, however, that the simple and convenient `AFINetHTTP` ingot is based on the functions integrated into the special Palm library, and therefore will not work with the Windows CE operating system. This is discussed in *Chapter 4*, when simply copying the application from one platform to another is impossible. Unfortunately, when creating the application for the Pocket PC, the application needs to be changed in some way. First, we should use the `AFClientSocket` communication ingot instead of the network `AFINetHTTP` one to provide for the connection with the Internet. Due to this, the `cmdGet_Click()` procedure shown in Listing 9.2 needs to be rewritten.

Listing 9.6. The `cmdGet_Click` procedure for the Pocket PC

```
Private Sub cmdGet_Click()
Dim IPAddress As String
' - first resolve the Host Name to the IP address
IPAddress = ctlSocket.ResolveHostName("mobile.go.com")

' - setting parameter values
ctlSocket.RemoteHostIP = IPAddress
ctlSocket.RemotePort = 80

' - executing the Connect method with parameters:
' - IP address, port number, timeout in milliseconds
ctlSocket.Connect IPAddress, 80, 3000

  Dim msg As String
  Dim strParams As String
  strParams = ""
```

Chapter 9: Internet Programming

```
    ' — preparing the server request string
    msg = "GET /pocketpc/AG_ABCNewsStory?category=int&i=" & _
            txtArticleNumber.Text & " HTTP/1.1" & vbCrLf _
          & "Host: " & IPAddress & vbCrLf _
          & "Content-Length: " & CStr(Len(strParams)) & vbCrLf _
          & vbCrLf & strParams & vbCrLf
    ' - sending request to server with a timeout of 10 sec
    ' - waiting for events: ctlSocket_DataWaiting or ctlSocket_Error
    ctlSocket.SendString msg, Len(msg), 10 * 1000
End Sub
```

Here, it is necessary to say a few words about query construction, since it is poorly explained in the **Help** menu. A query is made using the standard scheme, with a structure that is clearly seen in the example. You should use the parameters when a query is made to ASP files with a query string. The parameter is the part of URL that comes after the "?" symbol, for example, `strParams = "language=English"`. When we query to a regular ASP or HTML file (as in this case), we use the `GET` method. When addressing a file and transferring parameters, the `POST` method should be used. Sometimes, after the name of the method, it is necessary to indicate the full URL of the file being searched for, including the name of the protocol (`"GET http://mobile.go.com/pocketpc/AG_ABCNewsStory?category= ..."`).

In the `SendString` method, a length that is equal to or less than that of the query is used as the second parameter.

If the connection with the host was successful, we expect the arrival of a reply in the `DataWaiting` event (Listing 9.7).

Listing 9.7. The `ctlSocket_DataWaiting` procedure

```
Private Sub ctlSocket_DataWaiting()
    Dim Response As String
    ctlSocket.GetString Response, 1000, 1 * 1000
    ' - strWholeText — global variable
    strWholeText = strWholeText & Response
    txtBrowser.Text = strWholeText
End Sub
```

The received information is placed in the `Response` variable using the `GetString` method. The length of the expected information should be indicated as the second parameter. The attempt to use the `Len(Response)` function, however, led to the application freezing, and so we chose to accumulate the data in the global variable in parts. In this case, the `DataWaiting` event is continued until all the information is downloaded. If the length of the second parameter exceeds the length of the expected text, the application will freeze a priori, since the ingot will wait for the receipt of all of the information for an unlimited period of time.

Unfortunately, `AFClientSocket` does not inform you of the status of its interaction with the server, and so there is nothing to send to the status label. Thus we removed this ingot from the form. We do, however, have the `Error` event, which informs us of possible problems related to the connection with the server. Above we have described how, using the Object Browser, you can identify the returned numeric values with a concrete error.

Finally, we do not receive the pure HTML file in the buffer variable, as is the case with `AFINetHTTP`. On the contrary, the received result contains not only tags, but also the Header of the file that we have to remove before the text is displayed in the browser. This is described in detail in the part that we dedicate completely to Pocket PC programming (see *Chapter 16*). The general view of our application for the Pocket PC does not differ much from that for Palm (see Figs. 9.4, *a* and 9.4, *b*).

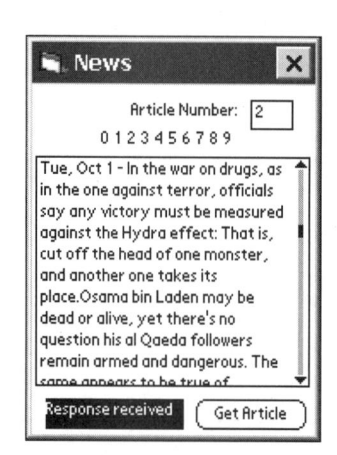

Fig. 9.4, *a*. The application for Palm

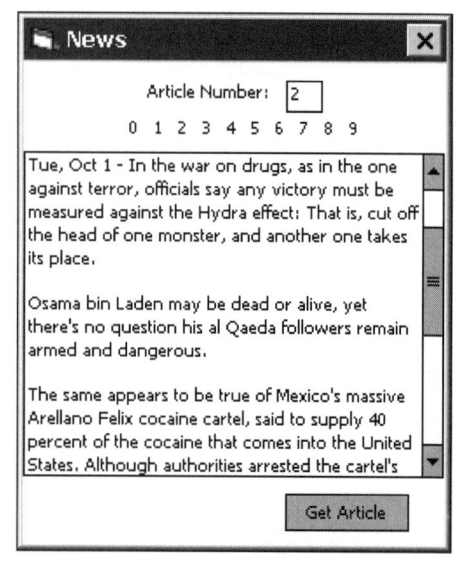

Fig. 9.4, *b*. The application for a pocket PC

Chapter 10

Creating Web Clipping Applications

The Technological Concept

This chapter is not directly related to AppForge MobileVB, but, without it, any book on Palm programming would be incomplete. The topic is important because, according to market research, the share of Internet users employing a wireless connection is constantly growing. Of course, a portable device is one of the tools used for a wireless connection with the Internet.

Although the previous chapter touched basically upon Internet programming for Palm, it was of more academic than practical interest, and was written with the specific character of the Palm PDA and its differences from the PC in mind. In fact, in the previous chapter, we developed an application for the Palm without taking into account its peculiarities. Moreover, we tried to reinvent the wheel by inventing the browser, since the latter is a very complex application, if we take into account at least some of the necessary requirements. The first and foremost distinct feature of Palm is the slowness of the PDA's wireless connection to the Internet.

Recently, Palm has developed a technology to create Internet applications for Palm with respect to this specific factor. The company's web site contains a long list of commercial applications that can be downloaded for free and installed on a Palm device (Fig. 10.1).

As an example, download the Weather.pqa application, which is just 11 KB. By dragging the file to the Palm emulator, we will see it in the **Application** section (Fig. 10.2). The new icon corresponding to this application is in the bottom right corner.

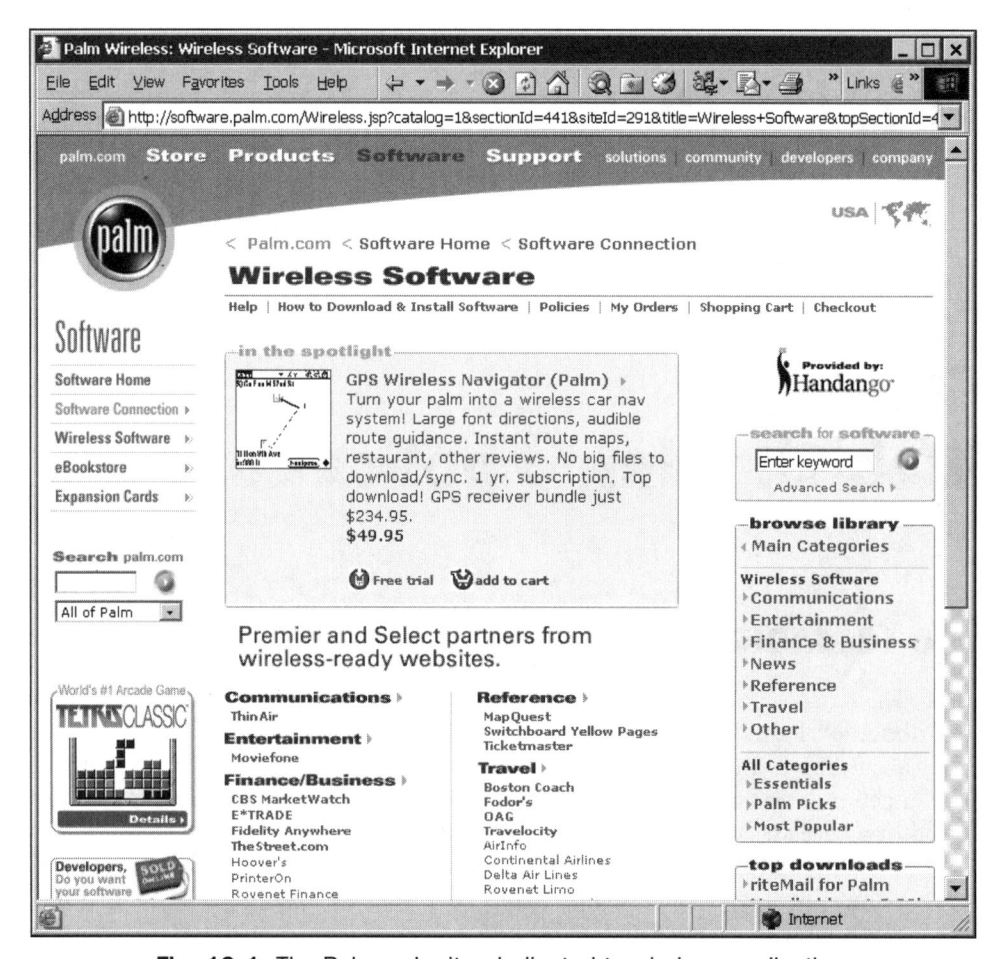

Fig. 10.1. The Palm web site, dedicated to wireless applications

As usual, if you click on the icon with the mouse (or press with the stylus on the actual device), the application will be opened (Fig. 10.3). The image and the whole file you see in the picture were loaded from the local Palm folder. There was no connection with the server at the time; it will be established after pressing the **Go** button.

However, before establishing an actual connection with the server and making a query, we have to adjust the emulator (without mentioning that your PC should be connected to the Internet while testing the application on the emulator). To do this, select the **Wireless** command from the pop-up menu on the **Preferences** tab as soon as the emulator is opened (Fig. 10.4, *a*).

Chapter 10: Creating Web Clipping Applications 171

Fig. 10.2. The weather application icon

Fig. 10.3. A typical Web Clipping application on Palm

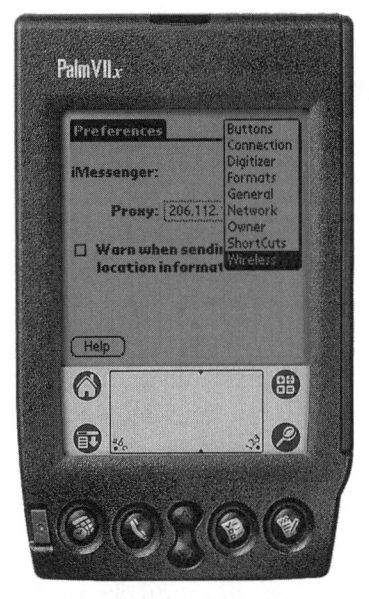

Fig. 10.4, a. Setting the emulator to work with the Internet

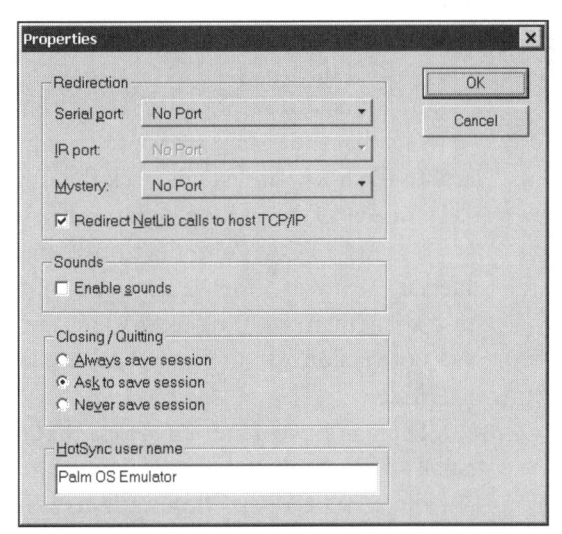

Fig. 10.4, b. Setting the emulator's properties to work with the Internet

Next, the proxy-server selection window will appear, and this server will be used for connecting to the **www.weather.com** server (in our example). It is the best to double check the value of the IP address indicated there using the Palm web site (**www.palm.com**) in the Development section. After the correct proxy IP address is indicated, click with the right mouse button on the emulator and select the **Settings/Properties** command from the pop-up menu. As a result, the window shown in Fig. 10.4, *b* will appear.

Here, check the **Redirect NetLab calls to host TCP/IP** checkbox. As a result, POSE will redirect all the queries to the network to which your PC is connected.

The applications described in this chapter are called Web Clipping Applications. Another commonly used term is Palm Query Application (PQA).

The core of the technology is as follows: A PQA is a set of HTML files (index.html, about.html, help.html, etc.) on the local Palm device in compressed format. In other words, a PQA is a mini web site saved on the PDA. The Index.html file may contain either the form or the list of hyperlinks to be sent to the server. Usually, after the query is received, the server sends back an HTML file, which can contain new text information and hyperlinks to other pages already present in the PQA. Therefore, Palm PDA actually receives only the text of the HTML file, but uses the images contained on Palm in the PQA, which saves both time and bandwidth during the Internet connection session. In fact, between your PDA and the server there is a Palm proxy server which further compresses transmitted data.

Of course, to create a PQA, a certain knowledge of HTML is needed. It is also obvious that the main task is writing applications for the server, which correctly reacts to the query and sends back the minimal necessary reply. And this all is left up to standard CGI or ASP programming.

To read a PQA, Palm developed an application called Clipper. Actually, this is a special browser for Palm OS used to decompress HTML files and to display them on the screen. This application is freely distributed with Palm devices of version VII and later, and can be downloaded for older models for a nominal price.

There are two general reasons that made Palm develop its own technology: the small display of the device, and the low speed of the Internet connection. So, the task of Web Clipping is to minimize as much as possible the volume of the displayed image, and minimize the use of the connection channel. The limited power of the Palm processor and the rather high cost of the Internet connection are the other important aspects to take into account.

Thus there are two key points that make up the core of Web Clipping:

- The typical and standard query is made from the Palm device with the PQA installed. If we are intereested in the weather in San Francisco, Washington D.C., or New York, then only the city is changed in the query. If we are concerned with the stock value of Microsoft or Rank Street, etc., then another Web Clipping application should be used (another query to another server), changing only the name of the company in the request. Having received the query, the server, using the CGI application, processes it and sends back a reply related to the specific query and nothing else. In other words, instead of surfing the site searching for the answer to the question, the user sends a specific query and receives a specific answer. This considerably reduces the connection time and limits the volume of information sent in both directions. Palm recommends that the query volume never exceed 40 bytes, and that the volume of the answer not exceed 360.

- Thus, the communication problem is solved using two parts of the application: the query (or the PQA) installed on the PDA as an application that can be opened and closed, and the CGI application installed on the server. Consequently, unlike the standard web situation, when the form from the server needs to be downloaded first, then filled in, and then the query sent, here the form itself is already localized on the device. All you have to do is to fill in the form and send the query. The resulting reply is minimal, since it does not contain the information to be displayed, but just the minimum of what is processed by the local application, and only then is displayed using the local file images, hyperlinks, and formatting rules.

Before considering this technology's architecture in even more detail, it is worth mentioning that the Palm application does not directly interact with the connecting company's web server, but via the intermediate server with the IP address specified on the previous pages, called Web Clipping Proxies — Palm.Net. First, the intermediate server receives the query from the Palm device via the UDP (User Datagram Protocol). Then this server connects with the company's web server via a standard HTTP connection (by uncompressing the request) and receives the necessary information. The proxy server then compresses the received information and sends it back to the Palm PDA.

The Limitations of Web Clipping

In order to implement the necessary functions, Web Clipping technology needs to follow certain rules. These first of all relate to reading HTML files. First, we'll look at hyperlinks, which are very simple.

```
<a href="http://www.internettrading.ru">financial market </a>
```

This leaves no place for links via the graphic file. They will simply be eliminated.

Another significant limitation is the lack of support for any user script languages. Clipper will completely ignore JavaScript, VBScript, Java Applets, and ActiveX controls.

Some standard text-formatting tags, or those for displaying the web-site information on the screen that cannot be accepted due to the small Palm display are also not supported. For example, the option of displaying frames is not supported. Another example of unsupported features may be tables within tables, etc. Finally, the use of cookies is not supported at all. These are usually used to identify the user and to accelerate his or her entry into sites requiring logins and passwords. Unfortunately, there is no such feature in the Clipper browser, and users are subject to authorization each time.

Specific Tags

At the same time, Clipper could not do without its own specific tags (which do not exist in HTML 3.2) that serve to accelerate information processing. We mentioned above, however, that since Clipper reads only local files installed on the Palm device, the application need only meet the requirements of Clipper, so as to be read by Clipper alone, and not by any other standard browser. There are four specific meta tags to be included into Web Clipping applications.

- PalmComputingPlatform. This tag identifies the page as specially developed for reading from Palm. In other words, this page is read well from a small screen, and does not waste the resources of the Internet connection. This tag guarantees that all images and the text of the file will be displayed on the screen. Ignoring this tag will lead to ignoring all image files, and only the first 1,024 bytes of text will be displayed on the screen. This tag should be used when all local and server pages are created. It is used as follows:

```
<meta name="PalmComputingPlatform" content="true">
```

- `HistoryListText`. This tag is needed to add this PQA application into the pop-up menu showing the history of the application's use. It is added in each required application as shown below:

    ```
    <meta name="HistoryListText" content="true">
    ```

- `Local Icon`. Developers of Web Clipping applications should avoid transmission of images. This not only hinders the information transmission, but also leads to excessive wear of the batteries and more quickly exhausting the monthly bandwidth provided. Therefore, it makes sense to keep the image files on the local Palm device within the specific Web Clipping application. This tag identifies the image files placed on the local Palm device that are to be displayed on the screen. The width of the displayed images should not exceed 153 pixels, and the length should not exceed 144 pixels. The focus depth is 2 bits per pixel. The image files may be in GIF or JPEG format. It is advisable to use this tag on the main page (index.html). The tag is used as follows:

    ```
    <meta name="LocalIcon" content="MyPicture.jpg">
    ```

- `PalmLauncherRevision`. This tag determines the version of the application. It should also be used on the main page. It is used as follows:

    ```
    <meta name="PalmLauncherRevision" content="2.1">
    ```

At the same time, if the page is to be shown both in a regular browser and in Clipper, there is a simple way of "clipping" part of the contents so that they are not shown in Clipper. To do this, place the unwanted part of the text within the frame of the `SmallScreenIgnore` tag.

There are three more special tags that allow interesting manipulations with the application on Palm. For example, if you need to open a local application from your PQA application, this can be done as follows:

```
<a href="palm: memo.appl">Memo Notes</a>
```

This hyperlink will open the Memo application. To open another Web Clipping application from the current one, you can use the tag as in the following example:

```
<a href="file: amazon.appl">Books</a>
```

Finally, to send e-mail (during the connection with the Internet and provided that the iMessanger application is installed on Palm) you can use the following tag:

```
<a href="mailto: not@real.com> Send Message</a>
```

Illustrated Examples

To create Web Clipping applications, you should have an HTML editor, which can be simply Notepad. Moreover, by the highest standards, this is the best solution, since Notepad does not add its own tags and does not modify the code, unlike, for example, Front Page. In addition, Notepad enables you to enter specific Palm tags painlessly.

Another necessary application for creating Web Clipping applications is Query Application Builder. It can be downloaded for free from the Palm web site, **www.palm.com**. Query Application Builder compiles the created HTML file into the PQA application, which can be viewed via Clipper on the Palm device.

To create a Web Clipping application, start with an HTML file. There may be several such files with hyperlinks, but the main one can have the name index.html (or another one associated with the name/purpose of the application). All files, including images, should be in one folder, or in nested folders. The maximum size of an application compressed by the wizard (Query Application Builder) must not exceed 64 KB, and so the use of images should be limited.

Let's start by creating a simple Web Clipping application. Open Notepad and enter the following code (Listing 10.1).

Listing 10.1. The index.html file

```
<html>
  <head>
    <title>First Web Clipping</title>
    <meta name="PalmComputingPlatform" content="true">
    <meta name="PalmLauncherRevision" content="1.0">
  </head>
  <body>
    <h1 align="center">Hello Palm World!</h1>
    <a href="second.html">Second file</a>
  </body>
</html>
```

The phrase "First Web Clipping" within the `<title>` tag will be seen on Palm as the title of the tab (see Fig. 10.7). Now save the file with the name "index.html", and create an analogous one, named "second.html" (Listing 10.2). In this file, we created a reference to another file — "second.html" — with the contents shown below (Listing 10.2).

Listing 10.2. The second.html file

```
<html>
  <head>
    <title>Second file Web Clipping</title>
    <meta name="PalmComputingPlatform" content="true">
    <meta name="PalmLauncherRevision" content="1.0">
  </head>
  <body>
    <h1 align="center">Second file</h1>
    <p align=center>Jenny's Picture </p>
    <center><img src="pics/jenny.jpg"></center>
  </body>
</html>
```

The second file has a reference to an image made in the usual way for HTML. Now you can compile all files into a single application using the wizard. Open the WCA Builder and select the **Open Index** submenu from the **File** menu. Find the first file and put the list of all files of the application in the wizard's window (Fig. 10.5). The wizard simply scans each file to find the references and finds all of them. If the reference is wrong or there is no such file, an error message appears. Actually, our file from Listing 10.1 could have any other name (for example, first.html), and the **Open Index** command would work in this case as well. Such name of a submenu indicates that it is makes sense to start from the initial file, which may have hyperlinks to other files to be found by the wizard and shown as a list in the window. Then select the **Build PQA** submenu from the **File** menu and go to the next step — the compilation window (Fig. 10.6).

At this stage, you can specify the resolution of the included image files. Of course, the better the quality and the more complicated the image, the bigger the application. It is also possible now to select the icon for the application that will appear in the list of applications on Palm. We used the standard version. Lastly, by clicking on the **Build** button, we have the "index.pqa" file in the selected folder. Note that Web Clipping applications do not work on Palm devices older than version VII. Since our emulator corresponds to version VII, by dragging the "index.pqa" file from Windows Explorer into the emulator window, we will have our application's icon in the list. Go to its first page by clicking with the mouse button on the icon — Fig. 10.7.

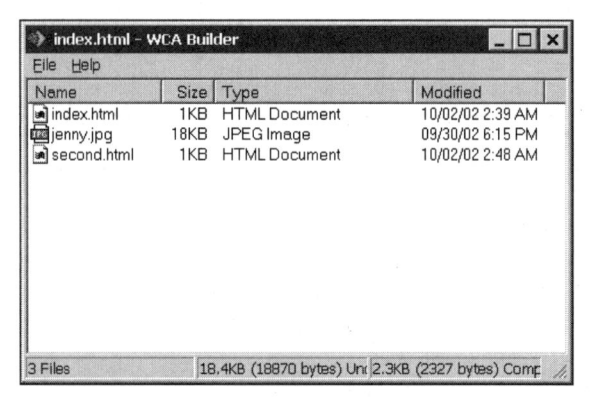

Fig 10.5. The wizard for creating PQA files

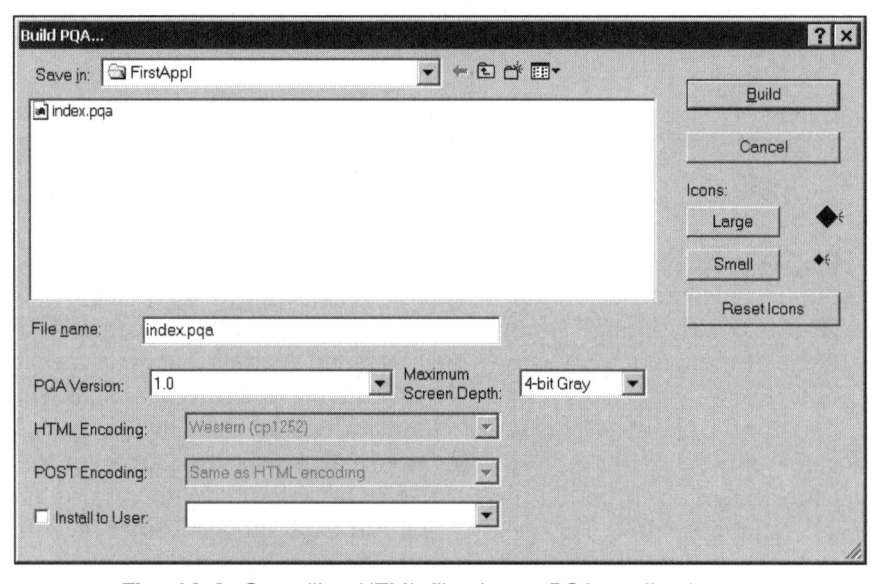

Fig. 10.6. Compiling HTML files into a PQA application

By clicking on the only hyperlink, we go to another local file (named "second.html" during development, and now an integral part of the single "index.pqa" application file). The second page of our application appears according to Listing 10.2 and is shown in Fig. 10.8.

Now, we'll briefly consider the prototype of a more useful application, which will make a query to the server as in the example we looked at above. Suppose that a CGI file on the server, after receiving the name of the city, sends back the current temperature, wind speed, and other local weather conditions. Usually, in order to collect data and send it to the server, the user has the `<form>` tag, which frames the form with the fields for information entry. The form may have controls that are in full correspondence with HTML 3.2 (Listing 10.3).

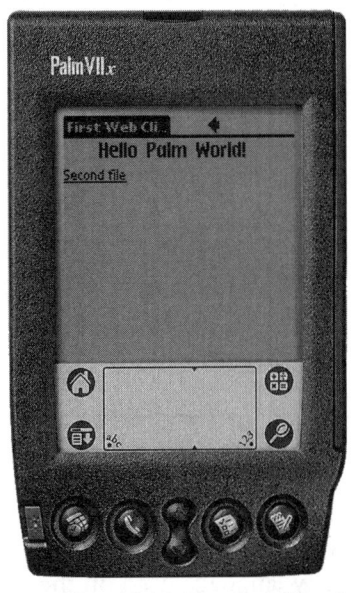

Fig. 10.7. The first file of our simple Web Clipping application

Fig. 10.8. The second page of "index.pqa"

Listing 10.3. An example of an information-entry form for a query

```
<html>
<head>
  <title>Weather</title>
  <meta name="palmcomputingplatform" content="true">
</head>
<body>
<h2 align=center>Select City</h2>
<center>
<form method="post" action="http://www.myserver.com/cgi-bin/weather.pl">
<select name="cmbCity">
  <option>New York
  <option>Washington
  <option>Santo Domingo
```

```
   <option>Tampa
   <option>London
   <option>Paris
   <option>Moscow
</select>
<br><br>
<p align=center>Or Type City Name: </p>
<input type="text" name="txtCity">
<input type="submit" value="Search" name="go">
</form>
<br>
<a href="about.html">About Us</a>
<a href="help.html">Help</a>
</center>
</body>
</html>
```

The two additional files, "about.html" and "help.html", have static contents, so they should be generated and stored locally. After the query is received, the CGI application on the server will generate a reply as an HTML file. How this is done is beyond the scope of this book. You can use any language used on the server: Perl, ASP, etc. The only requirement of the HTML file being generated is that it can be read by Clipper, i.e., it must comply with the rules discussed above. Developers can find more details on the Palm web site, where you can enter the key phrase "web clipping" to search for the required pages.

Part III

Programming Pocket PC with eMbedded Visual Basic

Chapter 11: Installing eMbedded Visual Tools 3.0

Chapter 12: Introduction to eMbedded Visual Basic

Chapter 13: Working with Controls

Chapter 14: Database Access Programming in eMbedded Visual Basic 3.0 Using ADOCE 3.0

Chapter 15: Database Access Using ADOCE 3.1, ADOXCE, and SQL Server CE 1.0

Chapter 16: Communication and the Infrared WinSock Control in Windows CE

Chapter 11

Installing eMbedded Visual Tools 3.0

The distribution package for eMbedded Visual Tools is available for free on **www.microsoft.com**. It currently can be downloaded from **www.microsoft.com/mobile/developer/downloads/emvt30/**. (The location of the files on **www.microsoft.com** often changes, so by the time this book is published, you may have to search the site). The size of the downloaded information is 304 MB, in the form of a single, self-unpacking archive. Before the download starts, you will be asked to register. Microsoft also distributes this software on CD ROM. The eMbedded Visual Tools software is available for free on CD ROM (plus shipping and handling — $7.50 in the U. S. and Canada, and $14.95 for the rest of the world if ordered from **http://developstore.com/devstore/product.asp?productID=7516&Store=Toolbox_INT**). Each user gets an individual product code (as a text file during the download, or as a sticker on the package if sent by mail).

The system requirements for installing eMbedded Visual Tools 3.0 are as follows:

- Pentium 150 MHz or higher is recommended.
- Microsoft Windows 98, Second Edition; Microsoft Windows NT Workstation 4.0 with Service Pack 5 (or a later one with Service Pack 5); Microsoft Windows 2000; or Microsoft Windows XP Workstation. (For Windows 98 SE, the installation is not as complete: portable-device emulators do not work.)

Part III: Programming Pocket PC with eMbedded Visual Basic

- 32 MB of RAM for Windows 98 SE and Windows NT Workstation 4.0 (48 MB or more is recommended).
- 64 MB of RAM for Windows 2000 (128 MB or more is recommended).
- Hard-disk space — 360 MB (minimum), 720 MB (maximum). (In addition, about 50 MB are used for the Windows folder.)
- VGA Monitor (640×480) or higher (SVGA is recommended).
- A mouse or compatible device.

When the archive is unpacked, 2 directories — Disk1 and Disk2 — are created. They are identical to the two mail-distributed CD ROMs: 735 MB total. The setup program is started by simply clicking on the Setup.exe file in the Disk1 directory. The key is in the cdkey.txt file.

Let's go step by step through the installation process.

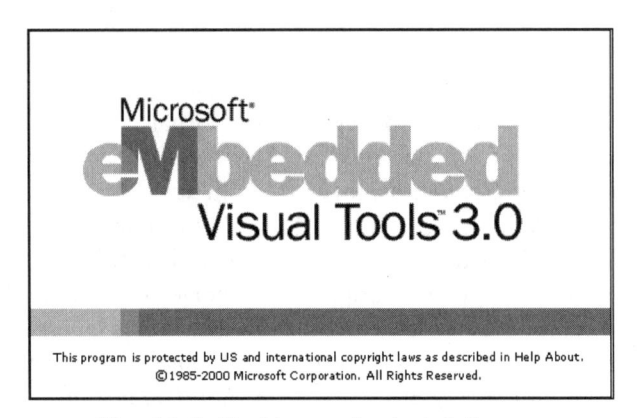

Fig. 11.1. Backing up the installation

After a short introduction (Fig. 11.1), you will be invited to begin the installation (Fig. 11.2).

The next window will request that you agree with the standard Microsoft license agreement (EULA, end user license agreement) (Fig. 11.3).

Then, enter the key (see the cdkey.txt file or the key on the CD ROM cover) — somewhat strange, since the software is supposed to be free (Fig. 11.4).

Then select the components to be installed (Fig. 11.5). If you select eMbedded Visual Tools, then the Platform Software Development Kit (SDK) needs a more detailed explanation. Microsoft uses the term "platform" to mean the Windows CE operating system and the specific hardware platform (screen size, keyboard, etc.). Within the eMbedded Visual Tools installation package, there are three Software Development Kits (SDKs) that include various tools and libraries for each of the three platforms.

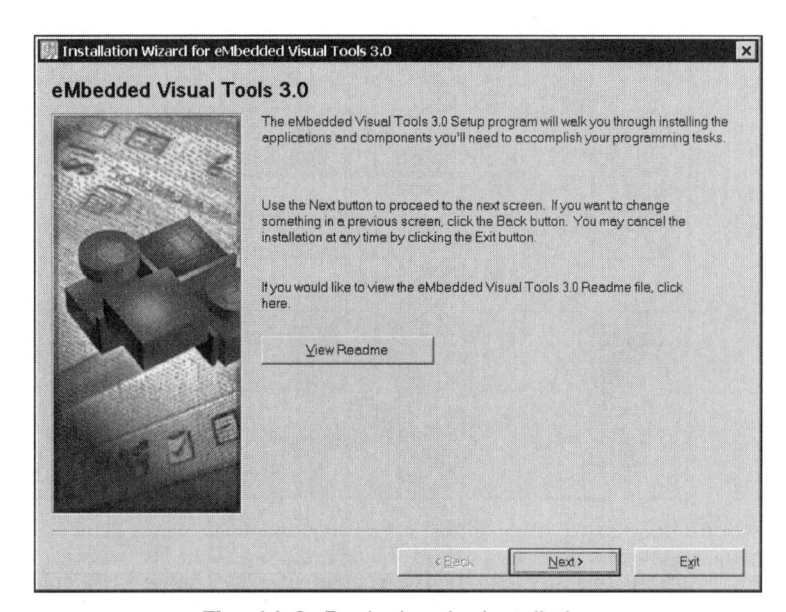

Fig. 11.2. Beginning the installation

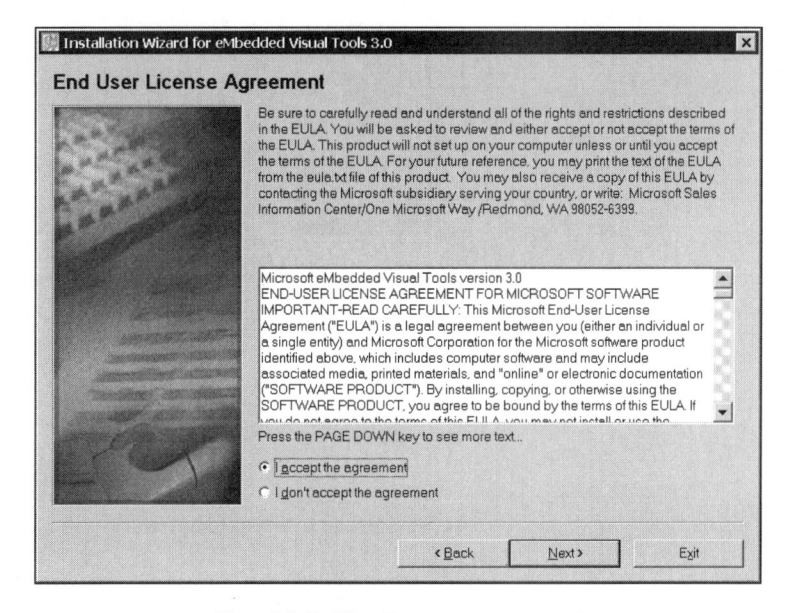

Fig. 11.3. The license agreement

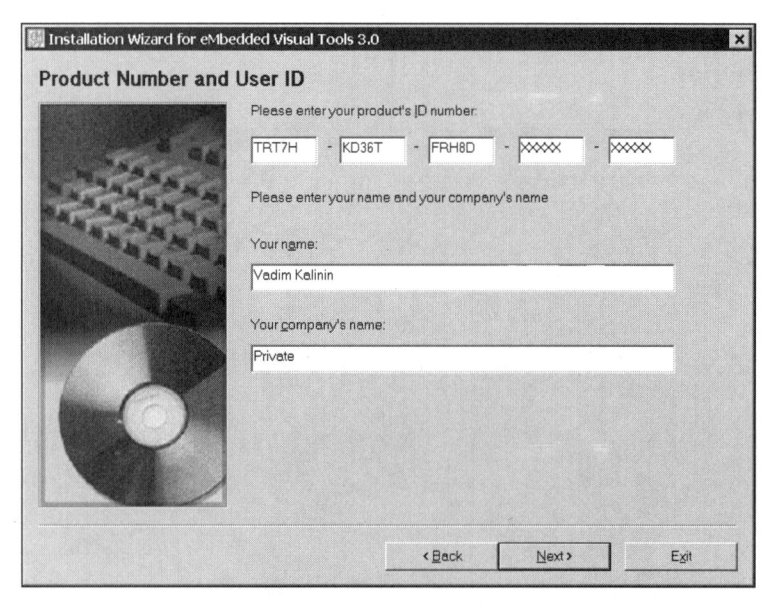

Fig. 11.4. The installation key

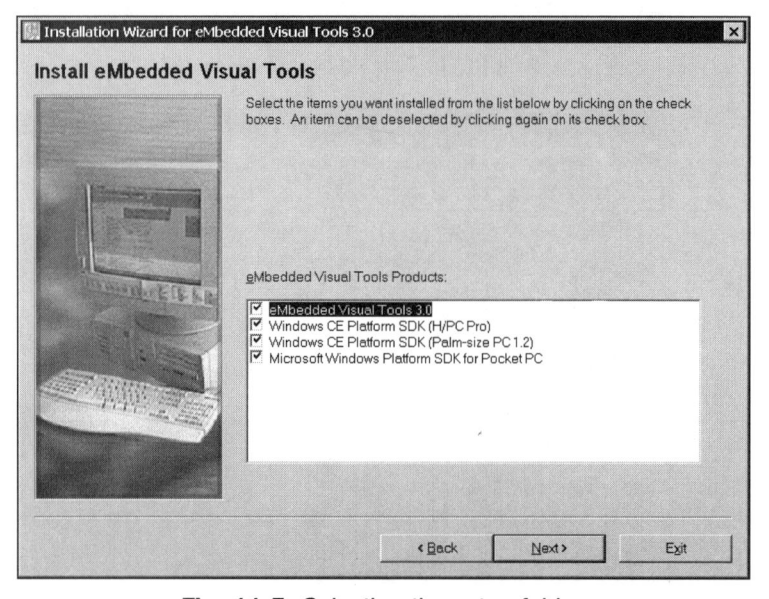

Fig. 11.5. Selecting the setup folder

Below are the characteristics of each platform in brief. The choice of platform depends on the devices for which the applications are to be developed. H/PC Pro

Chapter 11: Installing eMbedded Visual Tools 3.0

and Handheld PC Pro are keyboard devices with a large display that are based on Windows CE 2.11.

Palm-size PC 1.2 is a device without a keyboard. It has a display of 240 × 320 based on Windows CE 2.11. Note the interesting name — Palm-size PC. This is actually the old name of portable devices based on Windows CE that appeared a bit later than the first models of Palm. This term was used to stress their size, since the Palm was already on the market. In reality, these are mini-computers (not PDAs!) running Windows CE.

And, finally, Pocket PCs are contemporary devices without keyboards, with a display of 240 × 320, that are based on Windows CE 3.0. Pocket PC 2002 support will be considered later in this chapter.

Then select the setup folder: in practice, you should select the folder to which the SDK is to be installed (Fig. 11.6). Selecting the setup folder for eMbedded Visual Tools (Visual Basic and Visual C++) is done later (by default, this is the Program Files folder on the disk on which Windows is installed). In this case, it is possible not to install Visual C++.

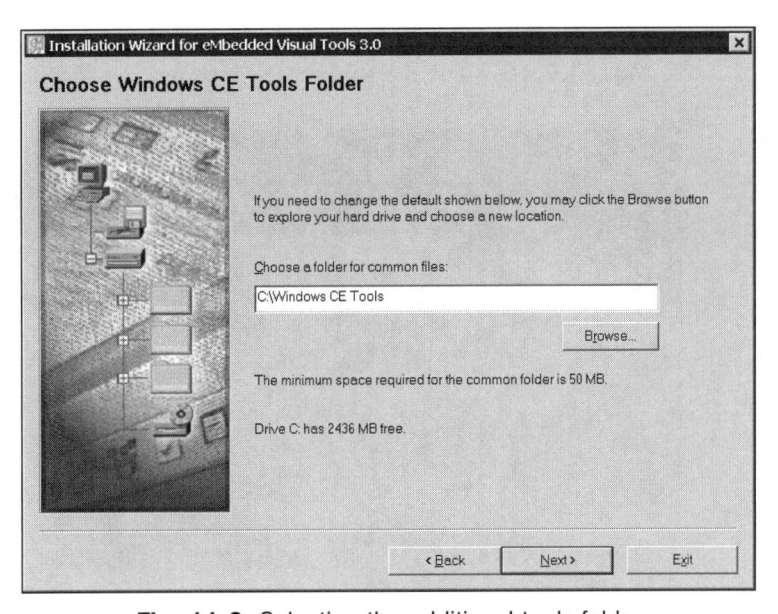

Fig. 11.6. Selecting the additional tools folder

The software will confirm the installation code.

Then comes the list of folders and the SDK (Fig. 11.7) (you can change the name of the root folder in which the main software is installed).

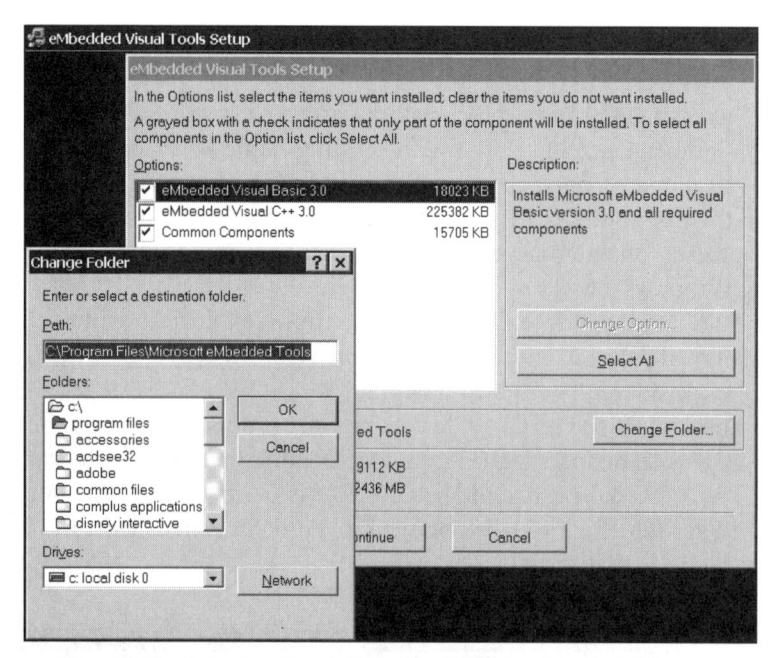

Fig. 11.7. Selecting the folder for eMbedded Visual Tools

Fig. 11.8. Installing the Microsoft Windows CE Platform SDK for the Handheld PC Pro Edition 3.0

Chapter 11: Installing eMbedded Visual Tools 3.0

The system files will then be updated, and the setup procedure for eMbedded Visual Tools will start.

Then the rest of the SDK will be installed (Fig. 11.8). Each SDK includes an emulator of the corresponding platform, libraries, and software tools.

Again the license agreement appears, and then you select the folder and the type of setup. You'll then see the list of the components for a custom setup (Fig. 11.9).

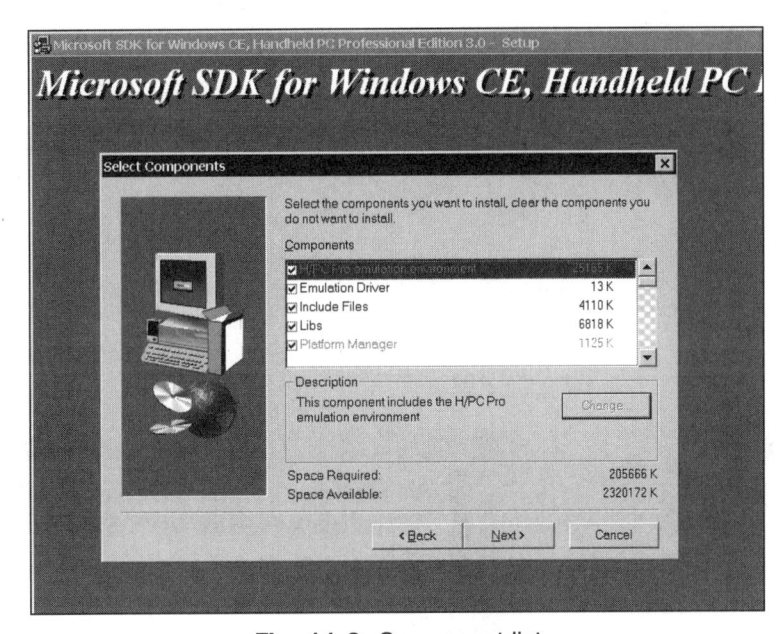

Fig. 11.9. Component list

Then we have a list of the installed parameters and applications, install the essential components and confirm the completion of the process.

The same operations are repeated for the Microsoft Windows CE Platform Software Development Kit version 2.11 Palm-size PC Edition 1.2 (Fig. 11.10).

Finally, Microsoft Windows Platform SDK for Pocket PC is installed.

The installation is slightly different in its design, but the operations performed are the same (Fig. 11.11).

After the installation is completed, several program folders will appear in the main menu.

So, now we have installed eMbedded Visual Tools 3.0.

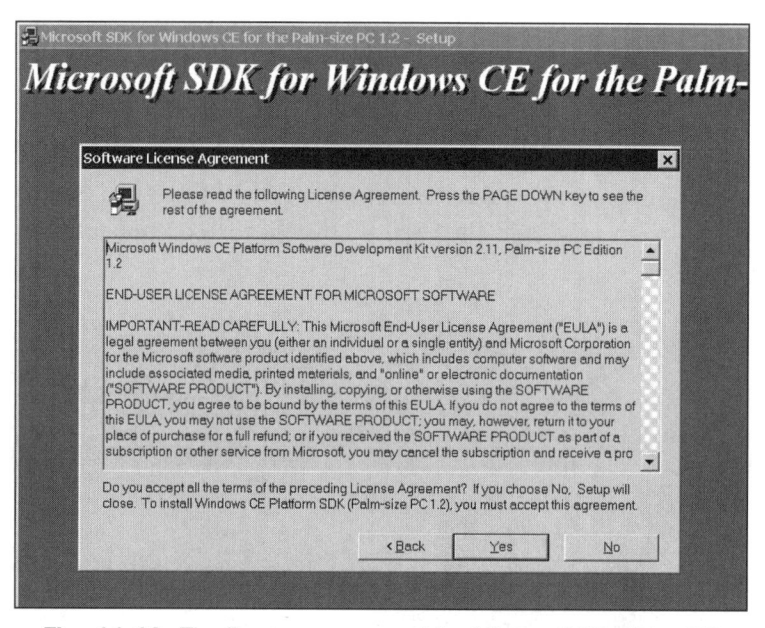

190   Part III: Programming Pocket PC with eMbedded Visual Basic

Fig. 11.10. The license agreement for Microsoft Windows CE Platform Software Development Kit version 2.11

Fig. 11.11. Beginning the setup of the Microsoft Windows Platform SDK for Pocket PC

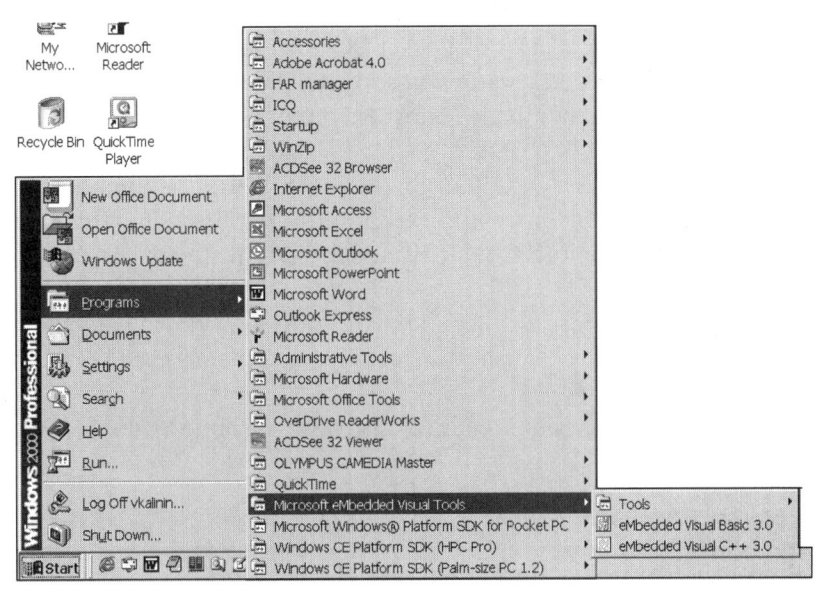

Fig. 11.12. Changes in the main menu

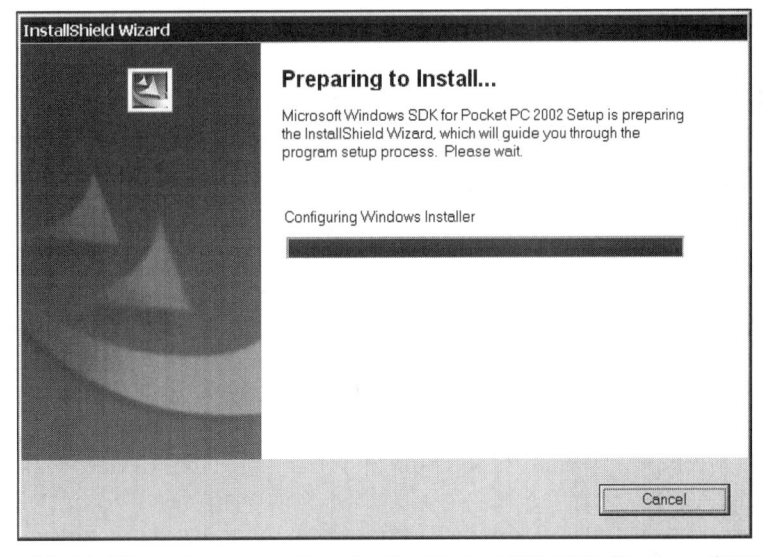

Fig. 11.13. The setup procedure for the Pocket PC 2002 Platform SDK

As soon as eMbedded Visual Tools 3.0 was put on the market, Microsoft released a new SDK supporting devices based on Pocket PC 2002 that contained the brand-new Pocket PC 2002 emulator and the libraries necessary for developing applications for this platform. Pocket PC 2002 is also based on Windows CE 3.0. It is recommended that you download this SDK from **http://www.microsoft.com/mobile/developer/downloads/**. Most examples in this book use the new emulator from the Pocket PC 2002 SDK.

After downloading PPC2002_SDK.exe (68 MB), it is unpacked into the folder indicated by the user. Start setup.exe in this folder. Installing this SDK is not much different from installing that of the Pocket PC platform. The start of the setup process is shown in Fig 11.13.

From the Microsoft web site, you can also download the SDK for the Handheld PC 2000 platform, which supports contemporary keyboard devices with Windows CE 3.0.

Microsoft states that eMbedded Visual Basic supports the following processors (Table 11.1).

Table 11.1. Types of Processors

Processor families	Supported types of processors
ARM	ARM720
Strong Arm	SA-1100 and later, in compatibility mode with SA-1100
MIPS	Supports MIPS39xx, MIPS41xx, and MIPS41xx in 16-bit mode
SHx	Hitachi SH3

Now we have successfully installed the eMbedded Visual Tools 3.0 development environment from Microsoft. It supports almost all devices running Windows CE.

This package, however, is not the only one from Microsoft or developing and compiling applications for portable devices. There is an earlier product — Windows CE Toolkit for Visual Basic 6.0. However, it requires Visual Basic 6.0 to develop applications for outdated portable devices with versions of Windows CE earlier than 2.11.

Developing Visual Basic applications for portable devices will also be possible using Visual Studio.Net. To do this, you also need to install Smart Device Extensions and .Net Compact Framework. At the time of writing, Microsoft was performing the beta testing of these products.

Chapter 12

Introduction to eMbedded Visual Basic

Creating a Demo Application

After launching eMbedded VB, you can clearly see that it closely resembles VB6 or other versions of Visual Basic. Here, however, it must be said that, as mentioned in the previous chapter, although eVB uses much the same system files as VB, it is independent software, which just looks like VB externally. If you glance over the menus and the toolbars, the difference in the features and their number when compared with the real VB will become obvious. We noted in *Chapter 4* that AppForge employs another philosophy, as if it were a VB Add-In.

We'll start by creating a demo application.

Launch eMbedded Visual Basic 3.0 (Fig. 12.1). During loading, a set of windows similar to those in VB6 appears (Fig. 12.1).

The differences, however, reveal themselves at the very start. Instead of the type of the project developed, you are asked to select one of 5 project types for various portable devices. We'll select a Windows CE for Pocket PC 2002 Project. Selecting a Windows CE Formless Project will open another dialog box in which you are asked to select the type of the project, and if you select another type, it will simply add some insignificant changes to the shell. If the Windows CE HPC HRO Project is selected, then the **Sub_Main** form will become the point of entry into the project. To begin with the same operations as in the other project types, you need to create the **Form1** form. If there are more developers' SDKs (Software Development Kits) installed, from Microsoft or from other manufacturers, then there will

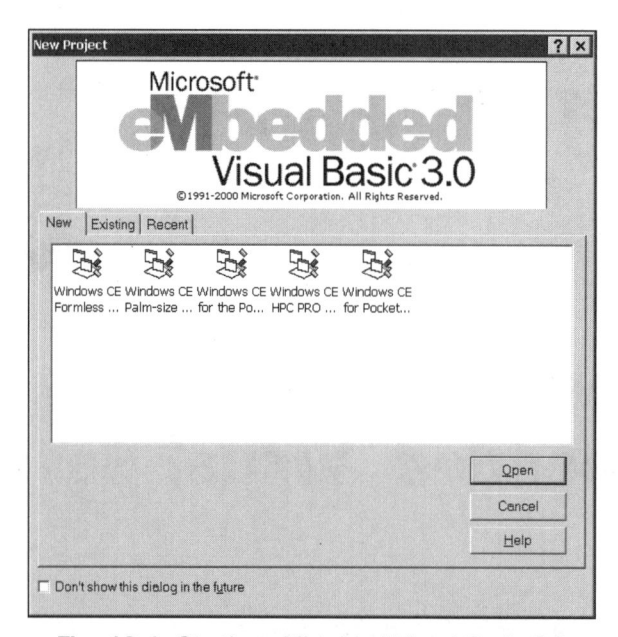

Fig. 12.1. Starting eMbedded Visual Basic 3.0

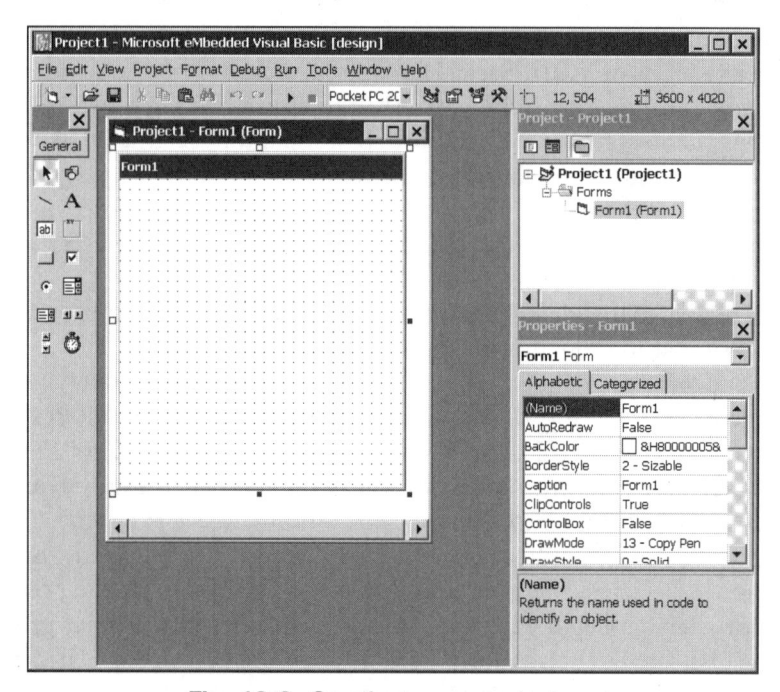

Fig. 12.2. Creating a new project

Chapter 12: Introduction to eMbedded Visual Basic   195

be more types of projects available. Note also the absence of the ActiveX.exe, ActiveX.dll, and ActiveX project types, since these options are not supported. Each type of project has a corresponding portable-device emulator, to debug the application and see approximately how it will look on a real device. In practice, it does not really matter what project is being developed, as long as options supported by each platform are used. Then you only have to change the type of portable device when the application is transferred: the differences will be automatically seen when the application is on the actual device. Now we will select only the type of the emulator on which the application will be tested during development.

As in the previous chapters dedicated to AppForge, let's start by developing a simple application that generates the message "Hello, World" when the **Hello** key is pressed. Design the form by dragging the text box and the command button from the toolbar into the **Form1** window, and change their attributes in the **Properties** window, e.g., pick a font, size 24, black, initial text — "Text Area". Change the button settings in the same way (Fig. 12.3).

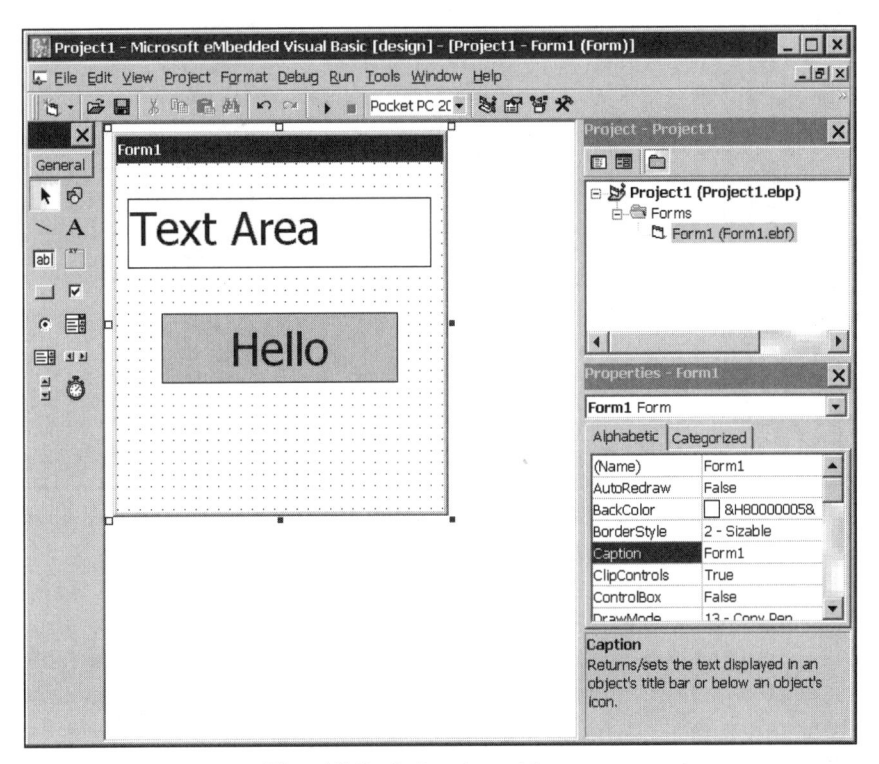

Fig. 12.3. A developed form

In order to evoke the events we want upon pressing the button, make some changes to the main program code. To do this, select **Code** from the **View** menu and make the necessary changes in the code.

When the new project is opened, the code already contains the "Close application" navigation button (Fig. 12.4).

Create a procedure that provides Click for Command1 in a similar manner.

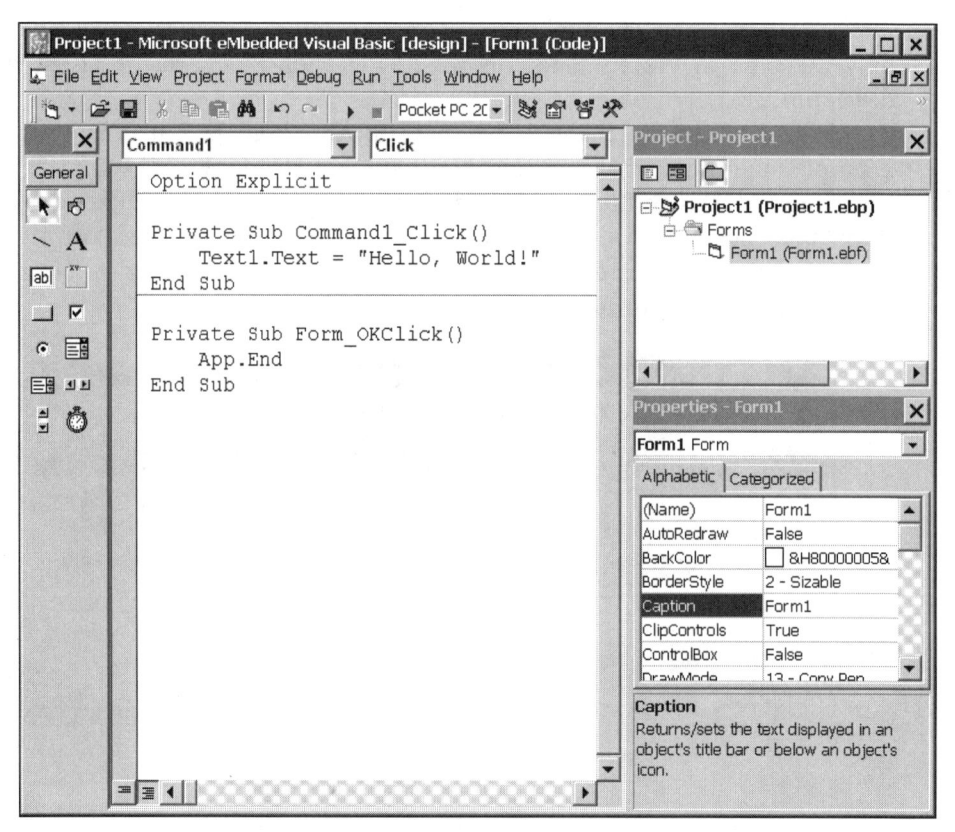

Fig. 12.4. Text of the procedures providing for the reaction of the button and window to the events

So, now we have created an application that, after the **Command1** button is pressed, generates the phrase "Hello, World!" in the **text1** box. The application is started by clicking on **Run** or ▶. The emulator is started automatically, in which you can watch the execution of the application. One of the phases of operation is shown in Fig. 12.5.

Chapter 12: Introduction to eMbedded Visual Basic   197

Fig. 12.5. The demo application at work

Our application is successfully implemented on the integrated emulator. To copy the application onto a real portable device, it is first necessary to create an executable version of the application using the **File/Make project.vb** menu, compile it using **Tools/Remote Tools/Application Install Wizard...**, and copy it to the portable device via the ActiveSync function (connecting the PC and portable device). Copying the created application to the portable device will be considered below, in the compilation stage of the next example.

While creating the test application, we used the same options as in VB6. In practice, however, there are a few differences, some of which will be considered below.

The Type of Variables in eVB

One of the main differences between eMbedded Visual Basic and its big brother is the impossibility of creating a binary executable program. Instead, a program code that comes with the corresponding interpreter settings is created. You have to install the eVB virtual machine on your portable device, and thus you must expand Pvbload.exe and all the components that enable its work. Many portable device manufacturers integrate the eVB virtual machine into ROM devices, which helps to minimize the installation package.

Each application is not just one executable file, but rather consists of the following set of files and libraries created during the work of the Remote tools wizard:

- Myfile.vb — the program itself
- pvbload.exe — interpreter
- pvbform2.dll
- pvbhost2.dll
- vbscript.dll

as well as other controls, libraries, and modules used during the development of the application.

This slows down the work of eVB applications. During the operation of an eVB application, the pseudocode needs to be interpreted during execution, which adds to the processor's load. This means that eVB is not suitable for complex mathematics, intensive graphics, and other applications that require substantial resources.

eVB compiles the project into a file with the extension VB. When registered, eVB connects the VB extension with the interpreter, and so, by clicking on a file with the extension VB, the eVB virtual machine is automatically called. The applications have the same icon as pvbload.exe. It is also possible to start pvbload.exe from the command line, with a parameter consisting of the name of the created application.

One positive difference is the absence of a dependence on the hardware. Unlike a compiled binary file, our VB file can be implemented on any supported processor without retranslation.

All Variables Are *Variants*

Another important difference between eVB and VB6, which makes eVB closer to VBScript, is that some variables are not supported. All variables in eVB are of the `Variant` type, even if you declare them otherwise. On the one hand, using the `variable_type` syntax simplifies the development of the application somewhat, and on the other hand, it forces the programmer to be careful. In addition, variables need to be initialized. For example, the phrase

```
Dim iMyInteger as Integer
```

Chapter 12: Introduction to eMbedded Visual Basic

automatically determines the value of this variable in VB as zero. It is still not defined in eVB. The developer should always check the assignation of initial values to variables, since they are not assigned automatically after the declaration.

Sometimes, this may cause logical errors that are difficult to debug. Therefore, all eVB variables should be initialized.

Consider this code fragment:

```
Dim MyForm As Form
Dim MyInteger As Integer
Dim MyBoolean As Boolean

MyBoolean=1
MyForm = True
MyForm = MyForm + MyBoolean
Set MyInteger = Form1
MyForm = MyInteger.Caption
MyInteger = MyInteger.Left + 1
```

In VB 6.0, this will not even be compiled, but in eVB this will be done with a result that is harder to predict than it is to write the code.

Mixing types may evoke logical errors that are too difficult to debug, and so this should be attended to very carefully when programming in eVB.

Other Differences between VB and eVB

There are a whole range of differences between Visual Basic and eVB that we will briefly describe below. However, these are just the main differences, since during work with the software, you are likely to notice others that are less obvious.

Another main difference between eVB and VB is the impossibility of creating classes in eVB. eVB projects support only two types of files: forms and regular modules. There is also no entire set of techniques and tools available in standard VB for working with classes.

eVB does not allow ActiveX controls or ActiveX libraries (files with the DLL extension) but provides the option of using libraries and ActiveX controls created using other software, e.g., eVC (eMbedded Visual C++).

A very annoying limitation of eVB is the extremely limited error handling. You cannot handle an error at the end of a procedure, using **GoTo** to return to it.

The only supported reaction to an error is the phrase: `"On Error Resume Next"`. Therefore, a good solution is line-by-line error handling. The following code may be useful in dubious cases:

```
Public Procedure abc()
On Error Resume Next
   If Err.Number <> 0 Then
    MsgBox Err.Description, vbCritical, "Error"
End If
End Procedure
```

The above example uses an `Err` object with the `Clear` and `Raise` methods, as well as `Number`, `Description`, `Source`, and other properties.

There is no menu editor in eVB. All menus are created in a programmatic way, and use an ActiveX component. Creating a menu is described in the next chapter.

Control arrays are not supported in eVB, which makes writing a general code for a number of controls a more creative task. The simplest way to solve this is to have all controls address one function.

eVB does not support User Defined Type (UDT) variables or structures. You can not use modal forms in eVB. This means that if you create an application with several forms, you should take into account the possibility that the user can move to another form at any moment by accidentally clicking on it instead of the active window. To avoid this problem, use only full, screen forms, or set the **Visible** checkbox on the background form to **False**.

No blocks with the key word "With" are supported. You must indicate the name of the object or its property or method every time.

Objects in eVB should be created only with `CreateObject` or `CreateObjectWithEvents`, and the last `WithEvents` part can not be used for variable declaration. The `New` operator is not supported in eVB.

Use `CreateObjectWithEvents` to create an object that has the option of changing its events. You should use the `CreateObjectWithEvents` method with two parameters: `ProgID` object and `Case` prefix. For example, to create the `WinSock` object with the option of controlling the handling of its events, use a construction like:

```
objSocket = CreateObjectWithEvents (" Winsock.Winsock ", " MySocket _ ")
```

This is the instruction for eVB to create an object, all of whose events start with `MySocket`. For example, `Connect` for our connection will be `MySocket_Connect()`.

Let's consider an example in eVB. You can create `WinSock` and immediately establish a connection with it. If no connection address is indicated, the query will not be executed, and the `Error` event of the `WinSock` object will be performed:

```
Sub Main()
   On Error Resume Next
   Dim objSocket As WinSock.WinSock
   Dim vData As String
   Set objSocket = CreateObjectWithEvents("Winsock.Winsock", "MySocket_")
   objSocket.Connect
End Sub


Public Sub MySocket_Error(Number As Integer, Description As String)
   MsgBox Description
End Sub
```

When using `CreateObject`, remember that this construction leads to some memory loss in eVB. When `CreateObject` is called to create any numbered object (a list, an array, etc), eVB allocates memory for all elements. If the actual dimension of the array turns out to be less than the reserved one, the memory is not released. This means that each call of `CreateObject` will allot memory sufficient for all elements, and keep it reserved until the application is closed. Microsoft has provided no solutions to this problem.

Despite the standard programming recommendations, we advise you to create objects once (but not when it is necessary to call them) and use them repeatedly as needed.

Using Windows CE Emulators

Each of the 4 types of Windows CE SDKs have their own emulators, which can be useful tools. You can use the emulator by starting any of its integrated applications (Fig. 12.6), as well as ones that you have developed on eVB. When additional Windows CE SDKs are used, it is possible to load additional emulators. This lets you test the applications you develop without the actual device. As a rule, loading the application on the emulator is faster than loading it on the device via ActiveSync, making it is more convenient to use emulators.

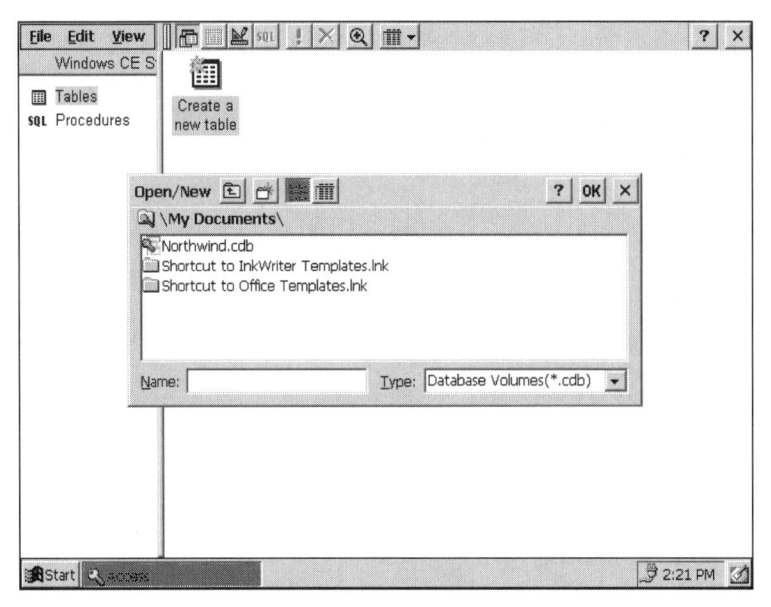

Fig. 12.6. The Handheld PC Pro emulator at the beginning of loading Pocket Access

Watch out, however, because the emulator is not error-free. An emulator created for a whole class of devices cannot work faultlessly with all of them, and it may be rather capricious. The emulator demonstrates about 80% accuracy in the imitation of the device. Obviously, there is no way to imitate, for example, the infrared socket of the COM port on the emulator, since it is physically impossible to connect to this device.

Even more annoying problems occur when the emulator behaves completely the opposite of the actual device.

Very often, these differences are revealed while working with databases. For example, pasting a large number of records into a table on the emulator will almost certainly end in an error, but the same code will work perfectly well on many real devices.

To avoid the trouble caused by specific emulator errors, it should be used only in the initial stages, e.g., to check the initial arrangement on the screen, the graphic interface's performance, on-screen menus, and moving around the screen. When you want to simulate a real application and its logic, however, try to use a real device. Try the application on the real device even if the emulator shows an error in a code of which you are sure. Reverse situations are also possible — when the application works well on the emulator, but gives errors on the actual device. Of course, these are special cases, but testing the application on the real device is always necessary, even if everything works fine on the emulator.

And More Differences between VB and eVB

Many differences between eVB and VB6 are obvious, and need no special description. Below is a list of most of the differences.

- Some project files change their extensions. Forms in eVB have the EBF extension, whereas project files have the EBP extention.
- eVB controls support only 256-color graphics. An attempt to load high-color or true-color graphics gives errors that are difficult to eliminate, so you should make sure that all pictures have a 256-color resolution or less.
- Since an application in eVB is interpreted, `AddressOf` is not supported. Also, it is not possible to use `VarPtr` or `StrPtr` to find a variable address.
- The `FORMAT()` function is not supported. Only a few new formatting procedures have been added: `FormatDateTime`, `FormatPercent`, `FormatNumber`, and `ForinatCurrency`. Any other type of formatting requires you to create a special procedure, because all variables are of the `Variant` type.
- The `Load` and `Unload` (e.g., `Load Form1`) commands are not supported.
- eVB does not support the creation of a function with additional parameters (although you can call C++ functions with additional parameters).
- Conditional clauses of directive comparison (`#If...Then...#Else`, `#Constant`) are not supported.
- The `Shell()` command is not supported. Use `CreateProcess` API instead.
- No static variables are supported.
- The `Left()` string function is not available in the code editor, but works perfectly well in the module.
- `DoEvents` is not supported.
- The Registry functions `SaveSetting` and `GetSetting` are not supported.
- eVB `ListBox` does not support the `CheckBox` style.
- eVB does not support the instruction `Timer`. Use the API function `GetTickCount`.
- The options `Base` and `Type` are not supported.
- Arrays always begin with the zero index element.
- Lists are not supported.
- The operator `!` (as in `objRs! Field1`) is not supported.
- `GoSub` is not supported.

- No string numbering is allowed.
- `GoTo` is not used in eVB.
- `End` is not supported. `App.End` is used instead.
- The following functions of type transformation are not allowed: `Str`, `Val`, `Cvar`. This is because all variables in eVB have the `Variant` type. `CStr`, `CInt`, `Cdate`, and other functions are used.
- eVB has no `Debug` object. For example, `Debug.Print` and `Debug.Assert` are not permitted.
- The function `TypeOf` is not supported.
- `Case` instructions using `Is` or `To` are not permitted (e.g., `Case obj Is Nothing` or `Case 1 To 5`).
- `Beep()` is not supported. Use `PlaySound` API instead.
- No string commands containing the symbol `$` (`Left$`, `Right$`) are supported.
- `LSet` and `RSet` are not supported.
- The operator `Like` is not supported.

Note

This chapter illustrates many (but not all) differences between eVB and Visual Basic 6. You encounter something not listed above. Moreover, the performance of some options depends on the platform on which the project will be implemented. When an unsupported option is compiled, it is possible to get an error message. In this case, use **Help**. If there is no such option in the **Help** menu, then it is most likely not supported. Be careful, though, because **Help** is created for all types of SDKs, and even if you found the description of the property you want, you still need to make sure that it is related to the relevant SDK type. This is typical for context help, since it often provides modules and procedures not supported by the given type of portable device. An even more bothersome situation may occur in which an unsupported option is wrongly compiled, but there is no error message. Different programming styles tend to use different methods. Knowing the limits of eVB will help you to create applications correctly and avoid an unsupported code.

Chapter 13

Working with Controls

The base set of controls and components is loaded upon first loading eVB. Using them is no different from VB6. Click once on the selected control on the toolbar and create a window of the required size on `YourFormName (Form)`. If you double-click on

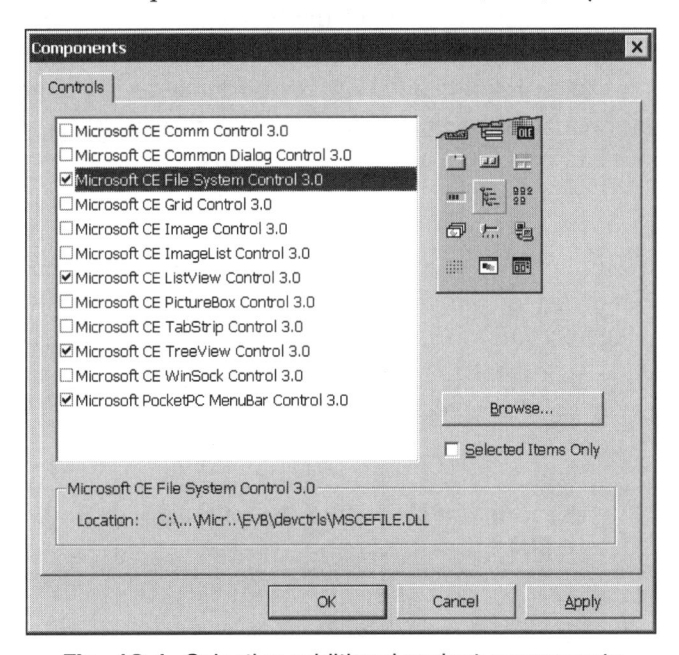

Fig. 13.1. Selecting additional project components

this control after it has been placed on the form, `Private Sub` will appear, which describes the default reaction to the event related to this control. Alternatively, you can go to the **View/Code** menu and select the name of the control and the event corresponding to it. If necessary, you can load additional components from other libraries, as in any other version of Visual Basic. To do this, select additional components (the **Components** command) from the **Project** menu (Fig. 13.1). The set of these components is more limited than in VB6. This chapter briefly deals with some of them.

To illustrate how the basic controls work, let's consider the development of a demo application.

Developing a Demo Application

Let's create a simple calculator as a demo application. Start eMbedded Visual Basic 3.0. Create a project for Windows CE for Pocket PC 2002. As previously noted, the differences between the projects are insignificant when implemented on the emulator integrated into the developer's package. When the project is compiled on the actual portable device, the support of some libraries and their functions depends on the processor type, the options of the corresponding Windows CE version, and the interpreter. If options not supported by the interpreter are used, the resulting application can be implemented on any portable device, although its appearance may be somewhat different. Here, we will disregard the differences between the versions and types of interpreters of portable devices.

The appearance of the form to be created is shown in Fig. 13.2. Any user can reproduce this appearance of the form by simply dragging the buttons and other controls from the toolbar: click on the required control in the toolbar, and choose the place and size for the control in the form field using the mouse. You should easily be able to create a form that meets your needs. If you need to specify the sizes more accurately, change the parameters of the controls. Or, simply to experiment, you can try to edit the corresponding EBF file. Below is a fragment of the code for this form (Listing 13.1).

Listing 13.1. The form developed for the calculator (a fragment of the frmCalc.ebf file)

```
VERSION 5.00
Object = "{F7DEA2C9-BA8F-446E-A292-B4840F3BD661}#1.0#0"; "mscemenubar.dll"
Begin VB.Form frmCalc
```

Chapter 13: Working with Controls

```
   Appearance     =   0  'Flat
   BackColor      =   &H80000005&
   Caption        =   "Calculator VB"
   ClientHeight   =   4332
   ClientLeft     =   60
   ClientTop      =   840
   ClientWidth    =   3600
   ForeColor      =   &H80000008&
   ScaleHeight    =   4332
   ScaleWidth     =   3600
   ShowOK         =   -1 'True
   Begin MenuBarLib.MenuBar MenuBar1
    Left          =   1080
    Top           =   33720
    _cx           =   2561
    _cy           =   656
    Enabled       =   -1 'True
    NewButton     =   -1 'True
   End
   Begin VBCE.CommandButton cmdMult
    Height        =   372
    Left          =   1920
    TabIndex      =   20
    Top           =   3120
    Width         =   372
    _cx           =   656
    _cy           =   656
    BackColor     =   12632256
    Caption       =   "*"
    Enabled       =   -1 'True
    BeginProperty Font {0BE35203-8F91-11CE-9DE3-00AA004BB851}
      Name        =   "Tahoma"
      Size        =   7.8
      Charset     =   204
      Weight      =   400
      Underline   =   0  'False
      Italic      =   0  'False
      Strikethrough = 0  'False
    EndProperty
    Style         =   0
   End
End
```

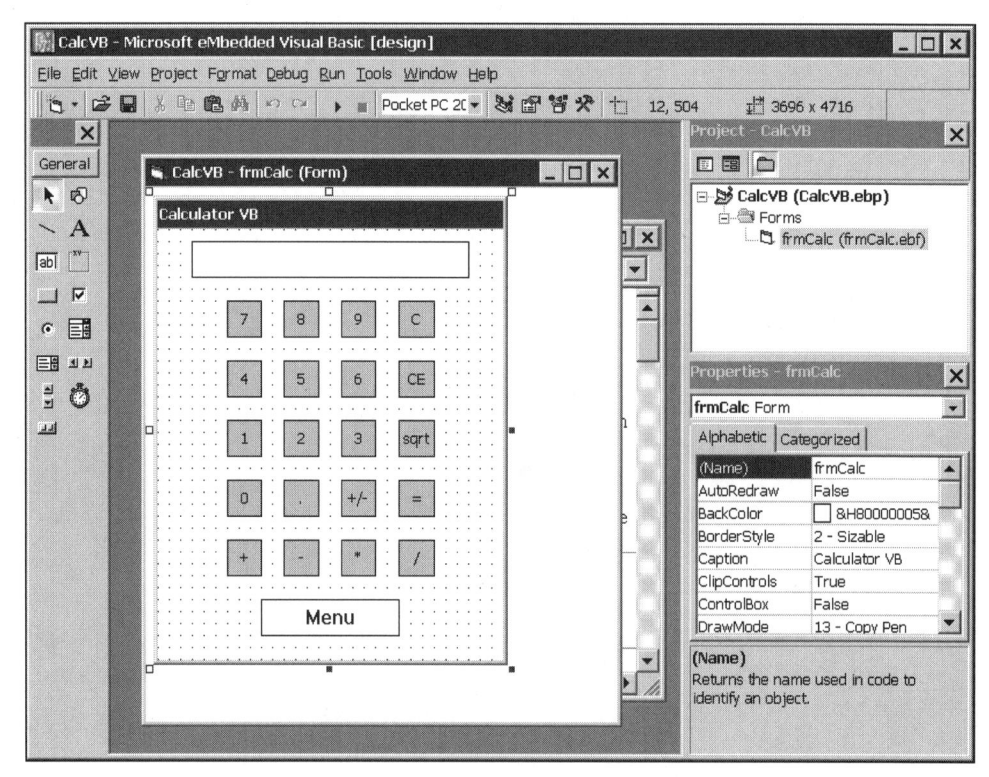

Fig. 13.2. A form developed for calculator

There are no problems with the form image, nor are there any significant differences from VB6 (note that each control now has fewer properties; many of the control properties available in VB6 are not supported here). To create a procedure responsible for each event of the form control, double-click on the required one, or select the name of the control and the event in the **Code** window from the **View** menu. The shell of the subprogram will then be created, which must be filled in with the certain contents, for example:

```
Private Sub cmd0_Click()
End Sub
```

The written program code will be different from that of VB6. Most of the differences were mentioned in the previous chapter. First of all, all variables are of the Variant type. This relates to another feature of eVB — the lack of the Val, Str, etc. types of transforming functions. Instead, use the analogous CInt, CLng, and CStr functions. This also means that performing the operations will be connected with the context of the variable of the `Variant` type (which is every variable, even if it was determined otherwise). In other words, if

```
Dim Var1 As Variant
Dim Var2 As Variant
Var1 = "1"
Var2 = "1",
```

Then the result of the calculation

```
Var3 = Var1 + Var2
```

will be 11, and

```
Var3 = Var1 * 1 + Var2
```

will accordingly be 2.

The use of variables of the `Variant` type is a powerful and convenient tool for users familiar with the system, but for adherents of strictly determined types, such as in, for example, Pascal, it is often the cause of getting the wrong answer as a result of the calculations. Other differences will be considered in subsequent chapters.

Project Description

Our goal is to write an application for the common calculator.

This application should have:

- ❐ Keys with the digits providing for the creation of the numbers with which the operations will be performed. The simplest way is to add the number to the string by pressing the number keys. The string is transformed into a variable of the `Double` type for further calculations, which is shown in Listing 13.2.
- ❐ Keys with one-variable functions (1/x, Sin, ±, and others) are simple to use in programming, and are represented in the application.
- ❐ The memory functions (M, M+, M–) are also simple to use (to implement them in our project, we used the **Copy Paste** menu to illustrate its options).
- ❐ Keys for arithmetic operations should be able to remember the code of the operation, save the number on the display in additional variables, and execute the selected operation after pressing "=" or the next symbol of the arithmetic operation.
- ❐ The procedure for the "=" key is a slightly amended variant of the subprograms for implementing the arithmetic operations.

- Finally, there are the "C" and "CE" keys, for cleaning the processed data and correcting wrongly entered information. "C" clears all, and "CE" clears just the last number.

Now, let's consider implementing each of the above items.

To implement entry using digits and the decimal point, string addition is sufficient. An example is shown below (Listing 13.2). Pressing each number key calls the `DigitPressed` subprogram with the corresponding parameter. The `strCurrentValue` string variable contains the number entered on the calculator.

Listing 13.2. Example of implementing the *Digit* button on the calculator

```
Private Sub cmd1_Click()
DigitPressed ("1")
End Sub

Private Sub DigitPressed(strDigit As String)
If boolNewValue = True Then
  boolNewValue = False
  intDigitsCount = 0
  strCurrentValue = "0"
  boolDecimalPressed = False
  boolEqualPressed = False
End If

If intDigitsCount < intMaxDigits Then
  intDigitsCount = intDigitsCount + 1
  If strCurrentValue = "0" Then
    strCurrentValue = strDigit
  Else
    strCurrentValue = strCurrentValue & strDigit
  End If
  dblDisplay = CDbl(strCurrentValue)
  dblEndValue = dblDisplay
  lblDisplay.Caption = CStr(dblDisplay)
End If
End Sub
```

Chapter 13: Working with Controls 211

Entering the decimal point is done by adding the period symbol in the string with the checkbox for preventing repeated entry of the decimal point activated (Listing 13.3).

Listing 13.3. Example of implementing the *Decimal* button

```
Private Sub cmdDecimal_Click()
If Not boolDecimalPressed Then
  boolDecimalPressed = True
   strCurrentValue = strCurrentValue & "."
   lblDisplay.Caption = strCurrentValue
End If
End Sub
```

Here, the `boolDecimalPressed` variable shows that the decimal point was pressed and cleared before the new digit is entered.

The keys for the arithmetic operations use the `Calculate` subprogram, which, depending on the `strCom` parameter, performs one of the arithmetic operations. This parameter contains the information on the previous time the arithmetic-operation key was pressed (Listing 13.4).

Listing 13.4. Subprogram performing arithmetic operations

```
Private Sub Calculate(strCom As String)
Dim dbltemp As Double
Select Case strCom
  Case "+"
    boolNewValue = True
    dblDisplay = dblResultValue + dblEndValue
    dblResultValue = dblDisplay
    lblDisplay.Caption = CStr(dblDisplay)
  Case "-"
    dblDisplay = dblResultValue - dblEndValue
    dblResultValue = dblDisplay
    lblDisplay.Caption = CStr(dblDisplay)
  Case "*"
    dblDisplay = dblResultValue * dblEndValue
    dblResultValue = dblDisplay
    lblDisplay.Caption = CStr(dblDisplay)
  Case "/"
```

```
      boolNewValue = True
      If CDbl(dblEndValue) <> 0 Then
        dblDisplay = dblResultValue / dblEndValue
        dblResultValue = dblDisplay
        lblDisplay.Caption = CStr(dblDisplay)
      Else
        lblDisplay.Caption = "Divide By Zero"
      End If
End Select
End Sub
```

The arithmetic-operation keys should remember the number in the text field in the additional variables, complete the previous operation, and determine the type of the next one. When arithmetic-operation keys are pressed, the `CommandPressed` subprogram is called, with the operation symbol as the parameter. Its implementation is shown in Listing 13.5.

Listing 13.5. Example of implementing the + button on the calculator

```
Private Sub cmdPlus_Click()
CommandPressed "+"
End Sub


Private Sub CommandPressed(strCom As String)
If boolEqualPressed Then
  strCommand = strCom
  boolNewValue = True
Else
  If strCommand = "" Then
    strCommand = strCom
    boolNewValue = True
    dblResultValue = dblDisplay
  Else
    Calculate strCommand
    strCommand = strCom
  End If
End If
End Sub
```

The procedure of the = operation differs only slightly from that of the arithmetic operations: the last arithmetic operation is performed if you press it (the value of the strCommand variable remains the same). After it is performed, the option of blocking the arithmetic operation keys until a new digit is entered is activated (Listing 13.6).

Listing 13.6. Example of implementing the = button on the calculator

```
Private Sub cmdEqual_Click()
  If strCommand <> "" Then
    Calculate strCommand
    boolEqualPressed = True
  End If
End Sub
```

The implementation of the rest of the module functions is shown in Listing 13.7.

Listing 13.7. The calculator module, other than the digits, arithmetic operations, and = buttons above, and the "Memory" menu, that will be considered in the next section

```
Option Explicit
'Variable declaration
Dim intMaxDigits As Integer
Dim intDigitsCount As Integer
Dim strCurrentValue As String
Dim strCommand As String
Dim boolDecimalPressed As Boolean
Dim boolNewValue As Boolean
Dim boolEqualPressed As Boolean
Dim dblResultValue As Double
Dim dblDisplay As Double
Dim dblEndValue As Double
Dim dblMemValue As Double
Dim KEY_BAR1_PROMPT1 As String
Dim KEY_BAR1_PROMPT2 As String
Dim KEY_ROOT1 As String
Dim objMenu As MenuBarLib.MenuBar
```

```
Dim objBar As MenuBarLib.MenuBar

'Form load - variable and menu initialization
Private Sub Form_Load()
intMaxDigits = 10
Clear
KEY_BAR1_PROMPT1 = "Copy"
KEY_BAR1_PROMPT2 = "Paste"
MenuBar1.Controls.Clear
Set objMenu = MenuBar1.Controls.AddMenu("Memory", KEY_ROOT1)
Set objBar = objMenu.Items.Add(, KEY_BAR1_PROMPT1, "Copy")
objBar.Tag = "Tag For Copy"
Set objBar = objMenu.Items.Add(, KEY_BAR1_PROMPT2, "Paste")
objBar.Tag = "Tag For Paste"
End Sub

'Square root calculation
Private Sub cmdSQRT_Click()
If dblDisplay > 0 Then
  dblDisplay = Sqr(dblDisplay)
  dblResultValue = dblDisplay
  lblDisplay.Caption = CStr(dblDisplay)
Else
  lblDisplay.Caption = "Negative Argument"
End If
End Sub

'Clear variables
Private Sub Clear()
boolDecimalPressed = False
strCommand = ""
lblDisplay.Caption = "0"
boolNewValue = True
dblResultValue = 0
dblDisplay = 0
dblEndValue = 0
boolEqualPressed = False
End Sub

'C button pressed
```

```
Private Sub cmdClear_Click()
Clear
End Sub

'CE button pressed
Private Sub cmdClearEnd_Click()
boolDecimalPressed = False
strCurrentValue = "0"
lblDisplay.Caption = strCurrentValue
intDigitsCount = 0
dblDisplay = 0
dblEndValue = 0
End Sub

'+/- button pressed
Private Sub cmdSign_Click()
strCurrentValue = CStr(-CDbl(strCurrentValue))
dblDisplay = -dblDisplay
lblDisplay.Caption = CStr(dblDisplay)
End Sub
```

You can supplement your calculator with the required functions, and have a newly updated and useful tool.

Compiling the Application and Copying It to the Portable Device

To create an application for a portable device, first use the **Make** command of the **File** menu to create the file CalcVB.vb, and then start the file-porting wizard using the **Remote Tools/Application Install Wizard** command from the **Tools** menu.

While the wizard is working, you are asked to answer the following questions:

- Path to the project
- Location of the compiled version
- Setup-files directory
- Types of supported processors
- Additional project components (coinciding with the list of libraries in **Project/Components**)

216 Part III: Programming Pocket PC with eMbedded Visual Basic

- Additional project files (e.g., modules created in other languages, e.g., eVC)
- Directory for installing on a portable device
- Project name, information about the project and author

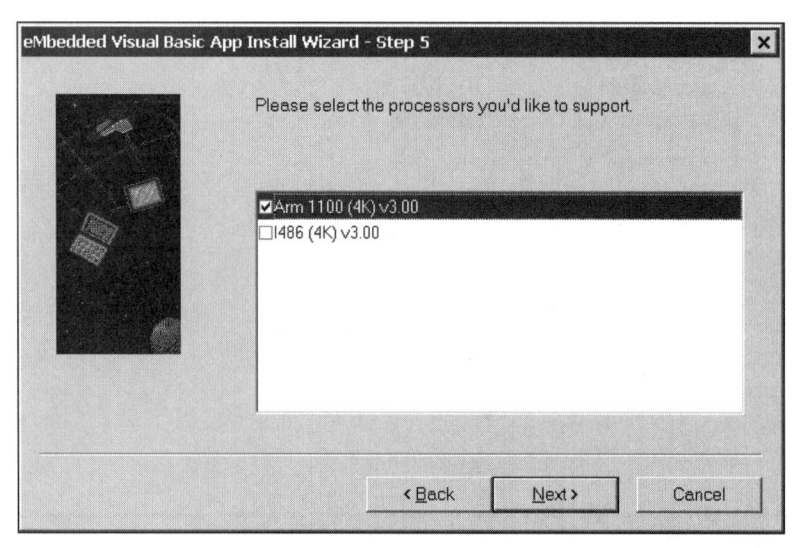

Fig. 13.3. The work of the porting wizard. Types of supported processors

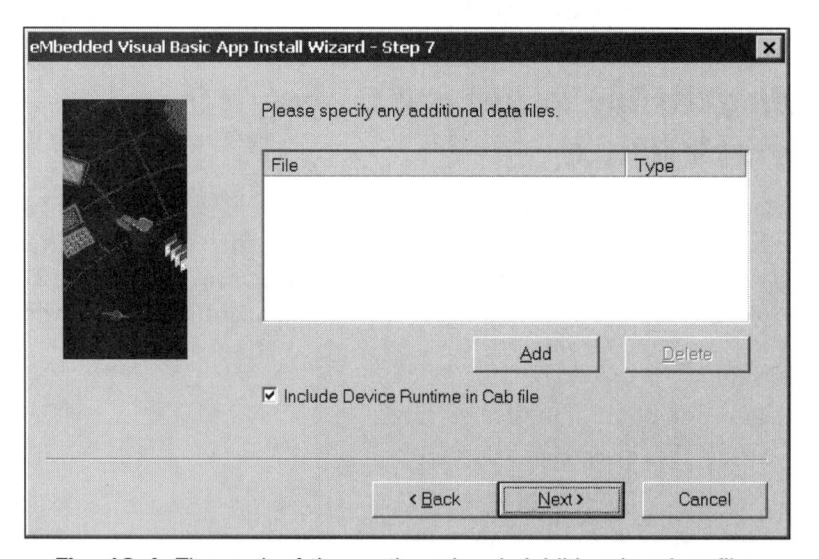

Fig. 13.4. The work of the porting wizard. Additional project files

After the readiness for setup is confirmed, the directories corresponding to all the selected types of processors are created, in which the full setup package of the developed application is stored. It consists of the loader `pvbload.exe` and several (no less than two) dll libraries in charge of the various control libraries. Also, the CD1 catalog is created, in which the Setup.exe file, necessary for installing the application on the portable device, is stored.

Working with the Menu

Unlike in VB6, there is no special tool for menu creation in eVB. Menus are created by programming methods using the special controls. To create a menu, you need to install additional controls using the **Project / Components** menu in the program shell (Fig. 13.5).

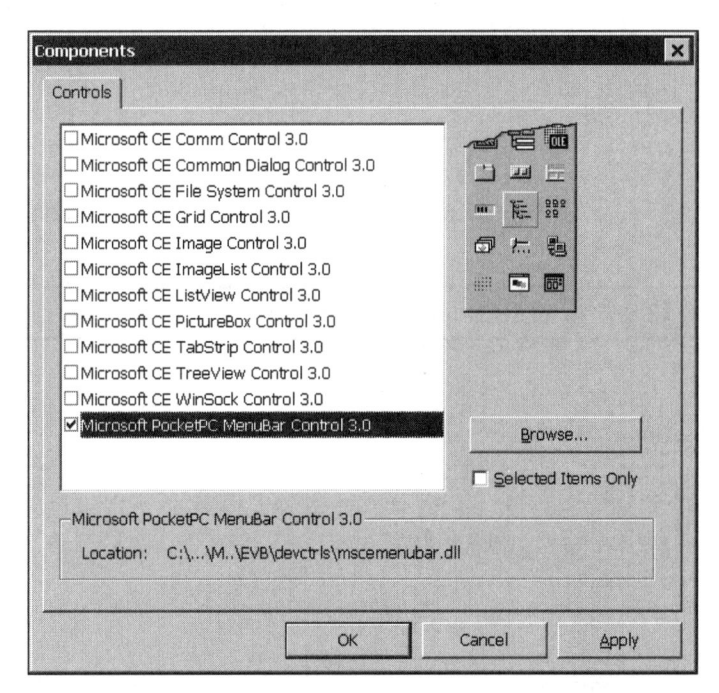

Fig. 13.5. Installing the additional menu component

Then, add the **MenuBar** button, which will activate the menu. To create the menu's items, use the MenuBarLib library with the variants of the menu buttons. Below is an example showing possible options. Create the form shown in Fig. 13.6. The procedure `cmd1` corresponds to the **Simple** command button, and the **Menu** is called `MenuBar`. We did our best to show various versions of the menu. The corresponding code is written in Listing 13.8.

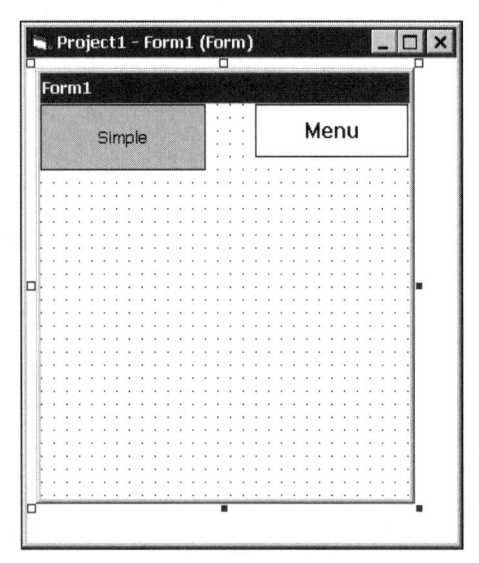

Fig. 13.6. The form of the example in question

Listing 13.8. The code creating the menu

```
Option Explicit
Dim KEY_SIMPLE_ROOT1, KEY_BAR1_PROMPT1, KEY_BAR1_PROMPT2, _
  KEY_BAR1_PROMPT3 As String
Dim KEY_COMPLEX_ROOT1, KEY_BAR3_PROMPT1, KEY_BAR3_PROMPT2, _
  KEY_COMPLEX_BAR1_PROMPT4, KEY_COMPLEX_BAR1_PROMPT3, _
  KEY_COMPLEX_BAR1_PROMPTS As String
'Names of menu items
KEY_BAR1_PROMPT1 = "Menu 1a"
KEY_BAR1_PROMPT2 = "Menu 1b"
KEY_BAR1_PROMPT3 = "Menu 1c"
KEY_BAR3_PROMPT1 = "Case 1"
KEY_BAR3_PROMPT2 = "Case 2"

Private Sub Form_OKClick()
  App.End
```

```
End Sub

Private Sub Cmd1_Click()
 Dim objMenu As MenuBarLib.MenuBar
 Dim objBar As MenuBarLib.MenuBar

 'Clear Menu
 MenuBar1.Controls.Clear

 'Define Menu item
 Set objMenu = MenuBar1.Controls.AddMenu("Prompt 1", KEY_SIMPLE_ROOT1)

 'Define Caption and Key of the Menu item
 Set objBar = objMenu.Items.Add(, KEY_BAR1_PROMPT1, "Bar 1a")
 objBar.Tag = "Tag For Bar 1a"

 Set objBar = objMenu.Items.Add(, KEY_BAR1_PROMPT2, "Bar 1b")
 objBar.Tag = "Tag For Bar 1b"
 Set objBar = objMenu.Items.Add(, "KEY_BAR1_PROMPT3", "Bar 1c")
 objBar.Tag = "Tag For Bar 1c"
 Set objBar = objMenu.Items.Add(, KEY_BAR3_PROMPT1, "Choice 1")
 'Define Menu item as checked
 objBar.Checked = True
 Set objBar = objMenu.Items.Add(, KEY_BAR3_PROMPT2, "Choice 1")
End Sub
```

The following procedure shows the characteristics of the menu item. You can use the printing functions to fill in the menu items:

Listing 13.9. The code printing the menu property

```
Private Sub MenuBar1_MenuClick(ByVal Item As MenuBarLib.Item)
 Dim strMessage As String
 strMessage = "Menu Item" & vbCr
 strMessage = strMessage & "Caption:" & Item.Caption & vbCr
 strMessage = strMessage & "Key:" & Item.Key & vbCr
 strMessage = strMessage & "Index:" & Item.Index & vbCr
 strMessage = strMessage & "Checked:" & Item.Checked & vbCr
 strMessage = strMessage & "Tag:" & Item.Tag & vbCr
 MsgBox strMessage
```

```
  Select Case Mid(Item.Key, 1, 1)
    Case "M"
      MsgBox "Bar"
    Case "C"
      MsgBox "Checked"
    Case Else
      MsgBox "Unknown Menu"
  End Select
End Sub
```

Apart from the menu buttons that appeared in the menu line, there is also the **New** button. You can activate it by going to the **Start** menu on the panel in the upper part of Form1, selecting **Settings**, and pressing the **Menus** element. If the checkbox is checked in the **Turn On New Button Menu** window (Fig. 13.7), then the triangle next to the **New** button will become available, enabling you to start one of the applications selected in the menu. The application selected is determined by the registered types of files. Since this registration is done by changing the corresponding dll files or having them appear, it can not be done with eVB tools only.

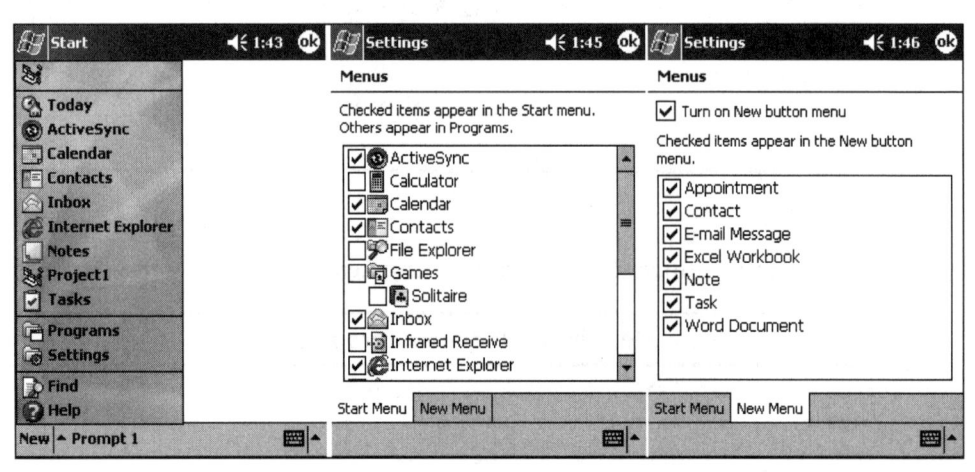

Fig. 13.7. Activating the **New** button

The next task is adding the **Menu** button to our application, the calculator. The button should show a menu with the **Copy** and **Paste** options. In our implementation, the contents of the clipboard are unavailable to other applications. The descriptions of the variables are included in Listing 13.7.

Listing 13.10 below contains the procedure for creating such a menu.

Listing 13.10. The *Memory* menu for the calculator

```
Private Sub MenuBar1_MenuClick(ByVal Item As MenuBarLib.Item)
 If Item.Key = "Copy" Then
  dblMemValue = dblDisplay
 ElseIf Item.Key = "Paste" Then
  dblDisplay = dblMemValue
  dblResultValue = dblMemValue
 End If
End Sub
```

The performance of the calculator with the menu is shown in Fig. 13.8.

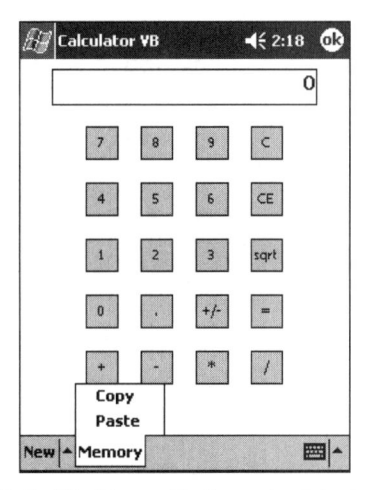

Fig. 13.8. Working with the calculator's menu

We have now considered the procedure for creating a menu on a portable device. The methods of programmatically creating all types of menus used here are more troublesome for developers than the VB6 menu editor, but in later projects, you will be able to amend already-developed modules for various types of menus, and the task becomes only slightly more complex than in VB6. A detailed list of objects, properties, and methods of the MenuBarControl library is given at the end of this chapter.

Working with Files and the File System

Now, we are going to consider working with files in an example of an application showing the directory tree and the contents of the directory, and enabling us to start the application or open a file of the registered type in the selected directory. To implement the project, we must supplement it with the Windows CE File System Control 3.0 and Windows CE TreeView Control 3.0 control libraries.

The MSCEFile.dll library enables you to systematize work with files and directories, and the MSCETreeview.dll library allows you to add a directory-view window, specify the properties of this window, and display the directory tree in it.

To create an application showing the directory tree and opening the contents of its files and directories with a click on any node, create the form described in Listing 13.11.

Listing 13.11. The form of the developed application

```
Begin VB.Form Form1
   Caption       =   "Form1"
   ClientHeight  =   3684
   ClientLeft    =   60
   ClientTop     =   840
   ClientWidth   =   3504
   ScaleHeight   =   3684
   ScaleWidth    =   3504
   ShowOK        =   -1  ' True
   Begin FILECTLCtl.FileSystem fsCtl
    Left   =   2160
    Top    =   2880
    _cx    =   2200
    _cy    =   1400
   End
   Begin MSCETREEVIEWLibCtl.TreeViewCtl tvFolderTree
    Height    =   1212
    Left      =   600
    TabIndex  =   0
    Top       =   0
    Width     =   2292
    _cx       =   4043
```

```
      _cy             =   2138
     PathSeparator =   "\"
     Enabled         =   -1  'True
  End
  Begin VBCE.Label Label1
     Caption         =   "Filter"
  End
  Begin VBCE.ComboBox cbFilter
     Height          =   240
     Left            =   120
     TabIndex        =   5
     Top             =   3240
     Width           =   1332
     _cx             =   2350
     _cy             =   423
     Text            =   "Combo1"
  End
  Begin VBCE.Label Folders
     Caption         =   "Folders"
  End
  Begin VBCE.Label Files
     Caption         =   "Files"
  End
  Begin VBCE.ListBox lbFolders
     Height          =   1560
     Left            =   120
     TabIndex        =   2
     Top             =   1440
     Width           =   1332
     _cx             =   2350
     _cy             =   2752
     Enabled         =   -1  'True
  End
  Begin VBCE.ListBox lbFiles
     Height          =   1560
     Left            =   1560
     TabIndex        =   1
     Top             =   1440
     Width           =   1332
  End
End
```

The default settings are skipped, as are the captions. The form in the development stage is shown in Fig. 13.9.

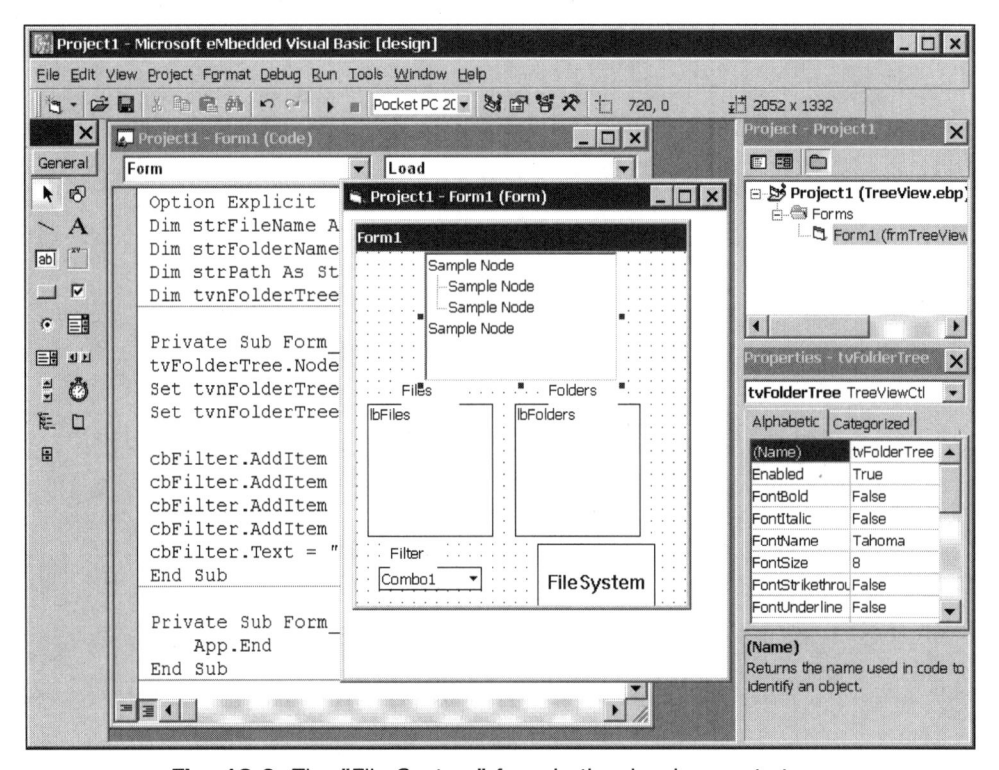

Fig. 13.9. The "File System" form in the development stage

Listings 13.12 and 13.13 describe the procedures for showing the directory tree and the list of files. During the loading of the form (`Sub Form_Load`), the initial values are set to the tree viewing window, and the `cbFilter` drop-down list containing the possible filters when viewing the file is determined.

Listing 13.12. Declaring variables

```
Option Explicit
Dim strFileName As String
Dim strFolderName As String
Dim strPath As String
```

Chapter 13: Working with Controls 225

```
Dim tvnFolderTreeNode As MSCETREEVIEWLibCtl.Node

Private Sub Form_Load()
'Adding a root node
tvFolderTree.Nodes.Clear
Set tvnFolderTreeNode = tvFolderTree.Nodes.Add(, , "Root", _
  "My Device", , "")
Set tvnFolderTreeNode = Nothing

'Defining the filter values
cbFilter.AddItem "*.*"
cbFilter.AddItem "*.txt"
cbFilter.AddItem "*.doc"
cbFilter.AddItem "*.exe"
cbFilter.Text = "*.*"
End Sub
```

The next procedure determines the reaction to clicking on the folder in the tree. `strPath` is specified by the `FullPath` method, and contains the full path to the selected folder. The `Add` method adds the folder to the directory-tree viewing window.

Listing 13.13. The procedure when clicking on the node

```
Private Sub tvFolderTree_NodeClick(ByVal Index As Long)

'Clearing the listboxes
lbFiles.Clear
lbFolders.Clear

strPath = Replace(tvFolderTree.SelectedItem.FullPath, "My Device", "")
If (Right(strPath, 1) <> "\") Then
  strPath = strPath & "\"
End If

'Filling the FolderName listbox using the fsAttrDirectory attribute
'to select folder names
```

```
  strFolderName = fsCtl.Dir(strPath & "*", fsAttrDirectory)
  Do While strFolderName <> ""
    lbFolders.AddItem strFolderName
    tvFolderTree.Nodes.Add tvFolderTree.SelectedItem.Key, _
      tvwChild, strFolderName, strFolderName
    strFolderName = fsCtl.Dir
  Loop

  'Filling the FileName listbox using the fsAttrNormal and
  'fsAttrReadOnly attributes to select the normal and r/o files
  strFileName = fsCtl.Dir(strPath & cbFilter.Text, _
    fsAttrNormal + fsAttrReadOnly)
  Do While strFileName <> ""
    lbFiles.AddItem strFileName
    strFileName = fsCtl.Dir
  Loop

End Sub
```

The interface of the application in operation is shown in Fig. 13.10.

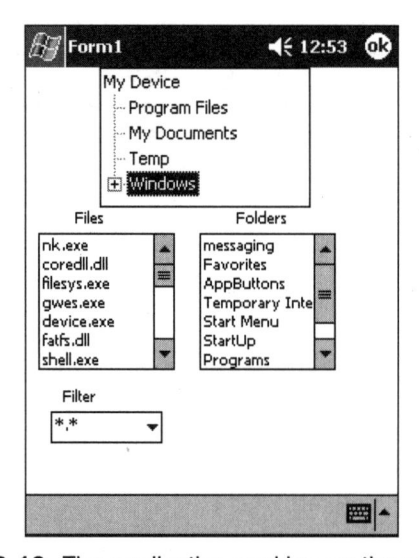

Fig. 13.10. The application working on the emulator

Events, Properties, Methods, and Additional Controls in eMbedded Visual Tools 3.0

The examples considered give an idea of eVB's features, and certain properties, methods, and constants of the additional libraries. The lists of methods, properties, constants, and some of the additional controls are shown below.

The Pocket PC MenuBar Control

The `MenuBar` control enables eVB applications to show the standard menu of a PC. To select this control, select `MenuBar` from the **Project / Components** menu of Microsoft Pocket PC Control 3.0. The library file is mscemenubar.dll.

Table 13.1. Properties of the `MenuBar` Control

Property	Type	Description
Controls	Collection	List of child objects of the first menu level. In using this list, you select from the list of objects of the first level that are related to the menu. Calling the methods enables you to manipulate the control by changing it
Enabled	Boolean	No effect
ImageList	Handle(Long)	Used when graphics are added to the menu
Name	String	Menu name
NewButton	Boolean	Used only in the project-development stage
Parent	Object	Parent object for the menu line. It should always be connected with the form
Tag	String	Used for a variable determined by the user

Table 13.2. Events of the `MenuBar` Control

Event	Description
NewClick	Appears after pressing the `New` button. Available only with `NewButton = True` (during development)
ButtonClick	Appears after pressing the `Button` button. Transfers control to the button selected as the parameter
MenuClick	Appears after pressing the `Menu` button. Transfers control to the menu item selected as the parameter

Table 13.3. Methods of the `MenuBar` Control

Method	Parameters	Returns	Description
AddButton	[key]{string} Value determining the menu button	Reference to the button (MenuBarButton)	Adds the menu button to the menu (parent object)
AddMenu	[caption](String) Caption of the menu line [key]{string} Value determining the item (button)	Pointer to the menu (MenuBar)	Adds a menu item to the menu (parent object)
Clear	None	None	Deletes all objects from the menu

Table 13.4. Properties of the `MenuBar` Control

Property	Type	Description
Count Item	Integer	Number of controls in the list Identifier of an individual control

Table 13.5. Properties of the `MenuBarMenu` Control

Property	Type	Description
Caption	String	Name of the menu item. Can not be changed after setting if it is in the root menu
Enabled	Boolean	`True` if the menu item is available to the user. Not used in the root menu
Index	Long	Index in the parent list
Items	Collection (MenuBarButton or MenuBarMenu)	List of the object components in the `MenuBar` root menu
Key	String	Object identifier in the parent list
Tag	String	Determined by the user
Type	MenuBarControlType	Read-only. Always equal to `mbrMenuBar` for the menu items
Visible	Boolean	Shows the menu's visibility

Table 13.6. Properties of the MenuBarMenu Items Control

Property	Type	Description
Count	Long	Not applicable in eVB
Item	Collection	Sub-item object of the item

Table 13.7. Methods of the MenuBarMenu Items

Method	Parameters	Returns	Description
Add	[index] (Long) Index of the item position	Object (item)	Enters the menu line in the list
	If the index value is in the list, the item is inserted before it		
	[key] (String) List item identifier		
	[caption] (String) Caption of the item being added		
	[style] (MenuStyleConstant)		
Clear	None	None	Deletes all the menu items from the list
Remove	Index	None	Deletes a fixed menu item from the list

Table 13.8. Properties of the MenuBarMenu Items

Property	Type	Description
Count	Long	Number of menu items in the list
Item	MenuBar	Returns a certain item of the list

Table 13.9. Properties of MenuBarButton

Property	Type	Description
Caption	String	Caption on the button

continues

Table 13.9 Continued

Property	Type	Description
`Enabled`	`Boolean`	Button availability
`Image`	`Long`	Control index in the list. The `ImageList` property of the item of the `MenuBarControl` object should be specified
`Index`	`Long`	Button index in the list
`Key`	`String`	Button identifier in the list
`MixedState`	`Boolean`	Button shaded or not
`Style`	`ButtonStyleConstants`	Determines the button style (switch, toggle, standard, or checkbox)
`Tag`	`String`	Determined by the user
`ToolTip`	`String`	The text appearing when the user holds the focus over the button
`Type`	`MenuBarControlType`	Shows if the item is a button or menu line
`Value`	`ButtonValueConstants`	Shows the current value of the item
`Visible`	`Boolean`	Shows the visibility of the item
`Width`	`Long`	Width of the item on the screen

Table 13.10. Properties of `Item`

Property	Type	Description
`Count Item`	`Long Enumerator`	Number of available items

Table 13.11. Methods of `Item`

Method	Parameters	Returns	Description
Add	`[index](Long)` Index of the location of the addition to the menu in the list `[key](String)` Menu identifier `[caption](String)` Menu line caption `[style](MenuStyleConstants)` Determines the menu type	`Item`	Adds `MenuBarMenu` to the list

continues

Table 13.11 Continued

Method	Parameters	Returns	Description
Clear	None	None	Deletes all items from the list
Remove	Index(String|Long) is connected with the index or the item identifier	None	Deletes a fixed item from the list

Table 13.12. Properties of Item

Property	Type	Description
Caption	String	Caption on the button or menu
Checked	Boolean	Applicable only to MenuBarMenu. It enables you to highlight the Checked mark. When applied to a button, an error message appears
Enabled	Boolean	If the MenuBarMenu item has no effect, setting the False value for MenuBarMenu provokes unexpected behavior from the application
Index	Long	The index of the item in the parent list is set when the item is added to the list
Key	String	Identifier of an item in the parent list
Parent	Object	Pointer to the object, where the item is the part of the parent list
Style	MenuStyleConstants	Applicable only to the MenuBarMenu class. It makes the (mbrMenuDefault) menu different from the (mbrMenuSeparator) toggle switch. Ignored when used with MenuBarButton
SubItems	Collection	Submenu list. Applicable only to the root menu
Tag	String	A value determined by the user
Visible	Boolean	Menu visibility for the user

Table 13.13. Style Constants — ButtonStyleConstants

Constant	Value	Description
mbrAutoSize	5	Size does not matter; the buttons automatically change their size

continues

Table 13.13 Continued

Constant	Value	Description
mbrButtonGroup	2	Creates a group of buttons for the toggle switch
inbrCheck	1	Creates a button working as a checkbox
mbrDefault	0	Standard button
mbrSeparator	3	Selection from several buttons or menu items. There can be several groups selected

Table 13.14. ButtonValueConstants

Constant	Value	Description
mbrPressed	1	Button is pressed
mbrllnPressed	0	Button is not pressed

Table 13.15. MenuBarControlType Constants

Constant	Value	Description
mbrButton	0	Button
mbrMenuBar	1	Menu

Table 13.16. MenuStyleConstants Constants

Constant	Value	Description
MbrMenuDefault	0	Standard menu
MbrMenuSeparator	1	Selection menu

The *File* Control

Below are the data for the Object Model for File control. MSCEFile.dll is the corresponding library.

Table 13.17. Methods of the File Control

Method	Returns	Description
Close	None	Closes an open file

continues

Table 13.17 Continued

Method	Returns	Description
Get	None	Reads the binary data into a variable of the `Variant` type. As a rule, used for data written using the `Put` method
Input	String	Reads the specified number of characters from the open text file
InputB	Byte array	Reads the specified number of characters from the open binary file
InputFields	Variant array	Reads the specified number of fields from the open file structured by commas
LineInputString	String	Reads one line (determined by `vbCr` or `vbCrLf`) from the open structured file
LinePrint	None	Inserts one line into the opened structured file and adds the vbCrLf line ending
Open	None	Opens the file for recording, reading, and adding in various modes
Put	None	Writes the binary data to the opened file
WriteFields	None	Writes numeric or text data to the open structured file

Table 13.18. Properties of the `File` Control

Property	Returns	Description
Attr	FileModeEnum	Shows the mode in which the file is opened
EOF	Boolean	Returns `True` when the end of the file is reached
Loc	Long	Shows the current position for recording/writing the open file
LOF	Long	File length in bytes
Name	String	Logical name of the `File` control as specified in the **Property** window
Parent	Object	Pointer to the `File` control parent object
Seek	Long	Sets or returns the current position for writing/reading the opened file. The search always returns `Loc + 1`, except for when the file is open
Tag	String	Sets or returns additional information the programmer wanted to save

The *FileSystem* Control

Below are the data for the Object Model for the `FileSystem` control. MSCEFile.dll is the corresponding library.

Table 13.19. Methods of the `FileSystem` Control

Method	Returns	Description
Dir	String	Returns the name of the next file that meets the condition specified in the Dir method. The first time addressing the Dir method, it should contain the required condition
FileCopy	None	Copies the existing file into a new one
FileDateTime	Date	Returns the date and time of the last modification of the file
FileLen	Long	Returns the file length in bytes
GetAttr	FileAttrEnum	Returns the number corresponding to the attributes of the file or directory. The file can have several attributes
Kill	None	Deletes the specified file
MkDir	None	Creates a new directory
MoveFile	None	Moves a file or directory (including subdirectories)
RmDir	None	Deletes the specified directory
SetAttr	None	Sets attributes for the file

Table 13.20. Properties of the `FileSystem` Control

Property	Returns	Description
Name	String	Indicates the name of the FileSystem control in the **Property** window
Parent	Object	Pointer to the FileSystem parent object, for example, the form
Tag	String	Sets or shows any additional information

MSCEFileCtl Constants

Below are the constant data for the `File` and `FileSystem` controls. MSCEFile.dll is the corresponding library.

Chapter 13: Working with Controls 235

Table 13.21. `FileAccessEnum` Constants

Constant	Value	Description
FsAccessRead	1	Indicates that the file is opened only for reading (read-only mode) — input
FsAccesWrite	2	Indicates that the file is opened only for writing (write-only mode) — output
FsAccessReadWrite	3	Indicates that the file is opened for reading/writing (read/write mode) — input/output

Table 13.22. `FileAttrEnum` Constants

Constant	Value	Description
FsAttrNormal	0	Indicates a normal file
FsAttrReadOnly	1	Indicates a read-only file
FsAttrHidden	2	Indicates a file or directory marked as "hidden"
FsAttrSystem	4	Indicates a system file
FsAftrVolume	8	Indicates file size
FsAttrDirectory	16	Indicates a directory
FsAttrArchive	32	Indicates a file modified since it was last saved

Table 13.23. `FileLockEnum` Constants

Constant	Value	Description
FsLockReadWrite	0	Indicates that the process can read or write in the file until it is opened
FsLockWrite	1	Indicates that the process can write in the file untill it is opened
FsLockRead	2	Indicates that the process can read in the file until it is opened
FsLockShared	3	Indicates that the file is opened by many processes (users)

Table 13.24. `FileModeEnum` Constants

Constant	Value	Description
`FsModeInput`	1	Used for opening a text file for reading only
`FsModeOutput`	2	Used for opening a text file for writing only. The beginning of the file is the point at which writing/recording begins
`FsModeRandom`	4	Used for opening a binary file for random access
`FsModeAppend`	8	Used for opening a text file for writing. The beginning of the file is the point at which writing/recording begins
`FsModeBinary`	32	Used for opening a file for binary access

The *TreeView* Control

The tables below are related to the `TreeView` control (CE Control TreeView Object Model). This control uses the MSCETreeview.dll library.

Table 13.25. `TreeViewCtl` Methods

Method	Returns	Description
`GetVisibleCount`	Long	The number of directory lines positioned vertically in the control window. Viewing the directory tree. **Warning! This number should exceed the real number of lines!**
`Move`	None	Moves the control to the specified position. `Left`, `Top`, `Height`, and `Width` can be used simultaneously
`Refresh`	None	Changes the color of the entire control
`SetFocus`	None	Sets the focus to the control
`StartLabelEdit`	None	Enables the user to edit the name of the line
`Zorder`	None	Moves the control before or after the Z–order

Table 13.26. `TreeViewCtl` Properties

Property	Returns	Description
`Container`	Object	Returns the pointer to the object containing the "Directory tree" control, e.g., the form

continues

Table 13.26 Continued

Property	Returns	Description
`Enabled`	`Boolean`	Sets or indicates if the control has something to do with the events called by the user
`EventCancel`	`Boolean`	Determines whether the control handles the event
`FontBold`	`Boolean`	Sets or indicates bold font
`FontItalic`	`Boolean`	Sets or indicates italics
`FontName`	`String`	Sets or indicates the font in the window
`FontSize`	`Long`	Sets or indicates the font size
`Font Strikethrough`	`Boolean`	Sets or indicates a struck-through font
`FontUnderline`	`Boolean`	Sets or indicates an underlined font
`Height`	`Long`	Sets or indicates the current font height
`HideSelection`	`Boolean`	Determines if the text remains selected after the control loses the focus
`ImageList`	`Long`	Sets or indicates the reference to the icon related to the control
`Indentation`	`Single`	Sets or indicates the distance between the child and parent directories
`LabelEdit`	`LabelEditEnum`	Determines if the user can edit the control captions
`Left`	`Long`	Sets or indicates the left position of the control
`LineStyle`	`LineStyleEnum`	Sets or indicates the style of the lines between the branches
`Name`	`String`	Control name in the **Properties** window
`Nodes`	`Nodes Collection`	Pointer to the Nodes Collection
`Parent`	`Object`	Returns a pointer to a parent object, e.g., to a form
`PathSeparator`	`String`	Sets or indicates the separator returning the `Full-Path` property
`SelectedItem`	`Node Object`	Pointer to the currently selected branch
`Sorted`	`Boolean`	Determines the parent directory and puts it in alphabetical order
`Style`	`TreeStyleEnum`	Sets or indicates the types of graphics, such as lines, "+", "−", for each branch

continues

Table 13.26 Continued

Property	Returns	Description
TabIndex	Long	Sets or indicates the order when the Tab key focuses the control relative to the other controls
TabStop	Boolean	Determines if the Tab key focuses the control
Tag	String	Sets or indicates the additional tags
Top	Long	Sets or indicates the current top position of the control
Visible	Boolean	Determines whether the user sees the control
Width	Long	Sets or indicates the current width of the control

Table 13.27. TreeViewControl Events

Event	Description
After-LabelEdit	Occurs after the user edits the label text
BeforeLabelEdit	Occurs before the user edits the label text
Collapse	Occurs at the moment of the directory's collapse
Expand	Occurs at the moment of the directory's expansion
GotFocus	Occurs when the control gets the focus
LostFocus	Occurs when the control loses the focus
NodeClick	Occurs at the click on the directory

Table 13.28. Node Object Methods

Method	Returns	Description
EnsureVisible	None	Ensures the visibility of the directory, if necessary by scrolling or expanding

Table 13.29. Node Object Properties

Property	Returns	Description
Child	Node Object	Indicates the first child directory
Children	Long	Number of child directories in the parent directory
Expanded	Boolean	Sets or indicates the option of directory expansion

continues

Chapter 13: Working with Controls   239

Table 13.29 Continued

Property	Returns	Description
ExpandedImage	Long	Sets or indicates the label index
FirstSibling	Node Object	Indicates the first sibling of the same level
FullPath	String	Returns the full path
Image	Long	Sets or indicates the index of the branch label in the control
Index	Long	Indicates the number that determines the node in TreeView
Key	String	Indicates the string variable that determines the current Node in TreeView
LastSibling	Node Object	Indicates the last sibling of the same level
Next	Node Object	Indicates the next sibling of the same level
Parent	Node Object	Indicates the parent directory
Previous	Node Object	Indicates the previous sibling of the same level
Root	Node Object	Indicates the root directory
Selected	Boolean	Sets or indicates whether the sibling is selected
SelectedImage	Long	Sets or indicates the number of the label that shows when the sibling is selected
Sorted	Boolean	Indicates alphabetical sorting of siblings
Text	String	Sets or indicates a text related to this sibling

Table 13.30. Node List Methods

Method	Returns	Description
Add	Node Object	A new object in the directory list
Clear	None	Deletes all items from the list
Remove	None	Deletes the selected directory from the list

Table 13.31. Node List Properties

Property	Returns	Description
Count	Long	Total number of items in the list of directories
Item	Node Object	Pointer to the item in the list of directories

Table 13.32. `TreeStyleEnum` **Constants**

Constant	Value	Description
`TvwTextOnly`	0	Does not show the non-text symbols (lines, "+", "–", labels)
`TvwPictureText`	1	Shows labels in each line of the tree
`TvwPlusMinusText`	2	The control shows +/– in each line of the tree
`TvwPlusPictureText`	3	Shows +/– labels in each line of the tree
`TvwTreelinesText`	4	Shows the lines between the branches of the directory
`TvwTreelinesPictureText`	5	Shows the lines between the branches and labels in each line of the tree
`TvwTreelinesPlusMinusText`	6	Shows the lines between the branches and +/– in each line of the tree
`TvwTreelinesPlusMinusPictureText`	7	Shows the lines between the branches, +/–, and labels in each line of the tree

Chapter 14

Database Access Programming in eMbedded Visual Basic 3.0 Using ADOCE 3.0

The Distinctive Features of Database Programming for Pocket PC. ADOCE Objects

For direct access to Windows CE databases, Microsoft developed ActiveX DataObjects for Windows CE (ADOCE). The initial version of ADOCE enabled eVB applications to gain access to Windows CE databases of the Object Store type. The requirements for this obsolete method of database design were inconvenient. For example, each table had to be assigned a unique names, even when they were in different applications. ADOCE 3.0, the software gained access to Pocket Access databases, a simplified version of Microsoft Access for portable devices with Windows CE. Microsoft, however, did not release Pocket Access for portable devices, but only for devices with a keyboard. Nevertheless, ADOCE 3.0 provided access to databases via applications created in eVB. SQL Server CE, released together with ADOCE 3.1, is an even more powerful tool for database access. ADOCE has its limitations as well, some related to the database architecture for pocket computers, and some to its own limitations. Some of these limitations were mentioned in *Chapter 12*. The present chapter deals with the peculiarities of portable device database access using the example of a currency exchange-rate calculator. Here we will use the special Windows CE database format — CEDB (Pocket Access). Files with data in this format have the extension CDB. Using Microsoft SQL Server CE will be considered in the next chapter.

Structure of a Windows CE Database

There are 3 methods of database access provided by Microsoft:

- The initial ADOCE method of database access — Windows CE Object Store
- Updated versions (ADOCE 3.0) with access to a CEDB database (CDB files) and the option of converting the Access Database Management System using ActiveSync
- ADOCE 3.1 with access to Microsoft SQL Server CE, or SQL servers of other developers, via OLEDBCE

Using Windows CE Object Store is obsolete, and with the appearance of ADOCE 3.0, there is really no need to discuss it any further.

There are 3 methods of creating databases for Pocket PC: using ActiveSync Microsoft Access database adaptation, creating databases using ADOCE connection, and importing the SQL Server CE database.

Using ActiveSync

To transmit and receive information on a portable device, it is necessary to use ActiveSync. At present, ActiveSync 3.1 and ActiveSync 3.5 are available at **www.microsoft.com/sql/downloads**. These applications are relatively small (about 4 MB), and can be downloaded to a desktop PC. After the connection is established with the portable device via the COM, USB, or IrDA port, data transmission between the portable device and the PC is possible in order to install applications, and transfer files, information, and databases. The version included in the standard set of Windows CE tools is connected with ActiveSync from the side of the portable device. The application converts Pocket Word files into Microsoft Word files and vice versa, Pocket Excel into Microsoft Excel files and vice versa, and Pocket Access into Microsoft Access files and vice versa. This option enables the creation of databases on the desktop PC and the viewing of the results of the update using Microsoft Access on the portable-device. Pocket Access does not work with portable-device emulators.

Database Objects

The ADOCE interface contains the Connection, Recordset, and Field objects, as well as the Fields collection. Their functions correspond to the purpose of

Chapter 14: Database Access Programming in eMbedded Visual Basic 3.0... 243

the objects used for working with databases in any system based on SQL, although their names in Microsoft eMbedded Visual Basic differ from those accepted by other developers, and sometimes even from other Microsoft products.

Connecting to the Database (the *Connection* Object)

This object determines all the rest of the objects, what makes up the database, which data sources are to be used, and how. The file or URL that corresponds to this object contains all the information stored in the database. The analog of this command in VB6 is the `Database` object.

`ConnectionString` is the most commonly used property.

The commands used are `Open`, `Execute`, and `Close`.

Query (the *Recordset* Object)

Queries allow the manipulation of data. The `Recordset` object lets you navigate the database, add and remove records, and set and save tabs. Its analog in VB6 has the same name.

The most important properties are `State` and `EOF`, as well as `Absolute Position`, `Bookmark`, `Source`, etc.

The commands used are `AddNew`, `Clone`, `Close`, `Delete`, `Find`, `GetRows`, `Move`, `MoveFirst`, `MoveLast MoveNext`, `MovePrevious`, `Open`, `Requery`, `Supports`, and `Update`.

Field (the *Field* Object)

Fields contain data. Users can gain access to them and change the format of the stored information.

Their properties are `ActualSize`, `Attributes`, `DefinedSize`, `Name`, `NumericScale`, `Precision`, `Type`, and `UnderlyingValue`.

The commands used are `AppendChunk` and `GetChunk`.

Fields (the *Fields* Collection)

Fields (a set of fields) are query columns, and provide access to specific data in the query or database using the index or its nickname.

Some Distinctive Features of ADOCE

We should take into account some of the peculiarities mentioned in *Chapter 12*.

Version Dependence

To use ADOCE, you need to have a reference to the corresponding library. When a new library is installed on a portable device, the references are not updated automatically, the software keeps using the libraries of the old version. Since the class names in ADOCE also contain information on the version, you have to write CreateObject ("ADOCE.Connection.3.0"). The command CreateObject ("ADOCE.Connection") will not work, and an error message will be given.

To simplify updating the software command, it is possible to enter the constants shown below:

```
Const ADOCE_CONNECTION = "ADOCE.Connection.3.0"
Const ADOCE_RECORDSET = "ADOCE.Recordset.3.0"
```

Features of the CEDB Database Processor

To reduce resource requirements, the CEDB database processor does not support the range of features familiar from MS Access. There are no unique indices and keys, no access-integrity check, and no option of sending SQL queries using GROUP BY. There are limitations on the number of records in the table, and the volume of data returned by the query cannot exceed 64 KB. Field names cannot contain more than 31 characters.

Currency Calculator: an Example of Using ADOCE

Project Description

Let's look at the development of a demo application. This application will have as its basis a CEDB database, which will contain information on the name of the currency and its exchange rate. The user will be able to enter exchange-rate information on the currencies, enter and delete currencies, specify the base currency with the units to be used to measure other currencies, and convert amounts from one currency into another.

A Description of the Database Structure

The database will contain the following two tables: Rates to store the list of currencies and rates, and Settings to save the values selected by the user (Tables 14.1 and 14.2).

Chapter 14: Database Access Programming in eMbedded Visual Basic 3.0... 245

Table 14.1. `Rates` — the List of Currencies

Field name	Type	Description
`CurrID`	`varchar (3)`	Currency code (a unique 3-symbol code)
`CurrName`	`varchar (64)`	Currency name
`CurrRate`	`float`	Currency rate (as related to the base currency)

Table 14.2. `Settings`

Field name	Type	Description
`BaseCurr`	`varchar (3)`	Base currency code
`Curr1`	`varchar (3)`	Currency code in the first drop-down list
`Curr1`	`varchar (3)`	Currency code in the second drop-down list

Now open eVB and select a Windows CE for Pocket PC 2002 project. Set the mouse cursor on the word `Project1` in the project objects list window, click on the right mouse button, and select the **Add/Module** command from the pop-up menu. This allows the addition of the module in which the global variables will be stored. These variables will be available in all the modules of the application.

The global variables are given in Listing 14.1.

Listing 14.1. Declaring the global variables

```
'All variables are to be declared before first use
Option Explicit

'Global variable ADOCE.Connection
Public objConnection As ADOCE.Connection

'Global variable ADOCE.Recordset
Public objRec As ADOCE.Recordset

'Database path
Const strDBPath = "\My Documents\CurrCalc.cdb"

'Base currency
```

```
Public strBaseCurr As String

'2 exchange rates to convert currencies on the main form
Public dblCurrRate1 As Double
Public dblCurrRate2 As Double
```

The Start Form for the Currency Converter

Name the available blank form `frmMainCalc`. This will be the start form for the project (Fig. 14.1), and will be used to enter an amount in any currency selected from the first drop-down currency list. When entered, the amount is converted into the currency selected from the second drop-down list.

The **Exchange Rates** button opens the second form of the "Exchange Rates" project (`frmCurrRates`), which enables the addition and deletion of currencies and to change their rates.

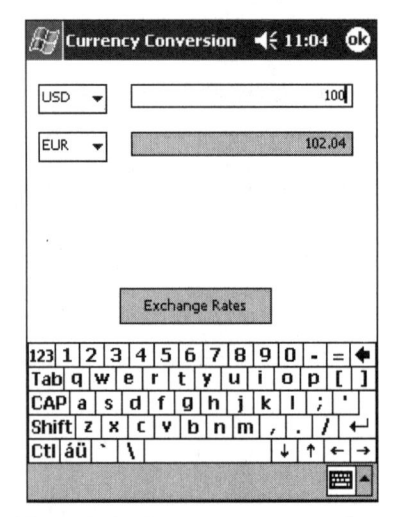

Fig. 14.1. The `frmMainCalc` form

The controls on the `frmMainCalc` form are shown in Table 14.3. The form itself in the development stage is shown in Fig. 14.2.

Chapter 14: Database Access Programming in eMbedded Visual Basic 3.0...

Table 14.3. Controls of the `frmMainCalc` Form

Name	Type	Label	Description
`txtCurr1`	`TextBox`		Field for entering the amount to be converted
`txtCurr2`	`TextBox`		Field for the result of the conversion
`cboCurr1`	`ComboBox` (`ComboDropDownList`)		The drop-down currency list for the amount being entered
`cboCurr2`	`ComboBox` (`ComboDropDownList`)		The drop-down currency list for the result
`fsCtl`	`FileSystem`		The component for working with the file system
`cmdCurrRates`	`CommandButton`	Exchange Rates	The "Exchange Rates" form button

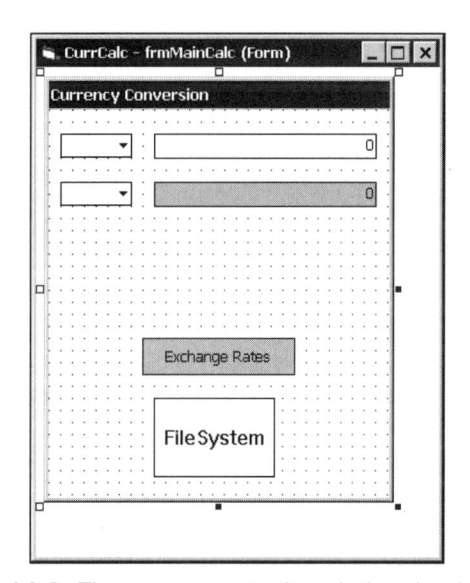

Fig. 14.2. The `frmMainCalc` form being developed

The first time you start the application, you have to create the database and tables and fill in the values. To create the database, use the `Open` command for the `Recordset` object with a parameter in the form of an SQL string:

```
CREATE DATABASE 'Database path'
```

An object of the Connection type is used to connect to the database, and using the Execute command enables you to create tables and indices and to enter values.

After the connection is complete, it should be closed using the command Close. Then clear the variable by assigning it the value Nothing.

Listing 14.2. Creating the database

```
Sub InitDB()
  'Creating a new database in the folder defined in the strDBPath
  'variable in this sample, in "My Documents"
  Set objRec = CreateObject("ADOCE.Recordset.3.0")
  objRec.Open "CREATE DATABASE '" & strDBPath & "'"
  'Database created. Clear variable
  Set objRec = Nothing

  'Connecting to the new database to create tables
  Set objConnection = CreateObject("ADOCE.Connection.3.0")
  objConnection.Open strDBPath
  'Creating the Rates table, with the fields:
  'CurrID — 3-character currency ID;
  'CurrName — currency name;
  'CurrRate — exchange rate as related to the base currency
  objConnection.Execute "CREATE TABLE Rates (CurrID varchar(3), " & _
  "CurrName varchar(64), CurrRate float)"
  'Creating index on the CurrID field in the table Rates
  objConnection.Execute "CREATE INDEX CurrIDIx on Rates (CurrID)"
  'Creating table Settings, to store program settings
  'as an alternative to storing settings in the Registry
  'BaseCurr — to store the base currency ID
  'Curr1 — currency selected in the fist combobox on the main form
  'Curr2 — currency selected in the second combobox
  objConnection.Execute "CREATE TABLE Settings (BaseCurr _
          varchar(3), Curr1 varchar(3), Curr2 varchar(3))"
  'Tables created

  'Filling in some initial values in these tables:
  'For Settings
  'Assume the base currency is USD, and values in the comboboxes as
  'USD and EUR
```

Chapter 14: Database Access Programming in eMbedded Visual Basic 3.0... 249

```
    objConnection.Execute "INSERT INTO Settings (BaseCurr, Curr1, Curr2) _
                VALUES ('USD', 'USD', 'EUR')"
    'Filling in the currency list in the Rates table with 2 currencies
    'USD — US dollars and EUR - European euros
    objConnection.Execute "INSERT INTO Rates (CurrID, CurrName, CurrRate) _
                VALUES ('USD', 'US dollars', 1)"
    objConnection.Execute "INSERT INTO Rates (CurrID, CurrName, CurrRate) _
                VALUES ('EUR', 'European euros', 0.98)"

    'Closing the connection and clearing the variable
    objConnection.Close
    Set objConnection = Nothing
End Sub
```

The first time you load the form in eVB, the `Form_Load` event is generated (forms are not unloaded from eVB, but hidden, and exist until the application is closed). For the initial form, this event is the first one handled, and is usually used to initialize the parameters in the event handler's code.

You have to determine whether there is a database that is necessary for the application to work. Use `FileSystem` to check the path to the database. If there is no database, call the described `InitDB` procedure.

You then have to fill in the drop-down currency lists. To do this, use `UpdateCurrCbo`, which will be considered below (Listing 14.4).

The application uses the global variable `strBaseCurr`, which stores the base-currency identifier. Its value is read from the `Settings` table. Establish a connection with the database, and perform the SQL query to the `Settings` table. The query returns the base-currency identifier value.

After work with the database is complete, close the objects of the `RecordSet` and `Connection` types using `Close`, and clear the variables by assigning them the value `Nothing`.

Listing 14.3. The first event of the application

```
Private Sub Form_Load()
    'Checking for the existence of the database using File System control
    If fsCtl.Dir(strDBPath) = "" Then
        'If there is none, creating a new database
        Call InitDB
```

```
    End If

    'Filling comboboxes with currency IDs
    Call UpdateCurrCbo

    'Setting the global variable with the base currency
    'Establishing a connection with database
    Set objConnection = CreateObject("ADOCE.Connection.3.0")
    objConnection.Open strDBPath
    'Using an SQL query to get the base currency ID
    Set objRec = objConnection.Execute("SELECT BaseCurr from Settings")

    'Setting the global variable with the base currency
    strBaseCurr = objRec(0).Value

    'Clearing the variables
    objRec.Close
    Set objRec = Nothing

    objConnection.Close
    Set objConnection = Nothing
End Sub
```

The `UpdateCurrCbo` procedure is used for filling in the drop-down currency lists and setting their current values in accordance with the data in the Settings table.

The drop-down lists are cleared using `Clear`.

Read the data from the Settings table and assign the values to the variables `strCurr1` and `strCurr2`.

Open the Rates table (by selecting two fields — `CurrID` and `CurrRate` — in the query) and, scanning its records, assign the currency identifiers' values to the elements of the drop-down lists. To go to the next record, use the `MoveNext` command in an object of the `Recordset` type. Adding new elements to the drop-down list is done using `AddItem`.

When a new currency identifier is added to a drop-down currency list, make sure that it is not the same as the value read from Settings (the `strCurr1` and `strCurr2` variables, respectively). If it is, set the property of the `ListIndex` drop-down list to the current number of the element being added. It is this element that will be displayed on the screen. Simultaneously assign values to the `dblCurrRate1`

Chapter 14: Database Access Programming in eMbedded Visual Basic 3.0... 251

or `dblCurrRate2` global variables. These variables contain the rate for the currency selected in the currency drop-down lists.

When you are finished, call the `CalculateConv` procedure (currency conversion recalculation).

Listing 14.4. The procedure for filling in the currency drop-down lists

```
Sub UpdateCurrCbo()
  Dim intIter As Integer
  Dim strCurr1 As String
  Dim strCurr2 As String

  'Filling comboboxes with currency IDs
  'First clearing comboboxes
  cboCurr1.Clear
  cboCurr2.Clear

  'Getting the last selected currency IDs for comboboxes from Settings
  'Establishing a connection with the database
  Set objConnection = CreateObject("ADOCE.Connection.3.0")
  objConnection.Open strDBPath
  'Executing an SQL query to get currency IDs
  Set objRec = objConnection.Execute("SELECT Curr1, Curr2 from Settings")

  'Storing currency IDs in the variables
  strCurr1 = objRec(0).Value
  strCurr2 = objRec(1).Value

  'Clearing the variable
  objRec.Close
  Set objRec = Nothing

  'Filling comboboxes with currency IDs
  'Executing an SQL query to get currency IDs and rates from the Rates
  'table
  Set objRec = objConnection.Execute("SELECT CurrID, _
                                      CurrRate from Rates")

  'Both comboboxes are filled with the same list of currencies
  intIter = 0
```

```
Do While Not objRec.EOF
   cboCurr1.AddItem (objRec(0).Value)
   If objRec(0).Value = strCurr1 Then
      cboCurr1.ListIndex = intIter
      dblCurrRate1 = objRec(1).Value
   End If
   cboCurr2.AddItem (objRec(0).Value)
   If objRec(0).Value = strCurr2 Then
      cboCurr2.ListIndex = intIter
      dblCurrRate2 = objRec(1).Value
   End If
   intIter = intIter + 1
   objRec.MoveNext
Loop

'Clearing the variables
objRec.Close
Set objRec = Nothing

objConnection.Close
Set objConnection = Nothing

'Calculating the currency conversion
Call CalculateConv
End Sub
```

The currency-conversion procedure updates the value in the txtCurr2 field by rounding off to two decimal places. If the txtCurr1 field is blank, then the txtCurr2 field is assigned a 0. The global variables dblCurrRate1 and dblCurrRate2 contain the currency rates used in the formula.

Listing 14.5. The CalculateConv **procedure for currency conversion**

```
Sub CalculateConv()
   'If the text field for entering the value to convert is empty,
   'then assume 0 as a result
   If txtCurr1 <> "" Then
      txtCurr2 = CStr(Round(CDbl(txtCurr1)*dblCurrRate1/dblCurrRate2, 2))
```

Chapter 14: Database Access Programming in eMbedded Visual Basic 3.0... 253

```
    Else
       txtCurr2 = "0"
    End If
End Sub
```

When the user enters the amount in the `txtCurr1` field, the `Change` event is generated, and the currency-conversion procedure `CalculateConv` is called.

Listing 14.6. The `txtCurr1_Change` event

```
Private Sub txtCurr1_Change()
   'Calculating the currency conversion
   Call CalculateConv
End Sub
```

Let's consider the procedures called as a result of a `Click` event performed on one of the two drop-down currency lists. In doing this, the user changes the current currency to another one selected from the list.

We must also update the values in the `Settings` table. Call the `UpdateSettings` procedure with two parameters: the currency identifier and the field number according to the `Settings` table (see details in the description of this procedure).

Next, update the values of the global variables `dblCurrRate1` and `dblCurrRate2` using the `GetCurrRate` function, with the currency identifier as a parameter.

Finally, update the currency conversion, using `CalculateConv`, described above.

Listing 14.7. The `cboCurr1_Click` and `cboCurr2_Click` procedures

```
Private Sub cboCurr1_Click()
   'Changing the selected currency in the first combobox
   'in the Settings table
   Call UpdateSettings(cboCurr1.Text, 1)
   'Updating the exchange rate
   dblCurrRate1 = GetCurrRate(cboCurr1.Text)
   'Calculating the currency conversion
   Call CalculateConv
End Sub

Private Sub cboCurr2_Click()
```

```
    'Changing the selected currency for the second combobox
    'in the Settings table
    Call UpdateSettings(cboCurr2.Text, 2)
    'Updating the exchange rate
    dblCurrRate2 = GetCurrRate(cboCurr2.Text)
    'Calculating the currency conversion
    Call CalculateConv
End Sub
```

`UpdateSettings` changes the `Curr1`, `Curr2`, or `BaseCurr` values in the `Settings` table. There are two parameters in the procedure: the first is the currency identifier, and the second shows which field is to be changed.

The `Recordset` object is opened using `Open`, with parameters that allow the records to be changed. After a new name is assigned to the field, you need to use `Update` in order to save the record.

Listing 14.8. The `UpdateSettings` procedure

```
Sub UpdateSettings(strCurr As String, intCboNum As Integer)
    Dim strSQL As String

    'Changing the value of Curr1, Curr2, or BaseCurr to strCurr, depending
    'on intCboNum (1, 2, or 3) in the Settings table
    'Establishing a connection
    Set objConnection = CreateObject("ADOCE.Connection.3.0")
    objConnection.Open strDBPath
    Set objRec = CreateObject("ADOCE.Recordset.3.0")
    'SQL string for selecting Curr1, Curr2, or BaseCurr from the Settings
    'table
    If intCboNum = 3 Then
        strSQL = "SELECT BaseCurr from Settings"
    Else
        strSQL = "SELECT Curr" & Trim(CStr(intCboNum)) & " from Settings"
    End If
    'addOpenKeyset used to open the recordset for reading, updating,
    'appending, and deleting records; adLockOptimistic locks records
    'only during update
    objRec.Open strSQL, objConnection, adOpenKeyset, adLockOptimistic

    objRec.MoveFirst
```

Chapter 14: Database Access Programming in eMbedded Visual Basic 3.0... 255

```
    'Storing strCurr in the selected field of the Settings table
    objRec(0).Value = strCurr
    objRec.Update

    'Clearing the variables
    objRec.Close
    Set objRec = Nothing

    objConnection.Close
    Set objConnection = Nothing
End Sub
```

The `GetCurrRate` function returns the rate for the currency with the identifier transmitted as a parameter. The SQL query to the `Rates` table uses the construction `WHERE CurrID = <Currency identifier>` to select the necessary currency.

Listing 14.9. The `GetCurrRate` procedure

```
Function GetCurrRate(strCurr As String) As Double
    'Getting the exchange rate for the currency ID
    'defined in the strCurr parameter
    'Establishing a connection
    Set objConnection = CreateObject("ADOCE.Connection.3.0")
    objConnection.Open strDBPath
    'The SQL query returns the CurrRate value
    Set objRec = objConnection.Execute _
            ("SELECT CurrRate from Rates WHERE CurrID = '" & _
    strCurr & "'")

    'The function returns the exchange rate
    GetCurrRate = objRec(0).Value

    'Clearing the variables
    objRec.Close
    Set objRec = Nothing

    objConnection.Close
    Set objConnection = Nothing
End Function
```

The `Activate` event is generated the first time you load the form and at each subsequent call. Note that, since the form is not unloaded from the memory of the portable device until the application is closed, the `Form_Load` event described in Listing 14.3 occurs only once. Set the focus and highlight the value in the text field.

Listing 14.10. The `Form_Activate` event

```
Private Sub Form_Activate()
  'For each form_activate event, set the focus on the
  'data entry field and select it
  txtCurr1.SetFocus
  txtCurr1.SelStart = 0
  txtCurr1.SelLength = 1000
End Sub
```

When the **OK** button in the upper right corner of the screen is pressed, the application is closed. But this event is already prepared by the project when it opens.

Listing 14.11. The `Form_Activate` event

```
Private Sub Form_OKClick()
  'Close the application
  App.End
End Sub
```

When you press the **Exchange Rates** button, the form of the application is hidden, and the **Exchange Rates** (`frmCurrRates`) form is opened.

Listing 14.12. The `Form_Activate` event

```
Private Sub cmdCurrRates_Click()
  'Hiding the Currency Conversion form and opening the
  'Exchange Rates form
  frmCurrRates.Show
  frmMainCalc.Hide
End Sub
```

The *Exchange Rates* Form

The **Exchange Rates** form shows the list of currencies and their rates as related to the base currency, allows the user to change the base currency, and to add, change, and delete the rate from the list. When the **OK** button is pressed, the user returns to the start form (Fig. 14.3).

Fig. 14.3. A general view of the **Exchange Rates** form (`frmCurrRates`)

The controls on the form are shown in Table 14.4, and the form in the development stage is shown in Fig. 14.4.

Table 14.4. Controls of the `frmCurrRates` Form

Name	Type	Label	Description
`LblBaseCurr`	`Label`	**Base Currency**	Label in front of the drop-down base-currency list
`CboBaseCurr`	`ComboBox` (`ComboDropDownList`)		Drop-down base-currency selection list
`LvCurrList`	`ListViewCtrl`		Component list — currencies and rates
`CmdAdd`	`CommandButton`	**Add**	**Add Currency** form button
`CmdChange`	`CommandButton`	**Change**	**Change Rate** form button

continues

Table 14.4 Continued

Name	Type	Label	Description
CmdRemove	CommandButton	**Delete**	The currency-deletion procedure button
CmdOK	CommandButton	**OK**	Button for returning to the **Currency Conversion** form

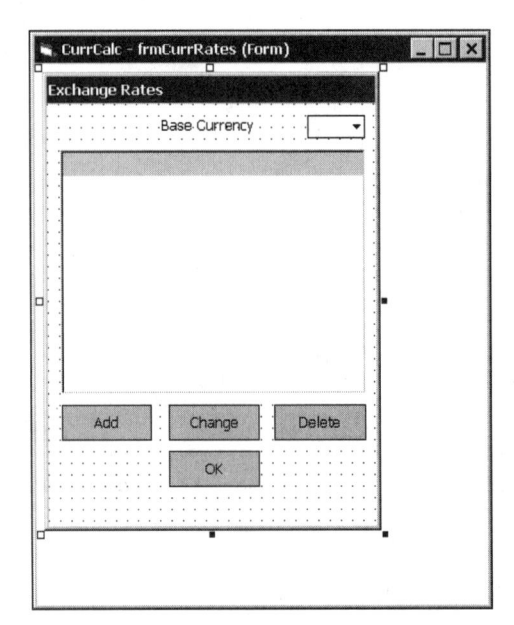

Fig. 14.4. The **Exchange Rates** form being developed

While the form in loading, initialize the drop-down list for selecting the base currency using the UpdateBaseCurrCbo procedure, and fill in the currency list.

The list control (LvCurrList) is used to show the list of currencies. If this object is missing on the toolbar, add it in the standard manner, via the **Project/ Components...** menu. There are three ways of viewing the list, and the Report version is used in our application. First of all, you have to describe the column headers, their width, and their alignment. A component of the ListView type has the ColumnHeaders property, which returns the collection of the column headers. Add the **ID**, **Currency Name**, and **Rate** columns using Add for this collection.

Call the UpdateList function to fill in the list of currencies.

Chapter 14: Database Access Programming in eMbedded Visual Basic 3.0... 259

Listing 14.13. The `Form_Load` event that occurs, the first time the form appears

```
Private Sub Form_Load()
  Dim objTempClmnHdr As ColumnHeader

  'Filling the base currency combobox with the list of currency IDs
  Call UpdateBaseCurrCbo

  'Setting the column names, sizes, and alignment
  'for the listview control with the currencies list — lvCurrList
  Set objTempClmnHdr = lvCurrList.ColumnHeaders.Add(, "chCurrID", _
                                         "ID", 540)
  Set objTempClmnHdr = lvCurrList.ColumnHeaders.Add(, "chCurrName", _
                                         "Currency Name", 1800)
  Set objTempClmnHdr = lvCurrList.ColumnHeaders.Add(, "chCurrRate", _
                                         "Rate", 860, 1)
  Set objTempClmnHdr = Nothing

  'Filling in the currency list
  Call UpdateList
End Sub
```

The `UpdateBaseCurrCbo` procedure fills in the drop-down list for selecting the base currency with the currency identifiers, and sets its current value equal to the global variable `strBaseCurr`. It is cleared before the list is filled in.

After filling it in, the list is checked for a value equal to `strBaseCurr`, and the position that is identical to it is set as the current one.

Listing 14.14. The `UpdateBaseCurrCbo` procedure

```
Sub UpdateBaseCurrCbo()
  Dim intIter As Integer

  'Filling in the base currency combobox with the currency IDs
  'Clearing the combobox first
  cboBaseCurr.Clear

  'Establishing a connection with the database
  Set objConnection = CreateObject("ADOCE.Connection.3.0")
```

```
objConnection.Open strDBPath
'An SQL query for returning the currency ID list
Set objRec = objConnection.Execute("SELECT CurrID from Rates")

'Filling in the base currency combobox with currency IDs
Do While Not objRec.EOF
  cboBaseCurr.AddItem (objRec(0).Value)
  objRec.MoveNext
Loop

'Clearing the variables
objRec.Close
Set objRec = Nothing

objConnection.Close
Set objConnection = Nothing

'Setting the base currency, comparing each item of the combobox
'with the base currency ID, and if equal, making
'this item the current one
For intIter = 0 To cboBaseCurr.ListCount - 1
  If cboBaseCurr.List(intIter) = strBaseCurr Then
    cboBaseCurr.ListIndex = intIter
    Exit For
  End If
Next
End Sub
```

The UpdateList procedure for filling in the control with the list reads the values of the CurrID, CurrName, and CurrRate fields from the Rates table ("SELECT * from Rates") and assigns them to the elements of the list. The list control contains the elements, each of them in this example having two additional elements. The main control (the ListItems property of a component of the ListView type) is assigned the CurrID value, and the additional elements (the Subitems() property of an element of the ListItem type) are assigned the CurrName and CurrRate values.

Select the first line from the list using the SelectedItem property of a component of the ListView type. Set the entry focus on the list of currencies using SetFocus.

Listing 14.15. The `UpdateList` procedure

```
Sub UpdateList()
  Dim itmTemp As ListItem

  'Clearing the ListView contol lvCurrList
  lvCurrList.ListItems.Clear

  'Establishing a connection to the database and
  'filling the list with the contents of the Rates table
  Set objConnection = CreateObject("ADOCE.Connection.3.0")
  objConnection.Open strDBPath
  Set objRec = objConnection.Execute("SELECT * from Rates")

  'List items are filled with currency IDs and
  'the 2 subitems are filled with the currency name and exchange rate
  Do While Not objRec.EOF
    Set itmTemp = lvCurrList.ListItems.Add(, , objRec(0).Value)
    itmTemp.SubItems(1) = objRec(1).Value
    itmTemp.SubItems(2) = CStr(objRec(2).Value)

    objRec.MoveNext
  Loop

  'Clearing the variables
  Set itmTemp = Nothing
  objRec.Close
  Set objRec = Nothing
  objConnection.Close
  Set objConnection = Nothing

  'Selecting the first line of the list
  lvCurrList.SelectedItem = lvCurrList.ListItems(1)
  'Setting the focus on the ListView control
  lvCurrList.SetFocus
End Sub
```

Let's look at the work of a procedure called by pressing the **Delete** button. (Pressing the **Add** and **Change** buttons calls separate forms, which will be considered below.)

The application does not allow the base currency to be deleted, although the mechanism for automatically, recalculating of rates when the base currency is changed is not demonstrated here.

Let's delete a record from the Rates table. Open an object of the Recordset type with the option of deleting a record. The SQL query chooses the record with the CurrID selected by the user from the list. Delete then deletes the record.

Then update the drop-down list of the base currency described above using UpdateBaseCurrCbo (Listing 14.14). Update the list of currencies using UpdateList.

You will have to update the drop-down lists on the start form, but the current value in one of them may be deleted. Check the Curr1 and Curr2 values in Settings and, if one is the same as the remote CurrID, make this value the first one in the list. To correct the value in Settings, use the UpdateSettings procedure described in the module of the frmMainCalc form. To call procedures from the other form, use a syntax of the *form_name.procedure_name* type.

Then update the drop-down lists for selecting the currency by the UpdateCurrCbo procedure from the module of the frmMainCalc form. The currency conversion is then recalculated.

Listing 14.16. The `cmdRemove_Click` event for deleting a currency

```
Private Sub cmdRemove_Click()
  Dim strSQL As String
  Dim strSelCurrID As String
  Dim intIter As Integer

  'Storing the selected currency ID value in the CurrID variable
  strSelCurrID = lvCurrList.SelectedItem.Text

  'Checking to see if we are trying to delete the base currency
  If strSelCurrID = strBaseCurr Then
    MsgBox "Base currency can't be deleted!", , "Error!"
    'Exiting procedure
    Exit Sub
  End If

  'Deleting a record from the database
  'Connecting
  Set objConnection = CreateObject("ADOCE.Connection.3.0")
```

Chapter 14: Database Access Programming in eMbedded Visual Basic 3.0...

```
objConnection.Open strDBPath
Set objRec = CreateObject("ADOCE.Recordset.3.0")
'An SQL string for selecting a record from the Rates table,
'where the CurrID value is equal to the currency ID
'of the selected line of the list
strSQL = "SELECT CurrRate from Rates WHERE CurrID = '" & strSelCurrID _
         & "'"
'addOpenKeyset is used to open the recordset for reading, updating,
'appending, and deleting records; adLockOptimistic is for locking
'records
'only during update
objRec.Open strSQL, objConnection, adOpenKeyset, adLockOptimistic

'Going to the first record (only 1 record in the recordset)
objRec.MoveFirst

'Deleting the record
objRec.Delete

'Clearing the variables
objRec.Close
Set objRec = Nothing
objConnection.Close
Set objConnection = Nothing

'Updating the base currency combobox
Call UpdateBaseCurrCbo
'Updating the currency list
Call UpdateList
'Checking to see if we have removed the currency selected
'in one of the two comboboxes on the main form
If strSelCurrID = frmMainCalc.cboCurr1.Text Then
   'If we are deleting the currency selected in the 1st combobox,
   'we change the value in the Settings table to the first one
   'in the list, other than the deleted one
   For intIter = 0 To cboBaseCurr.ListCount — 1
     If frmMainCalc.cboCurr1.List(intIter) <> strSelCurrID Then
```

```
      Call _
frmMainCalc.UpdateSettings(frmMainCalc.cboCurr1.List(intIter), 1)
        Exit For
      End If
    Next
  End If
  If strSelCurrID = frmMainCalc.cboCurr2.Text Then
    'If we are deleting the currency selected in the 2nd combobox,
    'we change the value in the Settings table to the first one
    'in the list, other than the deleted one
    For intIter = 0 To cboBaseCurr.ListCount - 1
      If frmMainCalc.cboCurr2.List(intIter) <> strSelCurrID Then
        Call _
frmMainCalc.UpdateSettings(frmMainCalc.cboCurr2.List(intIter), 2)
        Exit For
      End If
    Next
  End If
  'Updating the comboboxes on the main form
  'The currency conversion is updated
  Call frmMainCalc.UpdateCurrCbo
End Sub
```

If the base currency is changed, the `UpdateSettings` procedure described in the module of the `frmMainCalc` form (Listing 14.8) is called from the drop-down list for selecting the base currency. The new `BaseCurr` value is recorded in the `Settings` table. No rate recalculation is done, in order to simplify the example.

Listing 14.17. Changing the base currency

```
Private Sub cboBaseCurr_Click()
  'Changing the BaseCurr value in the Settings table to a new one
  'Argument 3 — changing BaseCurr
  Call frmMainCalc.UpdateSettings(cboBaseCurr.Text, 3)
End Sub
```

Let's describe the form's reaction to the `Activate` event. Set the focus to the currency list, making the selected line of the list visible.

Chapter 14: Database Access Programming in eMbedded Visual Basic 3.0...

Listing 14.18. The `Form_Activate` event

```
Private Sub Form_Activate()
  'For each form_activate event, set the focus on the ListView control
  lvCurrList.SetFocus
End Sub
```

When the **OK** buttons are pressed at the bottom of the form and in the upper right corner of the screen, the form is hidden, and the initial **Currency Conversion** form appears.

Listing 14.19. The closing event for the *Currency Rate* form

```
Private Sub cmdOK_Click()
  'Hiding the Exchange Rates form and returning to the main form
  frmMainCalc.Show
  frmCurrRates.Hide
End Sub

Private Sub Form_OKClick()
  'Hiding the Exchange Rates form and returning to the main form
  frmMainCalc.Show
  frmCurrRates.Hide
End Sub
```

When the **Add** and **Change** buttons are pressed, the **Exchange Rates** form is hidden, and the **Add Currency** and **Change Rate** forms appear.

Listing 14.20. Opening the *Add Currency* and *Change Rate* forms

```
Private Sub cmdAdd_Click()
  'Hiding the Exchange Rates form and showing the Add Currency form
  frmAdd.Show
  frmCurrRates.Hide
End Sub

Private Sub cmdChange_Click()
  'Hiding the Exchange Rates form and showing  the Change Rate form
  frmChange.Show
  frmCurrRates.Hide
End Sub
```

The Add Currency Form

The **Add Currency** form (Fig. 14.5) provides the option of entering a new currency by specifying its code, name, and rate, as well as of exiting this form without saving, using the **Cancel** button. The controls of this form are shown in Table 14.5.

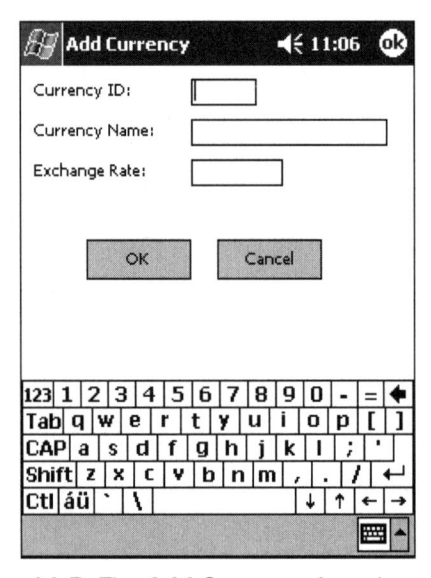

Fig. 14.5. The **Add Currency** form (`frmAdd`)

Table 14.5. Controls of the `frmAdd` Form

Name	Type	Label	Description
lblCurrID	Label	**Currency ID**	Label in front of the currency-code field
txtCurrID	TextBox		Currency-code field (maximum three characters)
lblCurrName	Label	**Currency Name**	Label in front of the currency-name field
txtCurrName	TextBox		Currency-name field
lblCurrRate	Label	**Exchange Rate**	Label in front of the currency-rate field
txtCurrRate	TextBox		Currency-rate field

continues

Chapter 14: Database Access Programming in eMbedded Visual Basic 3.0... 267

Table 14.5 Continued

Name	Type	Label	Description
cmdCancel	CommandButton	**Cancel**	Button for exiting without saving
cmdOK	CommandButton	**OK**	The **Add new currency** button

Each activation of the `frmAdd` form clears the fields of the old values and sets the focus to the currency-code field.

Listing 14.21. Activating the *Add currency* form

```
Private Sub Form_Activate()
  'Clearing the text fields at each activation of the form
  txtCurrID.Text = ""
  txtCurrName.Text = ""
  txtCurrRate.Text = ""
  'Setting the focus on the Currency ID field
  txtCurrID.SetFocus
End Sub
```

When the **OK** buttons at the bottom of the form and in the upper right corner of the screen are pressed, the `AddNewCurr` procedure for adding a new currency is started.

Listing 14.22. Activating the `AddNewCurr` procedure

```
Private Sub cmdOK_Click()
  'Adding a new currency
  Call AddNewCurr
End Sub

Private Sub Form_OKClick()
  'Adding new currency
  Call AddNewCurr
End Sub
```

The `AddNewCurr` procedure adds a new currency to the `Rates` table and updates the drop-down lists (Listing 14.23). Make sure that all fields are filled in. If not, exit the procedure.

Part III: Programming Pocket PC with eMbedded Basic

Add a record to the `Rates` table. Open the object of the `Recordset` type with the option of adding records. `AddNew` adds a new record. Fill in the fields in this record with values from the corresponding text boxes of the form. Use `Update` to save the new record.

Update the drop-down list of the base currency using the `UpdateBaseCurrCbo` function from the module of the `frmCurrRates` form, update the currency list using the `UpdateList` function from the module of the `frmCurrRates` form, and update the drop-down lists of the currency selection start form using the `UpdateCurrCbo` procedure from the module of the `frmMainCalc` form.

Hide the **Add Currency** form, and show the **Exchange Rates** form.

Listing 14.23. The `AddNewCurr` procedure

```
Sub AddNewCurr()
  Dim strSQL As String

  'Checking that no fields are empty
  If txtCurrID.Text = "" Or txtCurrName.Text = "" Or _
                    txtCurrRate.Text = "" Then
    MsgBox "All fields have to be filled", , "Error!"
    'Exiting procedure
    Exit Sub
  End If

  'Adding a record to the database
  'Connecting
  Set objConnection = CreateObject("ADOCE.Connection.3.0")
  objConnection.Open strDBPath
  Set objRec = CreateObject("ADOCE.Recordset.3.0")
  'An SQL string for selecting all fields and all records from Rates
  strSQL = "SELECT * from Rates"
  'addOpenKeyset is used to open a recordset for reading, updating,
  'appending, and deleting records; adLockOptimistic is for locking
  'records only during update
  objRec.Open strSQL, objConnection, adOpenKeyset, adLockOptimistic

  'Adding a new record
  objRec.AddNew
```

Chapter 14: Database Access Programming in eMbedded Visual Basic 3.0... 269

```
    'Setting the field values
    objRec(0) = txtCurrID.Text
    objRec(1) = txtCurrName.Text
    objRec(2) = CDbl(txtCurrRate.Text)
    'Storing the new record
    objRec.Update

    'Clearing the variables
    objRec.Close
    Set objRec = Nothing
    objConnection.Close
    Set objConnection = Nothing

    'Updating the base currency combobox
    Call frmCurrRates.UpdateBaseCurrCbo
    'Updating the currency list
    Call frmCurrRates.UpdateList
    'Updating the comboboxes on the main form
    Call frmMainCalc.UpdateCurrCbo

    'Hiding the Add Currency form and returning
    'to Exchange Rates
    frmCurrRates.Show
    frmAdd.Hide
End Sub
```

When the **Cancel** button is pressed, the form is hidden, and **Exchange Rates** is shown without adding a new currency.

Listing 14.24. The cmdCancel_Click event

```
Private Sub cmdCancel_Click()
    'Hiding the Add Currency form and returning
    'to Exchange Rates without making any changes
    frmCurrRates.Show
    frmAdd.Hide
End Sub
```

The Change Rate Form

The **Change Rate** form (`frmChange`) provides the option of changing the rate of the selected currency, or of leaving this form without saving, using the **Cancel** button (Fig. 14.6).

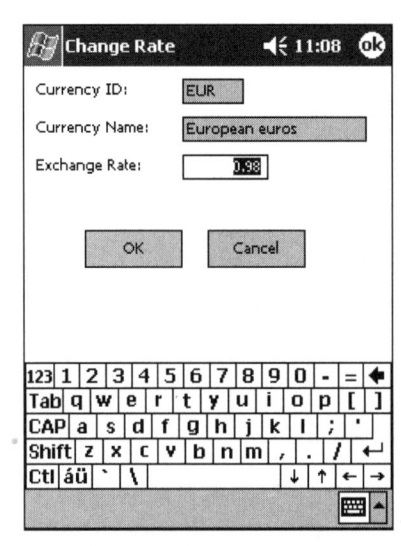

Fig. 14.6. The **Change Rate** form (`frmChange`)

The controls of this form (`frmChange`) are shown in Table 14.6.

Table 14.6. Controls of the `frmChange` Form

Name	Type	Label	Description
`lblCurrID`	Label	**Currency ID**	Label in front of the currency-code field
`txtCurrID`	TextBox		Currency-code field (maximum three characters). Not to be edited
`lblCurrName`	Label	**Currency Name**	Label in front of the currency-name field
`txtCurrName`	TextBox		Currency-name field. Not to be edited
`lblCurrRate`	Label	**Exchange Rate**	Label in front of the currency-rate field
`txtCurrRate`	TextBox		Currency-rate field
`cmdCancel`	CommandButton	**Cancel**	The button for exiting without saving
`cmdOK`	CommandButton	**OK**	The **Add new currency** button

Chapter 14: Database Access Programming in eMbedded Visual Basic 3.0...

Each time you activate the `frmChange` form, fill in the fields on the form with the values from the currency list selected in the **Currency Rate** form, and set the focus on the currency-code field after selecting its value.

Listing 14.25. The `Activate` event

```
Private Sub Form_Activate()
  'Filling in textboxes on the form with values from
  'the selected line of the ListView control on the Exchange Rates form
  txtCurrID.Text = frmCurrRates.lvCurrList.SelectedItem.Text
  txtCurrName.Text = frmCurrRates.lvCurrList.SelectedItem.SubItems(1)
  txtCurrRate.Text = frmCurrRates.lvCurrList.SelectedItem.SubItems(2)

  'Setting the focus on the exchange rate textbox and
  'selecting the contents of the textbox
  txtCurrRate.SetFocus
  txtCurrRate.SelStart = 0
  txtCurrRate.SelLength = 1000
End Sub
```

When the **OK** buttons at the bottom of the form and in the upper right corner of the screen are pressed, the `ChangeCurrRate` procedure for changing the rate of the selected currency is started.

Listing 14.26. Events upon pressing the OK button

```
Private Sub cmdOK_Click()
  'Changing the exchange rate for the selected currency
  Call ChangeCurrRate
End Sub

Private Sub Form_OKClick()
  'Changing the exchange rate for the selected currency
  Call ChangeCurrRate
End Sub
```

The `ChangeCurrRate` procedure changes the rate of the selected currency in the `Rates` table and updates the list of currencies and the drop-down lists on the start form. Make sure that the **Exchange Rate** field is filled in. Exit the procedure if it is not.

Add a record to the `Rates` table. Open an object of the `Recordset` type with the option of changing the records. The SQL query

```
SELECT CurrRate from Rates WHERE CurrID = <selected value from the
currency list>
```

selects just one record. Fill in the `CurrRate` field in this record with the value from the corresponding text box. Use `Update` to save the record.

Update the currency list using the `UpdateList` function from the module of the `frmCurrRates` form, and update the currency-selection drop-down lists using the `UpdateCurrCbo` procedure from the module of the `frmMainCalc` form. At the same time, the global variables with the rates of two currencies are updated — `dblCurrRate1` and `dblCurrRate2` — and the currency conversion is recalculated.

Hide the **Change Rate** form and show the **Exchange Rates** form.

Listing 14.27. Activating the `ChangeCurrRate` function

```
Sub ChangeCurrRate()
  Dim strSQL As String

  'Checking that the exchange rate textbox is not empty
  If txtCurrRate.Text = "" Then
    MsgBox "Exchange rate has to be entered!", , "Error!"
    'Exiting procedure
    Exit Sub
  End If

  'Changing a record in the database
  'Connecting
  Set objConnection = CreateObject("ADOCE.Connection.3.0")
  objConnection.Open strDBPath
  Set objRec = CreateObject("ADOCE.Recordset.3.0")
  'An SQL string for selecting a record in the Rates table,
  'where the value of CurrID is equal to txtCurrID
    strSQL = "SELECT CurrRate from Rates WHERE CurrID = '" &_
            txtCurrID.Text & "'"
  'addOpenKeyset is used to open a recordset for reading, updating,
  'appending, and deleting records; adLockOptimistic is for locking
  'records only during update
```

Chapter 14: Database Access Programming in eMbedded Visual Basic 3.0... 273

```
    objRec.Open strSQL, objConnection, adOpenKeyset, adLockOptimistic

    'Going to the first record (only 1 record in the recordset)
    objRec.MoveFirst

    'Setting values for the record fields
    objRec(0) = CDbl(txtCurrRate.Text)

    'Storing the updated record
    objRec.Update

    'Clearing the variables
    objRec.Close
    Set objRec = Nothing
    objConnection.Close
    Set objConnection = Nothing

    'Updating the currency list
    Call frmCurrRates.UpdateList
    'Updating the comboboxes on the main form
    'The rates in the global variables are also updated
    Call frmMainCalc.UpdateCurrCbo

    'Hiding the Change Rate form and returning
    'to Exchange Rates
    frmCurrRates.Show
    frmChange.Hide
End Sub
```

When the **Cancel** button is pressed, the form is hidden, and the **Exchange Rates** form is shown without changing the currency rate.

Listing 14.28. The event for closing the *Change Rate* form

```
Private Sub cmdCancel_Click()
    'Hiding the Change Rate form and returning
    'to Exchange Rates
    frmCurrRates.Show
    frmChange.Hide
End Sub
```

Events, Properties, and Methods of Microsoft CE ADO Control 3.0 and eMbedded Visual Tools 3.0

The ADOCE library is used to create and handle the Pocket Access and SQL Server CE databases. This object can be added to a project via the **Project/References** menu. Depending on the version, this can be "Microsoft CE ADO Control 3.0" or "Microsoft CE ADO Control 3.1". The latest version of the ADOCE library — 3.1 — is the file adocedt31.dll.

Table 14.7. Database Properties (ADOCE.Connection)

Constant	Value	Description
Attributes	Long	Only when OLEDBCE databases are used
ConnectionString	String	Where and how the database should be opened. For Pocket Access, it contains the filename and path, for example, ConnectionString = "\Program Files\My Application\MyPocketAccess.cdb". **Be careful! Make sure that the application can find the Program Files directory**
Errors	Collection	List all ADOCE.Errors of the Connection object from the moment that the Connection.Errors query was opened. Also see *Table 23*
Properties	Collection	List the Connection properties. Not used with Pocket Access
Provider	String	Name of the technology supplier. For Pocket Access, it is "CEDB"
State	ADOCE.ObjectStateEnum	Shows the status (open/closed) of the Connection object
Version	String	Version of the DLL libraries of the ADOCE server

Table 14.8. ADOCE Connection Methods

Method	Parameters	Description
BeginTrans	None	Starts transactions. Not used with Pocket Access
Close	None	Closes an opened database

continues

Table 14.8 Continued

Method	Parameters	Description
CommitTrans	None	Commits the changes made since the last BeginTrans. Not used with Pocket Access
Execute	CommandText;String	Performs the SQL command and returns the result
	[RecordsAffected]; Long	
	(ByRef) Number of records affected by the command (Does not work with Pocket Access)	
	[Options]; Long, Does not work with Pocket Access.	
Open	[ConnectionString]; String, ConnectionString for access to the database. If left blank, Windows CE Object Store will be opened in ADOCE.	Opens the database for data access
	[UserId]; String ID of the database user (Does not work with Pocket Access or Windows CE Object Store)	
	[Password]; String, Password of the database user (Does not work with Pocket Access or Windows CE Object Store)	
RollbackTrans	None	Cancels the changes made since the last BeginTrans. Doesn not work with Pocket Access

Table 14.9. ADOCE.Field Properties

Property	Type	Description
ActualSize	Integer	Length of record in the database. Be careful with variables of the String type, since in Windows CE they are always Unicode, and therefore, the ActualSize of this field should have twice as many characters as the variable length
Attributes	Long	

continues

Table 14.9 Continued

Property	Type	Description
`DefinedSize`	`Integer`	The field length when created
`Name`	`String`	Field name
`NumericScale` (Float).	`Byte`	Number of decimal places
`Precision`	`Integer`	Total number of decimal places
`Type`	`ADOCE.DataTypeEnum`	Value indicating `DataTypeEnum`. Field type, e.g., `adDate`, `adInt`, `adVarChar`
`UnderlyingValue`	`Variant`	Field value before changing

Table 14.10. `ADOCE.Field` Methods

Method	Parameters	Description
`AppendChunk`	`Data`; Information to be added to the field	Adds information in binary or text form. Only with OLEDBCE, version 3.1 or later
`GetChunk`	`Size`; `Long` number of bytes to be returned	Returns information in binary or text form. Only with OLEDBCE, version 3.1 or later

Table 14.11. `ADOCE.Recordset` Properties

Property	Type	Description
`AbsolutePage` `AbsolutePosition`	`Long`; Read/Write `Long`; Read/Write	Records the page position among the records
		Records the position in the group of records (recordset)
`ActiveConnection`	`Object`; `ADOCE.Connection`	Returns the cursor to the connection used for record access. Returns the connection when used directly. `ConnectionString` as `ConnectionString` is a default property of the ADOCE object
`BOF`	`Boolean`; Read-only	Returns `True` if `AbsolutePosition` is before the first record in the recordset
`Bookmark`	`Variant`; Read/Write	At the query, returns the `Variant` variable, which, after being placed in the recordset, will return the same record. When assigned, indicates the `AbsolutePosition` of the record

continues

Table 14.11 Continues

Property	Type	Description
`CursorType`	`Long;` `ADOCE.CursorTypeEnum`	For Windows CE Object Store or Pocket Access only `adOpenForwardOnly` and `adOpenKeyset` are available
`EditMode`	`Long; ADOCE EditModeEnum` Read-Only	Determines the current status of the record. See `ADOCE.EditModeEnum`
`EOF`	`Boolean;` Read-Only	Returns `True` if `AbsolutePosition` is after the last record in the recordset
`Fields Collection;`	`ADOCE.Fields`	A list of all fields in the record See `ADOCE.Fields`
`Filter`	`Variant`	Returns the set of current filters. Supported only by bookmarks and `adFilterNone`. Not used by Windows CE Object Store or Pocket Access
`Index`	`String / Long`	Sets or returns the current index. Can only be used with the base record table (`adCmdTableDirect`). May be a name or a number of indices. Not used by Windows CE Object Store or Pocket Access
`LockType`	`Long;`	`ADOCE.LockTypeEnum`
`PageCount`	`Long;` Read-Only	Number of pages in the recordset
`PageSize`	`Long;` Read/Write	Number of records on the page
`Properties`	`Collection;` `ADOCE.Properties`	Not used by Windows CE Object Store or Pocket Access
`RecordCount`	`Long`	Number of records in recordset. May return `adUnknown`
`Source`	`String;` Read-only before the database is opened, may be used for opening the database	The SQL command that creates (or has created) the database. Determines the source of records before the database is opened, or can be read when the database is opened
`State`	`Long;` `ADOCE.ObjectStateEnum` Read-Only	Returns the status (opened/closed) of the database

Table 14.12. `ADOCE.Recordset` **Methods**

Property	Type	Description
AddNew	`[Fields]` Array of fields to be assigned values	Adds the necessary record to the database. Assigns values to the fields if the array of values is indicated as a parameter
	`[Values]` Array of values corresponding to the fields	
CancelUpdate	None	Cancels all changes in the current database
Clone	`[LockType]`, `ADOCE.LockType`	Returns a copy of the database
Close	None	Closes the database
Delete	`[AffectRecords]` only assigns the value 1 to `adAffectCurrent`.	Deletes the current record
Find	`Criteria: String` — String contains the search field and the search string	Detects the first record that is the same as the search row
	`[SkipRows]; Long` — the row from which the search is started in the current record	
	`[searchDirection], ADOCE.SearchDirectionEnum` — search direction: forward or backward	
	`[start]. Variant` — Bookmark of the search's start	
GetRows	`[Rows]; Long` — number of returned rows	Returns the array of values from the record
	`[Start]; Long / Variant` — number or Bookmark of the row from which the selected fragment is started	
	`[ Fields ]; Array` — the fields to which the records are returned	
Move	`[Rows]; Long` — number of deleted rows	Deletes the value of arrays from the record

continues

Chapter 14: Database Access Programming in eMbedded Visual Basic 3.0...

Table 14.12 Continued

Property	Type	Description
`Move`	`[Start]; Long / Variant` — number or Bookmark of the row from which the selected fragment is started	
`MoveFirst`	None	Moves to the first record in the database
`MoveLast`	None	Moves to the last record in the database
`MoveNext`	None	Moves to the next record in the database
`MovePrevious`	None	Moves to the previous record in the database
`Open`	`Source; String` — name of the table or SQL command	Opens a new database
	`[ActiveConnection]; ADOCE.Connection` — the connection used.	
	`[CursorType]; ADOCE.CursorType` — cursor type	
	`[Loc/cType]; ADOCE.LockType` — Lock type	
	`[Options]; Long` — `AdCmdTableDirect` uses SQL Server CE to create and update the database	
`Seek`	`KeyValues` — Array	Performs a search in the indexed query and makes the found record the current one
	`Options` — SeekEnum	
`Requery`	None	Resets the database
`Supports`	`CursorOptions; ADOCE.CursorOptionEnum`	Returns a Boolean that shows if the database supports the option selected for the cursor (`adAddNew`)
`Update;`	`[Fields]` Array of fields for data recording	Record to the database
	`[Values]` Array of values for recording to the corresponding fields	

Table 14.13. `ADOCE.Error` **Properties**

Property	Type	Description
`Description`	`String; Read-Only`	Error description
`ErrorParaineters`	`Collection; String`	List of errors at the last attempt of execution. Not used by Windows CE Object Store and Pocket Access
`HelpContext`	`Long`	Not used by Windows CE
`HelpFile`	`String; Read-Only`	The path to the help file related to the error
`NativeError`	`Long; Read-Only`	Native error returned from the data provider. Limited use with Windows CE Object Store and Pocket Access
`Number`	`Long; Read-Only`	Number of the error according to the OLE classification
`Source`	`String`	Name of the object that caused the error. Limited use with Windows CE Object Store or Pocket Access

Some Features of Microsoft Jet Core's SQL Language as Used by ADOCE

ADOCE object supports some of the DML options of the ANSI Structured Query Language (SQL). The ADOXCE library supports some of the DDL options of this language. These options enable the use of SQL queries for creation, modification and query creation from tables, queries, and databases.

Windows CE supports some of the properties that are missing in standard databases, such as the arrangement of blank characters at the beginning and end of the table, and unsigned numerical data. You can also create indices from data of non-standard type and position, although this is not recommended. ADOCE SQL supports the display of these properties in the volume necessary for correct transmission of information to the port of the desktop PC.

The table below shows the main SQL queries in the versions supported by ADOCE 3.1.

Chapter 14: Database Access Programming in eMbedded Visual Basic 3.0... 281

Table 14.14. Main SQL Queries

Data Manipulation Language (DML)	
INSERT	**INSERT INTO** tablename columnname [(columnname , ...)] **VALUES** (constant ,...)
DELETE	**DELETE [FROM]** tablename [**WHERE** expression]
Variants of the SELECT query:	
SELECT — Join	SELECT [tablename.]fieldname, [tablename.]fieldname... FROM tablename INNER JOIN tablename2 ON = tablename.fieldname= tablename2.fieldname2
SELECT — Like	match_expression [NOT] LIKE pattern
SELECT — Order By	SELECT * FROM tablename ORDER BY fieldname
SELECT — Projection	**SELECT [**tablename.fieldname**][,** tablename.fieldname**] FROM** tablename
SELECT — Restricted	SELECT * FROM tablename WHERE fieldname-expression [AND|OR fieldname-expression]
SELECT — Simple	SELECT * FROM tablename
Data Definition Language (DDL)	
ALTER TABLE	ALTER TABLE tablename TO tablename2 ALTER TABLE tablename ADD fieldname fieldtype [BEFORE] fieldname2 ALTER TABLE tablename DROP fieldname ALTER TABLE tablename MOVE fieldname [BEFORE] fieldname2 ALTER TABLE tablename RENAME fieldname TO fieldname2
CREATE DATABASE*	CREATE DATABASE 'database_name.cdb'
CREATE INDEX	CREATE INDEX indexname ON tablename (fieldname [DESC] [CASESENSITIVE] [UNKNOWNFIRST])

continues

Table 14.14 Continued

CREATE TABLE	CREATE TABLE tablename (fieldname Fieldtype[,fieldname Fieldtype])
DROP DATABASE*	DROP DATABASE database_name.cdb' [,... n]
DROP INDEX	DROP INDEX tablename, indexname
DROP TABLE	DROP TABLE tablename

* CREATE DATABASE and DROP DATABASE are supported only by the CEDB provider, and do not work with other providers.

Explanations of Certain Types of Queries

Below are the explanations of the most frequertly used types of queries with the most difficult syntaxes.

The SELECT – Join Query

This query combines two tables using a field common to these tables.

```
SELECT [tablename.]fieldname [, [tablename.] fieldname...]
FROM tablename
INNER JOIN tablename2
ON tablename. fieldname = tablename 2. fieldname 2
```

Parameters:

- *tablename*—table name — data-source name
- *fieldname*— field name in the table included in the query

The SELECT – Like Query

Enables you to search for a text string in database fields or a combination of them. Returns the records in which the searched string was found.

```
expression_to_compare [NOT] LIKE string_to_compare
```

Parameters:

- *expression_to_compare* — the SQL expression that is to be compared with *string_to_compare*. Only the string data type is allowed
- *string_to_compare* — the object of the search in the *expression_to_compare*, which can use "%" as a replacement for any character or group of characters. Variants: *text%*; *%text* and *%text%*.

The *SELECT – Order By* Query

Returns records sorted by the selected fields.

```
SELECT * FROM tablename
ORDER BY fieldname [ASC | DESC] [,fieldname [ASC | DESC]...]
```

Parameters:

- `tablename` — name of the table
- `fieldname` — name of the field by which the sorting is performed

The *SELECT – Projection* Query

This query returns a partial set of fields from the table. It enables you to reduce the volume of information transmitted.

```
SELECT [tablename.] fieldname [, [tablename.] fieldname... ] FROM tablename
```

Parameters:

- `tablename` — name of the table
- `fieldname` — name of the field included in the query

The *SELECT – Restricted* Query

This type of SQL query is the kind used most often for complex queries. It returns a set of records limited by the condition `Where`.

```
SELECT * FROM tablename
WHERE fieldname_expression [AND|OR fieldname_expression]
```

Parameters:

- `tablename` — name of the table
- `fieldname_expression` — may have one of the following forms:
  - `[NOT] fieldname operator constant`
  - `fieldname IS [NOT] NULL`
  - `fieldname IS [NOT] TRUE`
  - `fieldname IS [NOT] FALSE`
  - `fieldname [NOT] LIKE "text%"`

Syntax	Description	
`Fieldname`	Fieldname to compare	
`Operator`	Comparison operator. The following types are possible:	
	Operator	**Description**
	=	Equal to *
	>	Greater than
	>=	Greater than or equal to
	<	Less than
	<=	Less than or equal to
	<>	Not equal*
`Constant`	Date limited by quotation marks	
`text%`	% — replaces any character or group of characters. Can be used at the end of a string variable. Using it in the beginning depends on the particular database processor	

* This operation gives an error when working with floating-point numbers.

Error messages:

- E_OUTOFMEMORY
- DB_E_ERRORSINCOMMAND
- DB_E_NOTABLE
- DB_E_BADCOLUMNID
- DB_E_CANTCONVERTVALUE
- DB_E_DATAOVERFLOW

Note

Using the equal (=) or not equal (<>) operators with floating point numbers in an SQL expression leads to an error. The comparison of numbers with a floating point is not accurate.

Limitations on Using *WHERE*

- No type transformation takes place in the comparison.
- BETWEEN is not supported.
- IN is not supported.
- LIKE works only with variables of the `varchar` type.
- WHERE does not work with unsigned integers.

Variables of the `varbinary` type can be used only with the IS [NOT] **NULL** construction.

Chapter 15

Database Access Using ADOCE 3.1, ADOXCE, and SQL Server CE 1.0

This chapter deals with Windows CE ADOCE (ActiveX Data Objects for Windows CE) version 3.1 database-access objects, the ADOXCE extension library (the eXtension to ADO), as well as Microsoft CE SQL Server 1.0. We will consider loading and installing Microsoft SQL Server CE, installing it on a portable device, and the additional features that appear when using these applications. Changes and additions related to other methods of access to databases and to those of the remote SQL server were introduced in the application written in *Chapter 14*. This chapter also deals with converting Microsoft Access databases into ADOCE databases.

Setting up Microsoft SQL Server

SQL Server CE uses Internet Information Services (IIS server) for access to a shared SQL server. Since CE applications are presumably mobile, HTTP is used to access the server.

SQL Server CE is available at **www.microsoft.com/sql/downloads** as a self-unpacking archive with a size of about 33 MB. You can install the package free of charge if you have a license for Microsoft SQL Server 2000; otherwise, a 120-day trial version is provided. To develop for the PPC 2002 (Pocket PC 2002) platform, you will need to download the update package from the Microsoft web site. The first step of installation is shown in Fig. 15.1.

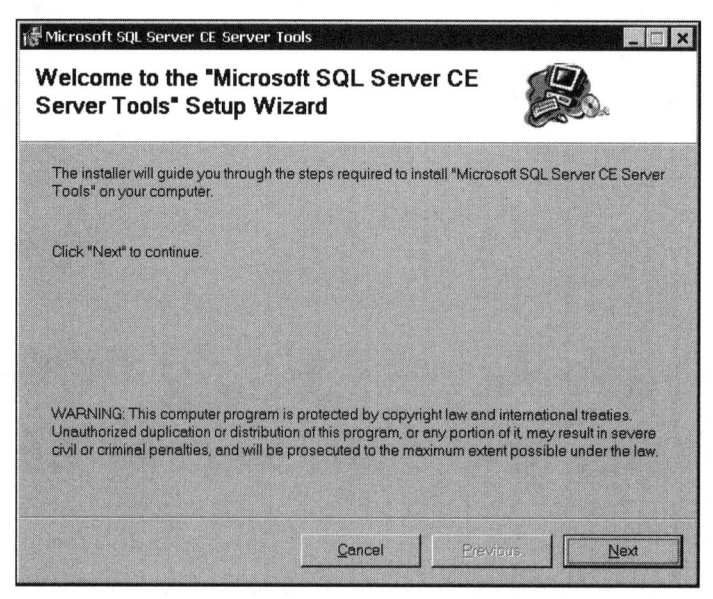

Fig. 15.1. The first step in installing SQL Server CE on a desktop PC

The system requirements for installation are basically the same as those for eMbedded Visual Tools, and the main ones are listed below.

SQL Server Windows CE Edition can be installed in one of four ways:

- On a system with a working SQL Server
- On a system with a working Microsoft Internet Information Services (IIS)
- Integrated into the developer's package
- On a device with the Windows CE, PPC 2002 operating system (and on a portable device emulator) including a combined installation on one computer

Each of the installation variants has its own system requirements.

- Hard-disk space:
  - SQL Server CE on a system with IIS or SQL Server 2000 — 120 MB
  - SQL Server CE on a developer's computer — 30 MB
  - SQL Server CE on a Windows CE device — from 1 to 3 MB of memory, depending on the processor type and the operating system

Chapter 15: Database Access Using ADOCE 3.1, ADOXCE, and SQL Server CE 1.0   287

❑ Operating system:
- On a system with IIS or SQL — Microsoft Windows NT 4.0 with Service Pack 5 or later, or Windows 2000 Professional. A working SQL Server or IIS is necessary
- On a developer's computer — Microsoft Windows 98, Windows Millennium Edition, Windows NT 4.0 with Service Pack 5 or later, Windows 2000, or Windows XP. Note: Windows 98 does not support portable device emulation
- On a device Windows CE running — Windows CE, version 2.11 or later for Handheld PC Pro (H/PC Pro) or Palm-size PC (P/PC); Windows CE 3.0 or later for Pocket PC, Pocket PC 2002, and Handheld PC 2000

❑ Other requirements:
- On a system with SQL Server CE on IIS — Microsoft Internet Explorer version 5.0 or later
- On a developer's computer — Internet Explorer 5.0 or later for viewing HTML help files

One Way of Installing on a Computer with Enterprise SQL Server

During installation, the user is asked to choose whether or not Server Tools and the developer's package should be installed (Fig. 15.2). Server Tools is necessary for work with a Microsoft SQL Server or IIS server that supports CE. To install a version that supports Server Tools, you have to have the Microsoft SQL Server 2000 package, which is also available at **www.microsoft.com/sql/downloads** as a self-unpacking archive with a size of about 400 MB (trial version). Like eMbedded Visual Tools 3.0, the package is also available by mail after you pay for shipping and handling.

If you do not have Microsoft SQL Server 2000 package (or 6.5 or 7.0 with a relatively recent Service Pack), you cannot install Server Tools. However, a package enabling such installation will be created later.

No changes to the main menu occur during installation except for the appearance of the HTML manual, called Books online.

Installing Server Tools makes it possible to configure Enterprise SQL Server to support CE. When the application is installed, you have to register sscerp10.dll and sscesa10.dll on the corresponding server. To do this, just enter the following commands in the **Run** window of the **Start** menu:

"C:\WINNT\system32\regsvr32.exe C:\Program Files\Microsoft SQL Server CE\Server\sscesa10.dll" followed by "C:\WINNT\system32\regsvr32.exe C:\Program Files\Microsoft SQL Server CE\Server\sscerp10.dll".

After the libraries are registered, start IIS Administration Tools and make the necessary changes, including giving permission to perform Scripts and Executables.

Installing a Developer's Package

If SQL Server is needed only for developing applications, then there is no need to install Server Tools, except to check the application's performance. After installation, Microsoft CE ADO Control 3.1, Microsoft ADO Ext. CE 3.1, and Microsoft CE SQL Server Control 1.0 (Fig. 14.2) will automatically become available. During installation, the corresponding library (named ca_mergex.tlb) will by default be set up in C:\Program Files\Microsoft SQL Server CE\Lib\. Make sure that it is installed.

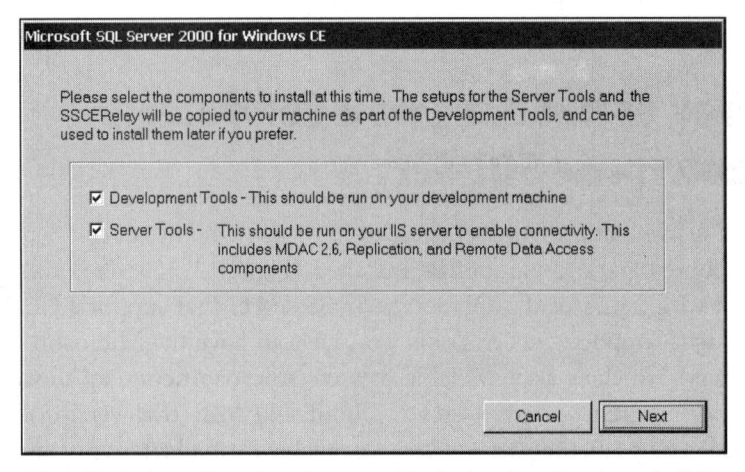

Fig. 15.2. Installing Development Tools (on the developer's PC) and Server Tools (on IIS Server)

Installing SQL Server 2000 Windows CE on a Portable Device

In a default installation, the folders containing SQL servers for the corresponding devices are found in C:\Program Files\Microsoft SQL Server CE\Device. To install

Chapter 15: Database Access Using ADOCE 3.1, ADOXCE, and SQL Server CE 1.0

them on your portable device, simply copy them there and start. The corresponding DLL libraries will be registered. This registration is automatic when starting and developing an application on the portable device.

Connecting to the SQL Server

The connection with the server is established via TCP/IP. There are several ways of establishing the connection:

- Establishing a direct connection between your portable device and the server using ActiveSync. Actually, as a rule, this is used on the developer's PC, since there is no reason to install IIS and SQL Server on each user's computer
- Using net cards, modems, or other means of access to the remote server via TCP/IP
- Using ActiveSync on the desktop PC as a proxy server, you can establish a connection with the remote SQL Server CE

Object Classes in the Libraries of the SQL Server

You can create three classes of objects:

- SSCE.Replication provides socket access to publications based on the SQL Server.
- SSCE.RemoteDataAccess enables you to manually enter and delete data from the tables using SQL queries.
- SSCE.Engine enables you to compress databases and eliminate errors in the databases.

The Main ADOXCE Objects

Compared to Pocket Access Model ADOCE 3.0, changes in version 3.1 are insignificant. One notable new feature, however, is Microsoft ActiveX Data Objects Extensions for Data Definition Language and Security (ADOXCE). Like SQL Server and Access on the desktop PC, now there are two ways of manipulating databases using SQL: Data Manipulation Language (DML) and Data Definition Language (DDL).

Let's take a look at creating and manipulating databases using ADOXCE 3.1.

Database Objects

The ADOXCE database controls contain the `Catalog`, `Table`, `Colunm`, `Index`, `Key`, and `Error` objects. Their functions correspond to the purpose of the objects used for manipulating databases within SQL, although their names in Microsoft eMbedded Visual Basic differ from those accepted by other developers.

The *Catalog* Object

The catalog contains a list of tables. This object is the database-description scheme using a database-management system (DBMS) based on the DDL language.

`Create` is the main method: it creates a new database and opens the ADOCE `Connection` to the data source.

`ActiveConnection` is the main property: it indicates the ADOCE `Connection` object to which the `Catalog` object belongs.

The *Table* Collection

This collection contains all tables described in the catalog.

Main methods and properties:

- `Append` (`Tables`) adds a new table.
- `Item` is a reference to a specific table.
- `Delete` deletes the table from the collection.
- `Refresh` refreshes the objects in the collection according to the database scheme.

The *Table* Object

This is a database object, and includes the `columns`, `indexes`, and `keys` collections.

Properties and collections of the object:

- `Name` is the table identifier.
- `Type` is the type of the table.
- `ParentCatalog` is the parent catalog or information about the provider.
- `DateCreated` is the date of the table's creation.
- `DateModified` is the date of the last modification.

Table Collections

- `Columns` — all of the table's `Column` objects
- `Indices` — all of the table's `Index` objects

- Keys — all of the table's Key objects
- Properties — all of the table's Property objects

The *Columns* Collection

This collection contains all Column objects of the Table, Index, and Key objects.

The Append method for the Columns collection has now appeared in ADOXCE, and adds a new column to the collection.

The standard ADOCE methods and properties for the collections are the following:

- Item provides access to the field.
- Delete deletes a column.
- Refresh updates the objects in the collection according to the database scheme.
- Count returns the number of columns in the collection.

The *Column* Object

This object is the column of the Table, Index, or Key objects.

The methods and properties of the Column object are the following:

- Name is the object identifier.
- Type is the data type.
- Attributes are the properties — the length and option of containing zero data.
- DefinedSize is the maximum size.
- NumericScale is the scale when numerical data are used.
- Precision is the accuracy of the numerical data.
- ParentCatalog is the parent catalog.
- RelatedColumn is the name of the corresponding column in another table (only for key columns).
- SortOrder is the order of sorting records (only for key columns).
- Properties supports the properties specific to the particular database processor.

Data Types

Table 15.1 shows the MS SQL Server CE data types and the corresponding ADOXCE constants.

Table 15.1. MS SQL Server CE Types of Data

Type of SQL Server	Description	ADOXCE Type
`bigint (INT 8)`	Integer from -2^{63} ($-9,223,372,036,854,775,808$) to $2^{63}-1$ ($9,223,372,036,854,775,807$). Size — 8 bytes.	`adBigInt`
`integer (INT 4)`	Integer from -2^{31} ($-2,147,483,648$) to $2^{31}-1$ ($2,147,483,647$).	`adInteger`
`smallint (INT 2)`	Integer from $-32,768$ to $32,767$. Size — 2 bytes.	`adSmallInt`
`tinyint (INT 1)`	Integer from 0 to 255. Size — 1 byte.	`adUnsignedTinyInt`
`bit`	Integer: 1 or 0.	`adBoolean`
`numeric (p, s)`	Fixed-precision and scale-numeric from $-10^{38}-1$ to $10^{38}-1$. p determines the length of the number and is between 1 and 38. s determines the number of symbols and is between 0 and p.	`adNumeric`
`money`	Monetary data values, from -2^{63} ($-922,337,203,685,477.5808$) to $2^{63}-1$ ($922,337,203,685,477.5807$, precise to 0.0001 unit. Size — 8 bytes.	`adCurrency`
`float(n)`	Floating-point number (approximate numerical) from $-1.79E+308$ to $1.79E+308$. n must be from 1 to 53. Size — 4 bytes if n is from 1 to 24, and 8 bytes if n is from 25 to 53.	`adDouble`
`real`	Floating precision number (approximate numerical) from $-3.40E+38$ to $3.40E+38$. Size — 4 bytes.	`adSingle`
`datetime`	Date and time from 1/1/1753 to 31/12/9999, precise to 0.00333 seconds.	`adDBTimestamp`

`NATIONAL CHARACTER (n)`
 	
Synonym
 	
`nchar(n)`
	Fixed-length Unicode data with a maximum length of 255 characters.	`adWChar`

continues

Table 15.1 Continued

Type of SQL Server	Description	ADOXCE Type
NATIONAL CHARACTER VARYING (n) Synonym nvarchar(n)	Variable-length Unicode data with a length from 1 to 255 characters.	AdVarWChar
ntext	Variable-length Unicode data with a maximum length of $(2^{30}-2)/2$ (536,870,911) characters. Size (in bytes) is twice the number of entered characters.	adLongVarWChar
binary(n)	Fixed-length binary data with a maximum length of 510 bytes.	adBinary
varbinary(n)	Variable-length binary data with a maximum length of 510 bytes.	adVarBinary
image	Variable-length binary data (image) with a maximum length of $2^{30}-1$ (1,073,741,823) bytes.	adLongVarBinary
uniqueidentifier	A globally unique identifier (GUID). Size — 16 bytes.	adGuid

Other Collections

In ADOXCE, we also have Index Collection and Key Collection. Both of them support the new Append method, as well as the standard ADOCE methods and properties for collections. The description is the same as for the column collection.

The *Index* Object

This object represents the Index tables in the database:

- Clustered — if the index is clustered.
- IndexNulls — if there are zero fields in the indices.
- Name is the index identifier.
- ParentCatalog is the parent catalog.
- PrimaryKey — if the index is the primary key of the table.
- Unique is the possibilty of repetition.

The *Key* Object

This object represents the primary, foreign, or unique key of the table.
Properties:

- `Name` is the name of the key.
- `Type` is the type of the key: primary, foreign, or unique.
- `RelatedTable` is the name of the corresponding table.
- `DeleteRule` are the rules for key deletion.
- `UpdateRule` are the rules for key updating.
- `Columns` are all `Column` objects related to this key.

Creating and Manipulating Databases Using SQL Server Tools

We'll use the example from *Chapter 14* to demonstrate working with SQL Server CE. We will need to make slight changes to the codes in order to use the features of SQL Server CE.

First of all, add the necessary libraries. The reference to SQL Server CE is done by the traditional for Visual Basic method (Fig. 15.3).

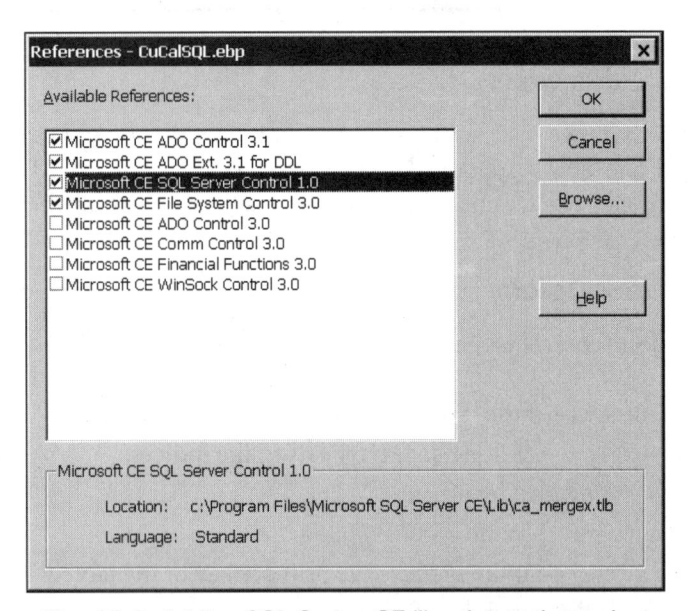

Fig. 15.3. Adding SQL Server CE libraries to the project

Chapter 15: Database Access Using ADOCE 3.1, ADOXCE, and SQL Server CE 1.0   295

Changes in the *GlobalVariables* Module

Let's introduce the new global variable `strConnStr`, which contains the information on the connection to the SQL Server (Listing 15.1). This variable will be used instead of `strDBPath` when connecting to the database in the previous example. The standard file extension with SQL is STF.

Listing 15.1. Adding a new constant to the module

```
...
'Database path
Const strDBPath = "\My Documents\CuCalSQL.sdf"

'String to connect to SQL server
Const strConnStr = "Provider=Microsoft.SQLSERVER.OLEDB.CE.1.0; _
         data source='\My Documents\CuCalSQL.sdf'"
...
```

Changes in the *frmMainCalc* Form

A new database is created using the ADOCE library extension ADOXCE, whose objects and methods allow you to manipulate the fields, indices, and keys (Listing 15.2). Determine the `Catalog`, `Table`, `Column`, and `Key` variables. The `Catalog` object represents the scheme of the database description, and contains the lists of tables. Create the new CuCalSQL.sdf database using the `Create` method for the `Catalog` object.

Connect to the created base via the `Open` method of the `Connection` object, and specify the `ActiveConnection` property of the `Catalog` object in accordance with this connection.

Then create an object of the `Table` type and name it `Rates` (the `Name` property). Create a series of objects of the `Column` type that are to be the fields in this table. Specify the name (`Name` property), data type (`Type` property) and, where necessary, the size (`DefinedSize` property) of each field. Each created field is added to the field collection of the `Rates` table using the `Append` method. When the fields are added to the table, add the table itself to the table collection of the catalog. Clear the variables.

SQL Server CE supports the primary key for tables that automatically require that the key field be unique. Create a primary key for the `CurrID` field of the `Primary` type. Add the `CurrID` field (which should already exist by the time the key is added) to the field collection of the key. Add the created key to the key collection of the `Rates` table. Clear the variable of the `Key` type.

Another way to create a table, without using ADOXCE, is to use an SQL query of the `CREATE TABLE` type. We will use this method to create the `Settings` table. The `Execute` method of the `Connection` object enables you to execute such a query. The difference between this and the previous example lies in the type names of the fields: `nvarchar` instead of `varchar` (Like `nvarchar`, `varchar` is a variable-length string of two-byte characters).

Fill in a few values in the tables in exactly the same way as in the previous example.

Listing 15.2. SQL Creating a server CE format database

```
Sub InitDB()
  Dim objCat As ADOXCE.Catalog
  Dim objTbl As ADOXCE.Table
  Dim objCol As ADOXCE.Column
  Dim objKey As ADOXCE.Key

  'Creating the database and tables using ADOXCE library
  'Creating a new database in the folder defined in the variable
  'strConnStr
  'in this sample - in "My Documents" - CuCalSQL.sdf
  Set objCat = CreateObject("ADOXCE.Catalog.3.1")
  objCat.Create strConnStr
  'Database created. Clearing the variable
  Set objCat = Nothing

  'Connecting to the new database to create tables
  Set objCat = CreateObject("ADOXCE.Catalog.3.1")
  Set objConnection = CreateObject("ADOCE.Connection.3.1")

  objConnection.Open strConnStr
  objCat.ActiveConnection = objConnection
  'Creating the Rates table, with the fields:
  'CurrID - 3-character currency ID;
  'CurrName - currency name;
  'CurrRate - exchange rate as related to the base currency
  Set objTbl = CreateObject("ADOXCE.TABLE.3.1")
  objTbl.Name = "Rates"
```

```
'Creating the CurrID field, type VarWChar(3)
Set objCol = CreateObject("ADOXCE.COLUMN.3.1")
objCol.Name = "CurrID"
objCol.Type = adVarWChar
objCol.DefinedSize = 3
'Adding a field to the table
objTbl.Columns.Append objCol
Set objCol = Nothing
'Creating the CurrName field, type VarWChar(64)
Set objCol = CreateObject("ADOXCE.COLUMN.3.1")
objCol.Name = "CurrName"
objCol.Type = adVarWChar
objCol.DefinedSize = 64
'Adding a field to the table
objTbl.Columns.Append objCol
Set objCol = Nothing
'Creating the CurrRate field, type Currency
Set objCol = CreateObject("ADOXCE.COLUMN.3.1")
objCol.Name = "CurrRate"
objCol.Type = adCurrency
'Adding a field to the table
objTbl.Columns.Append objCol
Set objCol = Nothing
'Adding a table to the catalog
objCat.Tables.Append objTbl
Set objTbl = Nothing

'Creating a primary key in the Rates table based on the CurrID field
Set objKey = CreateObject("ADOXCE.KEY.3.1")
objKey.Name = "PrimCurrID"
objKey.Type = adKeyPrimary
'Adding the CurrID field to the fields collection of the PrimCurrID key
objKey.Columns.Append "CurrID"
'Adding a key to the keys collection of the Rates table
objCat.Tables("Rates").Keys.Append objKey

'Clearing the variables
Set objKey = Nothing
Set objCat = Nothing

'Creating the Settings table to store the program settings,
```

```
'as an alternative to storing the settings in the Registry
'BaseCurr – to store the base currency ID;
'Curr1 – the currency selected in the fist combobox on the main form;
'Curr2 – the currency selected in the second combobox
'Using the SQL request method, the same as in the previous chapter
objConnection.Execute "CREATE TABLE Settings (BaseCurr nvarchar(3), _
            Curr1 nvarchar(3), Curr2 nvarchar(3))"
'Tables created

'Filling in some initial values in these tables:
'For Settings
'Assume the base currency to be USD, and values in the comboboxes to be
'USD and EUR
objConnection.Execute "INSERT INTO Settings (BaseCurr, Curr1, Curr2) _
            VALUES ('USD', 'USD', 'EUR')"
'Filling in the currency list in the Rates table with two currencies,
'USD – US dollars and EUR – European euros, at certaim rates
objConnection.Execute "INSERT INTO Rates (CurrID, CurrName, CurrRate) _
            VALUES ('USD', 'US dollars', 1)"
objConnection.Execute "INSERT INTO Rates (CurrID, CurrName, CurrRate) _
            VALUES ('EUR', 'European euros', 0.98)"

'Closing the connection and clearing the variable
objConnection.Close
Set objConnection = Nothing
End Sub
```

The only difference in the event handling of the form loading here lies in the establishment of a connection with the database using the strConnStr global variable, in which the description of the connection with the SQL Server is stored (Listing 15.3).

Listing 15.3. Codes additional to Listing 14.3

```
Private Sub Form_Load()
  ...
  Set objConnection = CreateObject("ADOCE.Connection.3.1")
  objConnection.Open strConnStr
  ...
End Sub
```

Chapter 15: Database Access Using ADOCE 3.1, ADOXCE, and SQL Server CE 1.0

Similarly, the `UpdateCurrCbo` procedure has undergone no changes, except for the establishment of a connection with the database (Listing 15.4).

Listing 15.4. Changes to the `UpdateCurrCbo` procedure

```
Private Sub UpdateCurrCbo ()
  ...
  Set objConnection = CreateObject("ADOCE.Connection.3.1")
  objConnection.Open strConnStr
  ...
End Sub
```

The fields of the Settings table are updated in the UpdateSettings procedure. Unlike in the example with access to CEDB, the implementation of database access in SQL CE does not update the fields that result from the SQL query. A special type of cursor is needed — direct access to the `adCmdTableDirect` table. All the fields are counted simultaneously. This method of changing the data is demonstrated in the procedure code (Listing 15.5), but it is not particularly convenient. When working with the SQL Server, it is recommended to use SQL queries that modify the data. This will be considered in an example of working with records in the Rates table.

Listing 15.5. Demonstrating direct access to the SQL CE table

```
Sub UpdateSettings(strCurr As String, intCboNum As Integer)
  'Changing the value of Curr1, Curr2, or BaseCurr to strCurr, depending
  'on intCboNum (1, 2, or 3) in the Settings table
  'Establishing the connection
  Set objConnection = CreateObject("ADOCE.Connection.3.1")
  objConnection.Open strConnStr
  'Opening the Settings recordset
  Set objRec = CreateObject("ADOCE.Recordset.3.1")
  'adOpenDynamic is used to open the recordset for reading, updating,
  'appending, and deleting records; adLockOptimistic is for locking
  'records only during update;
  'adCmdTableDirect evaluates CommandText
  'as a table name whose columns are all returned (update possible)
  objRec.Open "Settings", objConnection, adOpenDynamic, _
```

```
                        adLockOptimistic, adCmdTableDirect

  objRec.MoveFirst
  'Storing a new value in the Settings table
  Select Case intCboNum
    Case 1
      objRec(1).Value = strCurr
    Case 2
      objRec(2).Value = strCurr
    Case 3
      objRec(0).Value = strCurr
  End Select

  objRec.Update
  ...
End Sub
```

Changes to the `GetCurrRate` function are only in the string for data connection (Listing 15.6).

Listing 15.6. Changes to the `GetCurrRate` function

```
Function GetCurrRate(strCurr As String) As Double
  ...
  Set objConnection = CreateObject("ADOCE.Connection.3.1")
  objConnection.Open strConnStr
  ...
End Sub
```

Changes in the *frmCurrRates* form

The procedures that only read data from the database do not differ greatly from the example in the previous chapter. Only the connection string is changed, all the rest remaining relevant for working with an SQL Server (Listing 15.7).

Listing 15.7. Changes to the `UpdateBaseCurrCbo` and `UpdateList` functions

```
Sub UpdateBaseCurrCbo()
  ...
  Set objConnection = CreateObject("ADOCE.Connection.3.1")
```

Chapter 15: Database Access Using ADOCE 3.1, ADOXCE, and SQL Server CE 1.0

```
   objConnection.Open strConnStr
   ...
End Sub

Sub UpdateList()
   ...
   Set objConnection = CreateObject("ADOCE.Connection.3.1")
   objConnection.Open strConnStr
   ...
End Sub
```

The procedure called when you press the **Delete** button deletes the currency record selected from the currency list. As mentioned above, direct access to the table returns all fields, and requires the enumeration of the records in order to search for the necessary one. For work with the SQL Server, it is best to use an SQL query to delete the required record (Listing 15.8). This procedure requires the following query:

```
DELETE FROM Rates WHERE CurrID = '<CurrID field
   of the string selected in the currency list>'
```
An object of the `Recordset` type is not used.

Listing 15.8. A demonstration of deleting a record from the SQL Server CE table

```
Private Sub cmdRemove_Click()
   ...
   Set objConnection = CreateObject("ADOCE.Connection.3.1")
   objConnection.Open strConnStr
   'Executing the SQL query for deleting the record with the selected
   'CurrID
   objConnection.Execute "DELETE FROM Rates WHERE CurrID = '" & _
strSelCurrID & "'"
   ...
End Sub
```

Changes to the *frmAdd* Form

In the `AddNewCurr` procedure, an SQL query will add a new record to the `Rates` currency tables. This query is analogous to those that entered the initial values in the tables of the `InitDB` functions of the start form.

Listing 15.9. Changes to the `AddNewCurr` procedure

```
Sub AddNewCurr()
  ...
  Set objConnection = CreateObject("ADOCE.Connection.3.1")
  objConnection.Open strConnStr
  'Executing the SQL query to add a new currency with the parameters
  'from the form's textboxes
  objConnection.Execute "INSERT INTO Rates (CurrID, CurrName, CurrRate) _
      VALUES ('" & txtCurrID.Text & "', '" & txtCurrName.Text & "', " _
              & txtCurrRate.Text & ")"
  ...
End Sub
```

Changes to the *frmChange* Form

Finally, the `ChangeCurrRate` procedure demonstrates the changing of a record with an SQL query (Listing 15.10). The following construction is used:

```
UPDATE Rates SET CurrRate = <rate value from the form> WHERE CurrID =
<currency identifier from the form>
```

Listing 15.10. Changes to the `ChangeCurrRate` procedure

```
Sub ChangeCurrRate()
  ...
  Set objConnection = CreateObject("ADOCE.Connection.3.1")
  objConnection.Open strConnStr
  'Executing the SQL query for changing the exchange rate for the record
  'with the selected CurrID
  objConnection.Execute "UPDATE Rates SET CurrRate = _
                    " & txtCurrRate.Text & _
                    " WHERE CurrID = '" & txtCurrID.Text & "'"
  ...
End Sub
```

Interaction with the External MS SQL Server

One option for the wireless interaction of a portable device with a corporate server should be of great interest to corporate users in particular. HTTP is used for this

Chapter 15: Database Access Using ADOCE 3.1, ADOXCE, and SQL Server CE 1.0   303

type of connection. Let's modify our example to demonstrate sharing currency-rate data between the database of the portable device and the SQL Server. We'll make some changes to the `frmCurrRates` form by adding three command buttons and one label (Fig. 15.4).

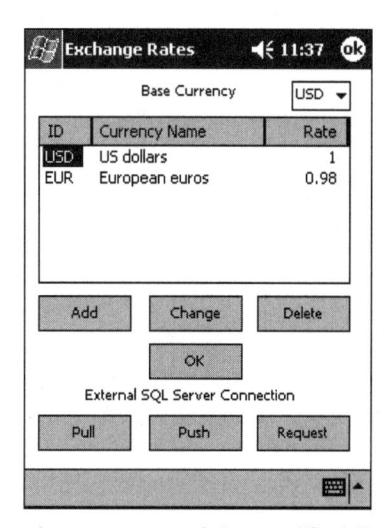

Fig. 15.4. The general appearance of the modified **Exchange Rates** form

The controls of the Exchange Rates form are shown in Table 15.2.

Table 15.2. Controls of the `frmCurrRates` Form

Name	Type	Label	Description
lblSQLServer	Label	**External SQL Server Connection**	The label in front of the group of buttons for working with the external server
cmdPull	CommandButton	**Pull**	Button for calling the procedure of receiving data from the server
cmdPush	CommandButton	**Push**	Button for calling the procedure of sending data to the server
cmdSubmitSQL	CommandButton	**Request**	Button for calling the procedure of sending a query to the server

The `cmdPull` button deletes the `Rates` table, and then calls and receives it from the external server. The `TrackingOn` checkbox is set for tracking further changes.

Listing 15.11. Transferring data from SQL to the portable device

```
Sub cmdPull_Click()
  Dim objRatesRDA As SSCE.RemoteDataAccess
  Dim objCat As ADOXCE.Catalog

  'Creating an RDA object (Remote Data Access)
  Set objRatesRDA = CreateObject("SSCE.RemoteDataAccess.1.0")
  Set objConnection = CreateObject("ADOCE.Connection.3.1")
  Set objRec = CreateObject("ADOCE.Recordset.3.1")
  objConnection.Open strConnStr
  'Before loading the Rates table from the external SQL server,
  'we have to remove it from the local server
  objRec.Open "SELECT * from mSysObjects WHERE Name = 'Rates'", _
              objConnection
  'Checking that Rates table exists on SQL CE
  If Not (objRec.BOF And objRec.EOF) Then
    'Removing Rates if it exists
    Set objCat = CreateObject("ADOXCE.Catalog.3.1")
    objCat.ActiveConnection = objConnection
    objCat.Tables.Delete "Rates"
    Set objCat = Nothing
  End If

  'Clearing the variables
  objRec.Close
  Set objRec = Nothing
  objConnection.Close
  Set objConnection = Nothing

  'Establishing a connection with the external SQL server
  'using the HTTP protocol
  objRatesRDA.InternetURL = "http://MyIIServer/SQLCE/sscesa10.dll"
  objRatesRDA.LocalConnectionString = "Data Source='" & strDBPath & "'"

  'Receiving the Rates table from the external server and
  'setting the TrackingOn parameter to track changes in the records
  objRatesRDA.Pull "Rates", "SELECT * from Rates", "Provider=sqloledb; _
            Data Source=MySQLServer;Initial Catalog=CurrCalc; _
      user id=CEUser;password=SamplePassword", TrackingOn, "tblErrRates"
  Set objRatesRDA = Nothing
End Sub
```

Chapter 15: Database Access Using ADOCE 3.1, ADOXCE, and SQL Server CE 1.0   305

The `cmdPush` button sends the `Rates` table to the external server. The set `TrackingOn` checkbox in the `Pull` procedure only transfers the modified data.

Listing 15.12. Transferring data transfer from the portable device to the external server

```
Sub PushRates()
  Dim objRatesRDA As SSCE.RemoteDataAccess

  'Creating an RDA object (Remote Data Access)
  Set objRatesRDA = CreateObject("SSCE.RemoteDataAccess.1.0")

  'Establishing a connection with the external SQL server
  'using the HTTP protocol
  objRatesRDA.InternetURL = "http://MyIIServer/SQLCE/sscesa10.dll"
  objRatesRDA.LocalConnectionString = "Data Source='" & strDBPath & "'"

  'Sending the Rates table to the external server
  'The TrackingOn parameter was set in the PullRates procedure
  'Only the changed records will be transferred
  objRatesRDA.Push "Rates", "SELECT * from Rates", "Provider=sqloledb; _
        Data Source=MySQLServer;Initial Catalog=CurrCalc; _
        user id=CEUser;password=SamplePassword"
  Set objRatesRDA = Nothing
End Sub
```

The `cmdSubmitSQL` query button executes the SQL query on the external server. The `INSERT`, `DELETE`, `UPDATE`, and DDL queries are permitted.

Listing 15.13. A query for executing a command on the SQL Server

```
Sub SubmitSQLtoServer()
  Dim objRatesRDA As SSCE.RemoteDataAccess

  'Creating the RDA object (Remote Data Access)
  Set objRatesRDA = CreateObject("SSCE.RemoteDataAccess.1.0")

  'Establishing a connection with the external SQL server
  'using the HTTP protocol
  objRatesRDA.InternetURL = "http://MyIIServer/SQLCE/sscesa10.dll"
  objRatesRDA.LocalConnectionString = "Data Source='" & strDBPath & "'"

  'Sending a request to the external server
```

```
'No data can be returned by this request
'Adding a new currency using the INSERT command
objRatesRDA.SubmitSQL "INSERT INTO Rates (CurrID, CurrName, CurrRate) _
           VALUES ('TTT', 'Test currency', 100)", _
           "Provider=sqloledb;Data Source=MySQLServer; _
           Initial Catalog=CurrCalc;user id=CEUser; _
           password=SamplePassword"
Set objRatesRDA = Nothing
End Sub
```

Additional Features of SQL Queries Supported by SQL Server CE

Compared to CEDB SQL, the CE server supports almost all queries that can be executed on the standard MS SQL Server. These new features include:

The *SELECT* Query

Let's look at the general query syntax with SELECT:

```
SELECT [ ALL | DISTINCT ] <list> [ FROM { < table_source > } [ ,...n ] ]
<list> =
{ *
| { tablename | tablename_label }.*
| { column_name | expression } [ [ AS ] column_name_label ]
} [ ,...n ]

< table_source > =
tablename [ [ AS ] tablename_label ] | < connected_table >

< connected_table > =
< table_source > [ INNER | { { LEFT | RIGHT } [ OUTER ] } ]
JOIN < table_source > ON search_condition | ( < connected_table > )
```

Parameters:

- [ALL | DISTINCT] — select all (All) or only unique fields (Distinct)
- * returns all columns
- *tablename* — name of the table
- *tablename_label* — the label used instead of the table name and determined via the AS operator after the From instruction

Chapter 15: Database Access Using ADOCE 3.1, ADOXCE, and SQL Server CE 1.0

- *column_name* — name of the table field
- *column_name_label* — the label used instead of the column name and determined via the AS operator
- *table_name* — name of the table

Types of table consolidation:

- INNER returns only identical pairs of strings. Used by default.
- LEFT [OUTER] returns all strings from the left table in addition to the identical strings. For these additional strings, the values in the right table columns are equal to Null.
- RIGHT [OUTER] returns all strings from the right table in addition to the identical strings. For these additional strings, the values in the left table columns are equal to Null.
- ON *search_condition* is the consolidation condition — the expression.

The *SELECT* Query – *GROUP BY*

When this instruction is executed, the table is divided into groups of strings according to the group expression value. If the group satisfies the logical expression in the HAVING construction, it is included in the result of the query's performance. The groups are returned without sorting. To sort them, you must use the ORDER BY construction. GROUP BY is used jointly with aggregation functions.

[**GROUP BY** *grouping_expression* [**HAVING** *search_condition*] [, ... *n*]]

Parameters:

- *grouping_expression* — the column name or the expression that does not use aggregation functions
- *search_condition* — logical expression

Functions Supported by SQL CE

The aggregation functions are shown in Table 15.3.

Table 15.3. Aggregation Functions of SQL Server CE

Function	Parameters	Description
AVG	[ALL] *expression*	Calculates the average value according to the expression
COUNT	[ALL] *expression* | *	Calculates the number of values in the group. * — total number of records, including Null

continues

Table 15.3 Continued

Function	Parameters	Description
MAX	expression >	The largest value in the expression
MIN	expression	The smallest value in the expression
SUM	[ALL] expression	Sum of the expression values

The functions for working with dates and times are shown in Table 15.4.

Table 15.4. Functions for Working with Dates and Times

Function	Parameters	Description
DATEADD	part_of_date, part, date	Adds the number of date parts to the date, where a part of date may have the following values: yy — year, qq — quarter, mm — month, dy — day of the year, dd — day, ww — week, hh — hour, mi — minute, ss — second, ms — millisecond
DATEDIFF	part_of_date, date1, date2	Number of date parts between two dates
DATENAME	part_of_date, date	Returns the text string of the date for the selected date
DATEPART	part_of_date, date	Returns the numerical value of the date for the selected date
GETDATE		Returns the current time and date in the SQL Server format

Logical Operators

In addition to the operators AND, OR, NOT, and LIKE, which we have already looked at, SQL CE also supports the operators listed in Table 15.5.

Table 15.5. Additional Operators Supported by SQL Server CE

Operator	Parameters	Description
BETWEEN	test_expression [NOT] BETWEEN initial_value AND final_value	Checks if the expression is in the range between the initial and final values
EXISTS	subquery	Checks if the subquery contains at least one string
IN	test_expression [NOT] IN (subquery | expression [, ... n])	Checks if the test expression is identical to at least one value in the subquery or with the expression from the list

Chapter 16

Communication and the Infrared WinSock Control in Windows CE

Creating Internet applications for a portable device running Windows CE has many special features compared to those that run Palm. First of all, the specific standard (Web Clipping) described in detail in *Chapter 10* is not available. Everything can be done using eVB and its controls — WinSock first and foremost. However, our general discussions about Internet programming for portable devices remain in force. Among these requirements, the most important one is the minimization of data transmitted via the Internet, since very often the connection turns out to be too slow and relatively expensive. Therefore, the general logic of application development is to create an interface that will make a query and receive data to be distributed among the controls.

Project Description

In essence and content, the project will be similar to the one considered in *Chapter 9*, but here we will define the task slightly differently, and implement it using eVB. Our application will enable users to determine the current price of shares on the stock market and all related information, such as the time of the last bid, the volume of shares sold, etc. The application will send to the server the minimal query, including the company's stock-exchange code, consisting of four letters (standard). As a result, we will receive minimal package of data, with the logical blocks separated by commas. Note that this approach crucially differs from the one implemented in *Chapter 9*, where the return of the inquired information was performed as an HTML file, which had to be processed before it was displayed on the screen. Now we will also have to process the received information, but it comes in standardized form, and of minimum volume. Another difference is that the version described in *Chapter 9* was universal, and would work with any web site and server. Generally speaking, it is difficult to find a suitable and concise data exchange here, since it would require the creation of a server corresponding to the user's application on the portable device. This, in turn, means that a considerable amount of work should be done on the server on which the requested information will be processed, and the maximally concise reply will be built so as to be recognized by the user of the portable device. We are in a sense dealing with an analog of Web Clipping.

The basis of the application will be the fact that the **http://quote.yahoo.com/download?format=sl&ext=.csv&symbols=xxxx** string, written in the URL address of the browser, returns a structurally determined set of data. In the upper message, "xxxx" indicates the alphabetical code of the company on the stock exchange. For example, if "xxxx" is replaced with "msft" (the code for Microsoft), then the following text string will be returned (November 25, 2002, 2:00 PM): "MSFT",58.16,"11/25/2002","2:17pm",-0.06,58.06,58.64,57.571,22336112.

First of all, we need to figure out what is what, and then we have to distribute this information correctly among the objects of the interface, so:

- "MSFT" (name) is the company symbol.
- 58.16 (current price) is the current price of one share in USD.
- "11/25/2002" (date) is the date of the last purchase and sale (at time of query).
- "2:17pm" (time) is the time of the last deal.
- −0.06 (change) is increase (or decrease) of the share price compared to the previous deal.
- 58.06 (open price) is the price of the share for the first deal of the day.
- 58.64 (hi price) is the maximum price of the share for today.
- 57.571 (low price) is the minimum price of the share for today.
- 22336112 (volume) is the volume of the last deal.

Note that the name of the server, the query string, and the reply returned by the server are only correct for the moment this book was being written, and can change.

Now let's move on to some real programming!

Creating the Interface

Open a new eVB project, and, as well as the standard controls, enter WinSock by selecting the **Components** command from the **Project** menu. Name the only form of the project frmMain, and place the controls on it according to Fig. 16.1.

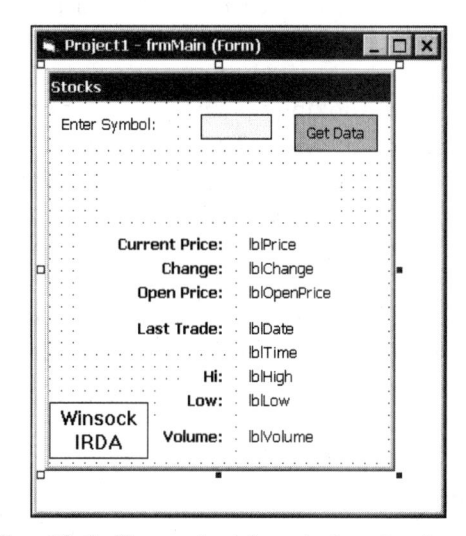

Fig. 16.1. The project form being developed

Labels are used to display the information on the screen. Only one field at the top will be the text: we will enter the stock exchange symbol of the company there. The button for sending the query to the server will be located next to it. WinSock1 will be the main control. Before going any further, let's briefly discuss the possible ways of establishing an Internet connection.

Infrared Port

The IrDA control can establish a connection using either TCP/IP, which will be used in our example, or Infrared Direct Access (IRDA). Each portable device has a special infrared port (IrDA) that can establish a wireless connection with a desktop PC using infrared radiation for a distance of up to 1 meter. The rate of data transfer can reach 115.2 KB/sec. The waveband used is 850–900 nm, and since the radiation level is relatively low, it does not require special FCC certification in the U.S. The session between the portable device and the desktop PC is performed as follows: first the device checks the availability of the band. If it is unavailable, then an error code is returned, which will be programmatically processed. If the band is available, then the connection starts. The desktop PC (from which HotSync is usually initialized) is the master during the connection session, and the portable device is the slave.

It follows that using this control makes sense only if the peripheral device with which the connection is established also has an infrared port.

As briefly mentioned above, the infrared port can be used, for example, for connection with the desktop PC during the data synchronization. Another use for the infrared port is hooking up a portable device to a cell phone to connect to the Internet. For this, the cell phone should be equipped with an infrared port (which all the latest models are). The portable device and the cell phone should be positioned in such a way so that the infrared port of the portable device is directly facing that of the cell phone (best done on a table). Activate the phone and find the option for Internet connection with a portable device (the cell phone should also have an integrated modem). It should be noted that this way of connecting has a low security level, so while doing this in public bear in mind that your neighbor with laptop and infrared port can access your data.

Creating the Code

The variables used on the level of the form module are declared in the `General` part, and shown in Listing 16.1.

Listing 16.1. Declaring variables

```
Option Explicit
'Stock Quote parameters
  Dim Name     As String
  Dim Current  As String
  Dim Date1    As String
  Dim Time1    As String
  Dim Change   As String
  Dim Low      As String
  Dim High     As String
  Dim OpenPrice As String
  Dim Volume   As String

Private Const OneSecond As Long = 1000
```

Chapter 16: Communication and the Infrared WinSock Control in Windows CE

```
Dim ipaddress As String
Dim port As Long
Dim sktError As Integer
```

After the application is started, the user should enter the company's abbreviation. According to the set standard, no symbol can have more than four characters. Therefore, it makes sense to accelerate the process of displaying the required information on the screen: having counted four characters, we automatically call the `cmdGet_Click` function, which can also be called independently by pressing the `cmdGet` button (Listing 16.2).

Listing 16.2. The function for checking the length of the entered symbol

```
Private Sub txtSymbolName_Change()
 If Len(txtSymbolName.Text) = 4 Then
   Call cmdGet_Click
 End If
End Sub
```

The `cmdGet_Click` procedure only contains the call of the `GetQuote` function. The process of recognizing the returned string is put into a separate function, since it can also be called, for example, from the menu. This `GetQuote` function is shown in Listing 16.3. First, specify all the necessary driver properties of the telecommunication port (winsock), such as the port number, the server name, and the protocol type (TCP/IP in our case). Then, call the `Connect` method to establish a connection with the server. If a connection is established, build the query and send it.

Listing 16.3. The main function of the application (GetQuote)

```
Public Sub GetQuote()
 'Close Winsock control before using
 WinSock1.Close

 'Initializing variables
 port = 80

 'Check to see if a symbol has been entered
```

```
If txtSymbolName.Text <> "" Then
   'Setting the socket parameters using the TCP/IP protocol
   WinSock1.Protocol = sckTCPProtocol
   WinSock1.RemoteHost = "quote.yahoo.com"
   WinSock1.RemotePort = port

   'Set the error state to 0 in order to check for any
   'errors that may occur when trying to connect.
   'If an error does occur, it will be set in the
   'WinSock1_Error event.
   sktError = 0

   'Connecting to "qoute.yahoo.com" on port 80
   WinSock1.Connect

   If (sktError = 0) Then
   'No errors - constructing the request
    Dim msg As String
    msg = "POST /d/quotes.csv HTTP/1.1" & vbCrLf & _
       "Host: 24.92.156.120" & vbCrLf & "Content-Length: " & _
       CStr(25 + Len(txtSymbolName.Text)) & vbCrLf & _
       vbCrLf & "s=" & txtSymbolName.Text & _
       "&f=sl1d1t1c1ohgv&e=.csv" & vbCrLf
    'Sending the request to the server
    WinSock1.SendData msg

   Else
    MsgBox "Error during connection."
   End If
  Else
   MsgBox "Please enter a symbol name.", vbExclamation
   txtSymbolName.SetFocus
  End If
End Sub
```

After the query is sent, process the `DataArrival` event (see Listing 16.4). The arriving data will be saved in the `Response` variable. Separate the informative part from the reply received from the server (without the header, which is separated from the main text by a "carriage return"). This is the task of the `StripHeader` function (Listing 16.5). Then, the `SplitData` function handles the contents of the pared-down

Chapter 16: Communication and the Infrared WinSock Control in Windows CE

buffer, distributing the data among the variables declared in `Option Explicit`. The data are then displayed on the screen.

Listing 16.4. The `WinSock1_DataArrival` procedure

```
Private Sub WinSock1_DataArrival(ByVal bytesTotal As Long)
 'Put the incoming data into the buffer
 Dim Response As String
 WinSock1.GetData Response
 'MsgBox Response
 'Removing the header
 Dim quote As String
 quote = StripHeader(Response)

 'Splitting the string into separate variables
 If SplitData(quote) Then
  'Showing the data on the screen
  DisplayData
 End If
End Sub
```

The function for cutting down the header lies in selecting the part of the buffer, after the "carriage is returned" (Listing 16.5). When the information from the server comes into the browser, along with the necessary data, it contains the system-protocol information in the header, and is separated from the main text by an invisible "carriage return" symbol (`vbCrLf & vbCrLf`). The following block is an example of the header's contents:

```
HTTP/1.1 200 OK
Date: Thu, 28 Mar 2002 15:22:12 GMT
P3P:
policyref="http://p3p.yahoo.com/w3c/p3p.xml"
Cache-Control: private
Connection: close
Transfer-Encoding: chunked
Content-Type: application/octet-stream
```

You can make sure of this if you show the buffer contents right after they are received in the `MsgBox` or in some other label in Listing 16.4, whereas the browser shows already processed information. Since we do not use the browser, we will have to perform this function separately (Listing 16.5).

Listing 16.5. Excluding system information

```
Private Function StripHeader(Response As String) As String
 Dim quotePosition As Long
 Dim delimiter As String
 Dim strTemp As String

 delimiter = vbCrLf & vbCrLf
 quotePosition = InStr(1, Response, delimiter) + Len(delimiter)
 strTemp = Mid(Response, quotePosition)

 'Removing the first line of the response after the header
 quotePosition = InStr(1, strTemp, vbCrLf) + Len(vbCrLf)
 StripHeader = Mid(strTemp, quotePosition)
End Function
```

A somewhat bulky but simple SplitData function is shown in Listing 16.6. Since the information coming from the server is strictly structured — each different token is separated from the next by a comma — then each block of the following procedure selects the data from the beginning of the string until the next comma, and assigns this value to the corresponding variable.

Listing 16.6. Splitting the received data into conceptual fragments

```
Private Function SplitData(ByVal strStringData As String) As Boolean
 Dim i As Long
 Dim temp As String

 temp = strStringData
 'We get back a comma delimited string, which consists of:
 '<name>, <current price>, <date>, <time>, <change>, <open price>,
 '<high price>, <low price>, <volume>

 'Assuming an error
 SplitData = False
 'Searching for the first comma
 i = InStr(1, temp, ",")

 If i > 0 Then
   'Highlighting the name from the beginning of the string until
```

Chapter 16: Communication and the Infrared WinSock Control in Windows CE 317

```
    'the first comma, and removing the quotation marks
    Name = Mid(temp, 2, i - 3)
    'The temp variable is set to the rest of the string
    temp = Right(temp, Len(temp) - i)
    'Searching for the first comma, etc...
    i = InStr(1, temp, ",")
    If i > 0 Then
     Current = Mid(temp, 1, i - 1)
     temp = Right(temp, Len(temp) - i)
     i = InStr(1, temp, ",")
     If i > 0 Then
      Date1 = Mid(temp, 2, i - 3)
      temp = Right(temp, Len(temp) - i)

      i = InStr(1, temp, ",")

      If i > 0 Then
       Time1 = Mid(temp, 2, i - 3)
       temp = Right(temp, Len(temp) - i)
       i = InStr(1, temp, ",")
       If i > 0 Then
        Change = Mid(temp, 1, i - 1)
        temp = Right(temp, Len(temp) - i)
        i = InStr(1, temp, ",")
        If i > 0 Then
         OpenPrice = Mid(temp, 1, i - 1)
         temp = Right(temp, Len(temp) - i)
         i = InStr(1, temp, ",")
         If i > 0 Then
          High = Mid(temp, 1, i - 1)
          temp = Right(temp, Len(temp) - i)
          i = InStr(1, temp, ",")
          If i > 0 Then
           Low = Mid(temp, 1, i - 1)
           temp = Right(temp, Len(temp) - i)
           Volume = temp
           'If we are here, then we have parsed the data correctly
           SplitData = True
          End If
         End If
```

Part III: Programming Pocket PC with eMbedded Visual Basic

```
      End If
     End If
    End If
   End If
  End If
 End If
End Function
```

If the `SplitData` function returned `True`, then, according to Listing 16.4, the next step will be to display the data on the screen. This is the job of the `DisplayData` procedure (Listing 16.7). First, all controls are cleared from previous values, and then the labels are assigned the corresponding values from the modular variables.

Listing 16.7. The procedure for displaying the data on the screen

```
Private Sub DisplayData()
 'Clearing the labels
 lblName.Caption = ""
 lblPrice.Caption = ""
 lblChange.Caption = ""
 lblOpenPrice.Caption = ""
 lblDate.Caption = ""
 lblTime.Caption = ""
 lblHigh.Caption = ""
 lblLow.Caption = ""
 lblVolume.Caption = ""
 'If a value is not found, then show the message
 If High = "N/A" Then
  MsgBox "Unable to find a match for: " & txtSymbolName.Text, vbOKOnly
  lblName.Caption = "(""" & txtSymbolName.Text & """ not found.)"
 Else
  lblName.Caption = Name
  lblPrice.Caption = Current
  lblChange.Caption = Change
  lblOpenPrice.Caaption = OpenPrice
  lblDate.Caption = Date1
  lblTime.Caption = Time1
  lblHigh.Caption = High
  lblLow.Caption = Low
```

Chapter 16: Communication and the Infrared WinSock Control in Windows CE 319

```
    lblVolume.Caption = Volume
  End If
  txtSymbolName.SetFocus
End Sub
```

The working application looks as shown in Fig. 16.2.

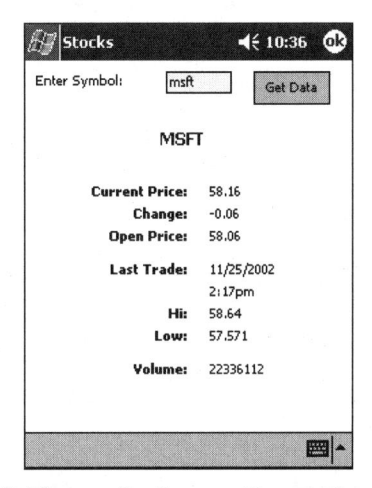

Fig. 16.2. The application working on the emulator

As usual, the eVB project will add the following procedure:

```
Private Sub Form_OKClick()
   App.End
End Sub
```

It closes the application by clicking on the **OK** button in the upper right corner (Fig. 16.2). As when developing an Internet application for Palm, it would be good to use Object Browser to find out the states that WinSock may have during the connection with the server. Since the connection with the Internet is quick and transient, however, there is no reason to display the current states of the session. Nevertheless, for more complex data handling, and for your own information, you can see them in Fig. 16.3.

Similarly, you should investigate the set of WinSock's possible errors. The `WinSock1_Error` event, however, is done well, and returns a brief explanation along with the error code. In this example we are interested only in the actual error, in which the `sktError` variable was assigned the value of the error code (Listing 16.4) in the `Error` event.

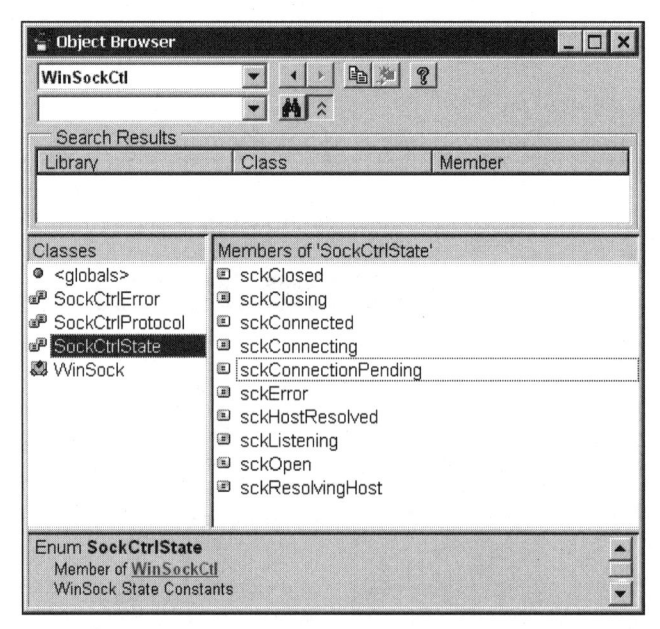

Fig. 16.3. States of WinSock control during the connection with the server

Properties, Methods, and Constants of the WinSock Control

The tables below contain the properties, methods, and constants of the Windows CE WinSock Control Object Model. They are contained in the MSCEWinsock.dll library.

Table 16.1. Methods of the `WinSock` control

Method	Returns	Description
Accept	None	Establishes the connection. Query for connection
Close	None	Closes reception or transmission
Connect	None	Inquires about the connection with the node specified in the RemoteHost property via the port specified in the RemotePort property
GetData	None	Gets the data from the buffer. Only the String and Integer array variables are supported. **Be careful! The `maxLen` parameter is ignored!**

continues

Table 16.1 Continued

Method	Returns	Description
Listen	None	Switches WinSock into the receipt mode via the protocol specified in the `Protocol` parameter
SendData	None	Transmits the data of the current WinSock to the remote host. Only the `String` and `Integer array` variables are supported

Table 16.2. Properties of `WinSock`

Property	Returns	Description
BytesReceived	Integer	Read only. The amount of data received by WinSock
LocalHostName	String	Read only. The name of the local device
LocalIP	String	Read only. The IP address of the local device
LocalPort	Integer	Sets or displays the local WinSock port
Name	String	Sets or displays the name of WinSock in the **Property** window
Parent	Object	Returns the pointer to the parent object of WinSock
Protocol	SockCtrlProtocol	Sets or displays the data transfer protocol. WinSock supports only TCP/IP and IrDA
RemoteHost	String	Sets or displays the name or IP of the remote device
RemoteHostIP	String	Read only. The IP of the remote device after a successful connection
RemotePort	Integer	Sets or displays the port of the remote device with which WinSock is or will be connected
SocketHandle	Long	Read only. The header of the open window used by WinSock
State	SockCtrlState	Read only. The current state of the WinSock control
ServiceName	String	Sets or displays the name of the IrDA connection
Tag	String	Sets or displays the additional information

Table 16.3. Events of the `WinSock` control

Event	Description
`Close`	Occurs when the connection is closed by the remote device
`ConnectionRequest`	Occurs when the request for connection in the comes in the receipt mode
`Connect`	Occurs upon a successful connection
`DataArrival`	Occurs when WinSock receives the information in an empty buffer
`Error`	Occurs when there is a connection error
`SendComplete`	Occurs at the end of data transmission using the `SendData` method
`SendProgress`	Occurs after each package is sent. Data with a volume exceeding 8 KB are automatically split into packages

Table 16.4. Constants of `WinSockCtlError`

Constant	Value	Description
`SckOutOfMemory`	7	Overfill
`SckInvalidPropertyValue`	380	Property error
`SckGetNotSupported`	394	Property unavailable
`SckSetNotSupported`	383	Read-only property
`SckBadState`	40006	Protocol, connection state, or query is erroneous
`SckInvalidArg`	40014	The parameter is in the wrong format or has the wrong value
`SckSuccess`	40017	Successful
`SckUnsupported`	40018	Unsupported type of variable
`SckInvalidOp`	40020	Operation incorrect
`SckOutOfRange`	40021	The parameter is outside the range
`SckWrongProtocol`	40026	Wrong send or query protocol
`SckOpCanceled`	10004	Operation interrupted
`SckInvalidArgument`	10014	The inquired address is broadcast, but no check-box is checked
`SckWouldBlock`	10035	The socket is not blocked, but the operation is
`SckInProgress`	10036	Blocking in progress

continues

Chapter 16: Communication and the Infrared WinSock Control in Windows CE

Table 16.4 Continued

Constant	Value	Description
SckAlreadyComplete	10037	Operation completed
SckNotSocket	10038	No connection
SckMsgTooBig	10040	The data volume does not fit into the buffer, and is cut
SckPortNotSupported	10043	The indicated port is not supported
SckAddressInUse	10048	Address is in use
SckAddressNotAvailable	10049	Address is not available from the local computer
SckNetworkSubsystem-Failed	10050	Network subsystem failed
SckNetworkUnreachable	10051	Network unavailable
SckNetReset	10052	Connection time expired
SckConnectAborted	10053	Connection failed
SckConnectionReset	10054	Connection is closed by the remote device
SckNoBufferSpace	10055	Buffer is unavailable
SckAlreadyConnected	10056	Connection is already established
SckNotConnected	10057	No connection
SckSocketShutdown	10058	Socket closed
SckTimedout	10060	No connection (timeout)
SckConnectionRefused	10061	Connection refused
SckNotInitialized	10093	WinSockInit is not initialized
SckHostNotFound	11001	Authorized reply: Host not found
SckHostNotFoundTryAgain	11002	Non-authorized reply: Host not found
SckNonRecoverableError	11003	Non-recoverable error
SckNoData	11004	Name correct, no data

Table 16.5. Constants of the SockCtrls protocol

Constant	Value	Description
SckIRDAProtocol	2	TCP/IP protocol
SckTCPProtocol	0	Infrared port protocol

Table 16.6. Constants of `SockCtrlState`

Constant	Value	Description
SckClosed	0	Closed (by default)
SckOpen	1	Open
SckListening	2	Reception
SckConnectionPending	3	Connection in progress
SckResolvingHost	4	Repeated call
SckHostResolved	5	Repeated connection with the device
SckConnecting	6	Connection
SckConnected	7	Connection established
SckClosing	8	Connection closed
SckError	9	Error

Conclusion

Having become acquainted with pocket-computer programming techniques, the reader should now have an idea of the wide range of options currently available.

So far, the technology is still in its early stages, and is only just starting to impact everyday life. Already, however, communication systems are starting to merge with information resources and organizers, in the shape of the latest smart phones and communicators, for example. Economists estimate that, in the next 10 years, the development of portable-communication technology will begin to gather speed, as the power of portable computers increases; even so, portable-computer processors are already running at speeds in excess of the first Pentium processors. After the next, inevitable, technological breakthrough reduces the cost of flash memory, portable computers will likely squeeze out the notebook, and will compete on equal terms with desktop computers, requiring a lot of new universal — not just corporate — software. Another trend is the use of pocket devices as terminals of desktop computers and corporate servers, which will enjoy their current king-of-the-hill status for some time.

Unfortunately, this book could not even begin to look at devices that, on the one hand, are portable and, on the other hand, require a processor, such as various gaming devices, digital cameras and GPS systems. These devices, until now separate, are already being combined with portable machines. Devices that appeared not long ago, such as electronic translators, are already losing their value as separate devices, as there is already a lot of portable-device software that performs the same functions.

Current trends highlight the extreme importance of the programming described in this book. All that remains is to wish the reader success in this captivating walk of life.

Appendix A

List of Useful Web Sites for Palm and Pocket PC Developers

http://www.appforge.com — the AppForge, Inc. web site. The *For Developers* section contains code samples, an informational database for developers, boosters for different devices, etc.

http://www.handango.com — a very popular site, which has a huge amount of software for different OSs. The site helps developers sell their products for small commissions.

http://www.devbuzz.com — a site for eVB developers. You can find news, articles, application samples, and so on.

http://www.microsoft.com/sql/CE/default.asp — the Microsoft site dedicated to a SQL CE server.

http://www.cewindows.net — a site dedicated to the Windows CE (Pocket PC) OS.

http://frankscaslpage.home.att.net — a very interesting site for programmers who use CASL.

http://www.caslsoft.com — the official CASL site. Contains a lot of information and provides trial versions for download.

http://www.microsoft.com/windowsxp/tabletpc — the part of Microsoft's web site dedicated to Tablet.

http://www.pocketpcmag.com — Pocket PC magazine's official web site.

http://geek.com/pdageek — a huge site with a lot of information and devices for sale. Also includes material on wireless technology, reviews, articles, news, and products.

http://www.wirelessdevnet.com/training/ — a site with training materials for different platforms and various tools.

http://www.irda.org — the site of the Infrared Data Association® (IrDA®), which sets standards for the infrared industry.

> **Note**
> More web sites useful for developers are mentioned in *Chapter 3*.

Appendix B

Advice on Further Actions

It is quite possible that many bought our book out of sheer curiosity but, no doubt, many were stimulated by professional interests, too. This category of readers will be interested to know that, after they have created their own useful application, they can try to sell it via the Internet and get real profit from the sales. Here we will explain how to do so using the Handango (**www.handango.com**) web site. Handango is the biggest Internet site devoted to portable devices of all operating systems. About one million people visit it monthly and so, it is no surprise that you can sell an interesting application from there.

First, you have to become a so-called "partner" of the company (Handango Software Partner). The position is absolutely free of charge and serves to help independent developers software for portable devices reach many millions of potential customers. As a result of registration in the Developer section, you will be able to:

- Upload your application to their web site as an on-line member
- Update your product
- Describe the product and specify its price

In addition, you can check the state of your account at any time, and receive an instantaneous e-mail when a copy is bought. You can have daily, weekly, or monthly reports generated on the selling activity and amounts you earned. Payments are performed either on a monthly basis, or as $100 are accumulated for programmers outside the U.S.A. The company's commission is 30%.

After then on-line registration is complete, the product can be uploaded to the site. Nothing else needs to be done. The only thing is to think over how to best market of your product.

There are other known web sites dedicated to PDAs. They also allow developers to distribute their programs for sale or as shareware:

- **www.palmgear.com** — the PalmGear site dedicated to the Palm PDA.
- **www.pdastreet.com** — a site dedicated to all OSs.
- **upload.com.com** — a site which belongs to Cnet.
- **www.tucows.com** — this site also allows you to distribute your program. But if you do not send the first payment, processing may take several weeks.

References

1. Basset T., Tacke C. eMbedded Visual Basic. — SAMS, 2001.
2. Crooks C. E. Palm Development. — QUE, 2002.
3. Kawa A. Develop Mobile & Wireless Solutions with SQL Server CE // Access, VB, SQL Advisor.
4. Kilburn J. Palm Programming in Basic. — Apress, 2002.
5. Perry C. Converging Technologies // Wireless Computing. — 2002 — No. 5.
6. Perry C. The Handheld Internet // Wireless Computing. — 2002 — No. 5.
7. Smith S. Palm vs. Pocket PC // Wireless Computing. — 2002 — No. 5.

Additional Resources

1. Palm-Size PC (User's Guide).
2. AppForge MobileVB Help.
3. eMbedded Visual Basic Help.
4. Internet Resources (Appendix 1).

Index

A
About:
  window, 65
About Info:
  Starting window, 65
AutoNumber:
  functions, 139

B
Build PQA
  File, 177
Button Text:
  Form Properties, 68
Buttons:
  menu, 220
  new, 220

C
Code:
  view, 206
  window, 208
Compile/Download:
  Compile into Fat App, 72
  Options, 71
Compile and Validate:
  MobileVB, 156
Compile into Fat App:
  Compile/Download, 72
Components:
  project, 206, 217, 227, 311
Conduit:
  Finish button, 139
  MobileVB, 134
Conduits, 58

D
Database converter:
  MobileVB, 130

Database Viewer:
  MobileVB, 130
  Person ID field, 130
  Unique ID field, 130

E
Edit:
  Starting window, 65
Emulator Preferences:
  Wireless command, 170
Event driven code, 57

F
File:
  Build PQA, 177
  make, 215
  Master, 177
  menu, 177, 215
  Open Index, 177
Finish button:
  Conduit, 139
Form Properties:
  Button Text, 68
  Main Form, 66
  Primary Database Form, 66
  window, 66
Functions:
  Auto Number, 139

G
General:
  Options, 71
Get Article:
  MobileVB, 162

H
Handheld pocket computer, 53

HistoryListText:
  Tags, 175

L
Local Icon:
  Tags, 175

M
Main Form:
  Form Properties, 66
Make:
  file, 215
Master:
  File, 177
  Query Application Builder, 176
Menu:
  button, 220
  file, 177
  file, 215
  MobileVB, 155
  new, 220
  NS Basic, 71
  project, 206, 217, 227, 311
  start, 220
  tools, 215
  Tools, 71
  view, 206, 208
MenuDraw:
  NS Basic, 71
MobileVB:
  Compile and Validate, 156
  Conduit, 134
  Database converter, 130
  Database Viewer, 130
  Get Article, 162
  menu, 155
  Palm OS, 156

Save Project Package..., 156
Settings, 155
Universal Conduit, 135
View, 163
Zoom, 162

N

New:
  button, 220
  menu, 220
NS Basic:
  Menu, 71
  MenuDraw, 71

O

Object Browser:
  View, 163
Open Index:
  File, 177
Options:
  General, 71
  Tools, 71
  Compile/Download, 71

P

Palm, 49
Palm operating system, 50
Palm OS:
  MobileVB, 156
PalmComputingPlatform:
  Tags, 174
PalmLauncherRevision:
  Tags, 175
Person ID field:
  Database Viewer, 130
Pocket PC, 49
Pocket PC 2002 operating system, 53
Primary Database Form:
  Form Properties, 66

Project:
  components, 206, 217, 227, 311
  menu, 206, 217, 227, 311

Q

Query Application Builder:
  Master, 176

R

Remote Tools/Application Install Wizard:
  tools, 215

S

Save Project Package…
  MobileVB, 156
Settings:
  MobileVB, 155
SmallScreenIgnore
  Tag, 175
Start:
  menu, 220
Starting window:
  About Info, 65
  Edit, 65

T

Tags:
  HistoryListText, 175
  Local Icon, 175
  PalmComputingPlatform, 174
  PalmLauncherRevision, 175
  SmallScreenIgnore, 175
Textbox Properties:
  window, 66
Tools:
  menu, 71, 215
  options, 71

remote tools/application install wizard, 215
Turn On New Button:
  menu
  window, 220

U

Unique ID field:
  Database Viewer, 130
Universal Conduit:
  MobileVB, 135
Universal Conduit Manager:
  window, 139

V

View:
  code, 206
  menu, 206, 208
  MobileVB, 163
  Object Browser, 163
Virtual machines, 57

W

Window:
  about, 65
  code, 208
  Field Properties, 66
  Form Properties, 66
  turn on New button menu, 220
  Universal Conduit Manager, 139
Windows CE, 49, 53
Wireless command:
  Emulator Preferences, 170

Z

Zoom:
  MobileVB, 162